THE GREAT WESTERN RAILWAY
In The Nineteenth Century
by O. S. Nock

THE GREAT WESTERN RAILWAY

RAILWAY

In The Nineteenth Century

By

O. S. NOCK

B.Sc., M.I.C.E., M.I.Mech.E., M.I.Loco.E.

LONDON

IAN ALLAN

First published 1962

This edition 1971

Second impression 1972

SBN 71 10 0226 6

Printed in Great Britain
By Unwin Brothers Limited
The Gresham Press, Old Woking, Surrey, England
A member of the Staples Printing Group

Contents

Bibliography

History of the Great Western Railway	:	E. T. MacDermot
The Armstrongs of the Great Western	:	H. Holcroft
An Outline of G.W.R. Locomotive Practice	:	H. Holcroft
Locos of the Royal Road	:	W. G. Chapman
Track Topics	:	W. G. Chapman
Isambard Kingdom Brunel	:	L. T. C. Rolt
Locomotive and Train Working in the Latter Part of the 19th Century (Vol. IV)	:	E. L. Ahrons
Centenary of the G.W.R. (Special Issue of the Railway Gazette)		
Express Trains English and Foreign	:	Foxwell & Farrer
Great Western Steam	:	W. A. Tuplin

Preface

AMONG the old railway companies of Great Britain none has been written up more thoroughly, or more appreciatively than the Great Western. There have been articles by the hundred, pamphlets, brochures, and a plethora of full length books – two indeed by your humble servant. And now here am I setting out to add yet another, and a book moreover that will run inevitably into a couple of volumes! What is there new to be written? The ground would appear to have been covered so thoroughly from the impartial scholarship of MacDermot to W. G. Chapman, and the boisterous controversialism of Professor Tuplin. It is perhaps inevitable that Brunel should be a favourite subject for biographers, and the intensely human story of this amazing man tends to dominate the stage, as we see it in retrospect, when actually he did not really do so at the time.

Today, unhappily, the Great Western Railway as an institution is receding into history, and one can perhaps make a better appraisal of its great men, its traffic and its engineering affairs than when it was a living entity in our midst. The anxious days of 1838, when Brunel was on the point of resignation, assume a new poignancy; the birth and development of 'New Swindon' assumes an added significance in these days of welfare state, and one can see the famous engines of Churchward and Collett in clearer perspective. The Great Western Railway during the nineteenth century was a concern of such multifarious and far flung activities that to write chronologically of the system would be to jump from one place to another in a way that would be confusing in the extreme. I have chosen instead to present a series of essays dealing with various well-defined aspects of its history, engineering topography and so on, much of which seemed at times to be no more than loosely connected with the fountain head at Paddington.

In preparing this first volume I have had the most invaluable help from a number of good friends, particularly among the present-day officers of the Western Region, who have put numerous drawings, photographs and other information at my disposal. I am also especially indebted to the Archivist of the British Transport Commission for making available to me the magnificent collection of photographs of broad gauge engines and trains taken by the late Rev. A. H. Malan. The detailed references to the work of the Dean locomotives was made possible by Mr. G. J. Aston, who sent me the relevant volumes from the train running notes compiled by the late R. E. Charlewood. In addition to all the above I have had considerable help from reference to the various works listed in the bibliography. To the Superintendent of H.M. Nautical Almanac Office of the Royal Greenwich Observatory I am indebted for the trouble he took to verify the feasibility of the sun's rays shining right through Box Tunnel on Brunel's birthday. To Mr. B. W. C. Cooke, Editor of *The Railway Magazine*, I am grateful for permission to quote the two passages from Ahrons included in Chapter IX.

O. S. Nock.

20 Sion Hill,
Bath, Somerset.
April 1962.

COAT OF ARMS OF THE
GREAT WESTERN RAILWAY COMPANY

A blending of the Arms of the cities of London and Bristol; the original limits of the Great Western Railway as contemplated by the GWR Act of 1835

I

Pioneer Days

THE Great Western always had a way of doing things differently from everyone else. Its birthplace was truly in Bristol, where, in the autumn of 1832, a strong committee of prominent merchants and other business men was formed to investigate the possibility of a railway to London. The Bristol Committee wasted no time. At its first meeting, on January 21st, 1833, it was agreed to obtain a preliminary survey and estimate, and within two months the Committee had appointed the youthful Isambard Kingdom Brunel as its engineer. How Brunel got the job is one of the best known stories in railway history, but it is important to realize that he was connected with this great enterprise before there was any support coming from the London end. The ground was surveyed, the route via Swindon and the Vale of the White Horse decided and the estimates presented to the Bristol Committee in time for an elaborate report to be presented to a public meeting at the Guildhall, Bristol on July 30th, 1833.

It was not until after the decision to form a company had been taken that support for the project was seriously solicited in the City of London. Support was readily obtained, and with the formation of a London Committee the latter body began making appointments of its own, just as the Bristol Committee had done in the case of Brunel. Their choice of a secretary was in many ways an appointment more momentous than that of the Bristol Committee in appointing Brunel as engineer, for in Charles Alexander Saunders they secured a man of quite exceptional talent, yet of talent combined with such a steadfast and level-headed temperament as to prove of priceless value to the company in many of the difficult years that were to come. It was on August 19th, 1833, that the Bristol and London Committees met together for the first time; they met in the counting house of Messrs Anthony Gibbs and Sons, in the City of London, and there, amid the Georgian splendour of 47 Lime Street, the name 'Great Western Railway' was adopted.

Between that time and the passing of the Act on August 31st, 1835, the project went through many vicissitudes, but the intervening

years revealed without any doubt the tremendous energy and
enthusiasm of the two men who were to do so much to carry the
Great Western forward in the ensuing twenty years. One could
understand the secretary of the London Committee being tireless in
his canvassing for financial support; but Brunel was likewise
indefatigable. Meetings in support of the project were organized in
almost every town of importance in the west. While Saunders was
working up enthusiasm in Bristol itself, in Gloucestershire and in
South Wales, Brunel was active as far away as Bridport and Truro.
At the very start of his association with the G.W.R. he showed that
he was not content merely to carry out his engineering commissions;
he must throw himself in, heart and soul, invest to the limit of his
purse, and urge everyone he met to do the same.

To Saunders and Brunel must be added a third outstanding
personality who was at first not on either the Bristol or the London
Committees; this was Charles Russell, Member of Parliament for
Reading, who was Chairman of the Parliamentary Committee of
1835 that examined the Bill in the minutest detail. It was before
Charles Russell that so much nonsense was talked by some of the
'expert' witnesses called to advise upon the Box Tunnel – apos-
trophised as 'monstrous and extraordinary', 'most dangerous and
impracticable'. Far from being impressed by the arguments to which
he had to listen, Russell became the strongest and most staunch
supporter Brunel ever had – even including Saunders. The most
severe testing time for them all, however, was still four years ahead,
for in 1835 Russell was not even a director of the Great Western
Railway. The Bill received the Royal Assent on August 31st, 1835,
and it is of interest to recall that although the line was primarily a
child of Bristolian enterprise the first general meeting of the new
company was held at the City of London Tavern, and one of the
leading members of the London Committee, Benjamin Shaw, was
the first Chairman.

While the surveys had been made in considerable detail at the
Bristol end of the line, and a vast amount of controversy had raged
over Box Tunnel, it seems strange that the route at the London end
was left in quite a vague manner. The original surveys that Brunel
carried out for the Bristol Committee seem to have gone no farther
eastwards than Kingston, and even after the Act had been obtained
there appears to have been some considerable doubt as to where the
Great Western would eventually terminate in London. At the first
general meeting of the company the Directors reported that they
were negotiating with the Board of the London and Birmingham

Railway for use of their line into London. Furthermore, they bought some premises in Prince's Street, in the heart of the City, and near to the Bank of England. It was intended these should form not only the administrative headquarters of the company, but should constitute the receiving station for passengers and light goods proceeding to and from the railway. Apparently the idea was that passengers from the west, having arrived in Euston, were to be whisked off willy-nilly, by private omnibus, and duly landed in the City.

As the line was actually laid out the route came very near to the London and Birmingham, at Kensal Green, and it would have needed no more than a slight swing to the north to make a junction just to the west of Kensal Green tunnels. Fortunately for both parties these negotiations came to nothing, else Euston would have been the scene of congestion and confusion worse than the approach to London Bridge, or on the line between Hitchin and Kings Cross during those difficult days when the Midland trains were exercising running powers. Negotiations with the London and Birmingham went on during the autumn of 1835. A factor of uncertainty was cast over them by the startling proposal of Brunel to use a rail gauge of 7 ft, in contrast to the 4 ft 8½ in. of the London and Birmingham, and most other railways under construction at that time. The advantages to be gained by the use of the broad gauge were outlined in a letter from Brunel to the Board of the Great Western Railway dated September 15th, 1835, and it can be truly said that from the time the contents of that letter became public every action by the Great Western was eyed with the gravest suspicion.

Brunel disliked the idea of a junction with the London and Birmingham, because of the difficulties that existed in the way of his carrying the seven-foot gauge into Euston. It is sometimes thought that the broad-gauge proposal killed the project for the joint line; although it undoubtedly brought a complication, the main cause of its abandonment was the complete failure of the two companies to come to terms over the land to be occupied by the Great Western at Camden, and in the neighbourhood of Euston itself. The Great Western wanted freehold rights if possible, and at the very least a 21-year lease. The best the London and Birmingham would offer was a 5-year tenancy, and this the Great Western somewhat naturally refused. The negotiations ended in acrimony on both sides. Robert Stephenson complained that his company had been left with land to spare, bought to accommodate the Great Western, while Saunders said the negotiations had broken down because the London and

Birmingham were afraid that the speed of the G.W.R. trains would
be so much greater than their own as to constitute a definite danger,
both at the junctions near Kensal Green and on the run into
Euston! Had they not had these fears, he felt, they might have been
more reasonable in negotiation.

In the meantime, as early as October 29th, 1835 in fact, the Board
had sanctioned the use of the broad gauge, but although the news
leaked out quite soon it was not until August 1836 that the decision was
made public officially. The collapse of the London and Birmingham
negotiations left the Great Western without a London terminus, but
fortunately the company was able to secure a piece of vacant ground
adjoining the Basin of the Paddington Canal. An additional Act of
Parliament had to be obtained for the abandonment of the line from
Acton to the junction with the London and Birmingham at Kensal
Green, and for the construction of $4\frac{1}{2}$ miles of new line from Acton
to Paddington. This Act was not obtained until 1837, and in the
meantime another complication had arisen. In the previous year a
short, but potentially important railway, with a high sounding name
had been authorized. This was the Birmingham, Bristol and Thames
Junction, which, believe it or not, ran no farther than from
Willesden Junction to Kensington. But it cut clean across the proposed Great Western deviation from Acton to Paddington, and
being first in the field could undoubtedly claim prior rights at the
crossing. As one of its objects was to collect traffic from Bristol the
Great Western did not have any very great difficulty in persuading
this little company to give up its prior rights at the junction, though
the inconveniences of the level crossing persisted for many years.

The Great Western was not a year old before it had given strong
evidence of its way of 'doing things differently' in the curious
proposals regarding its headquarters in the City of London, and in
its adoption of the broad gauge. When construction of the line
commenced another unusual practice became evident. Although the
Company had a single Board of Directors the London and Bristol
Committees remained strong and influential, so much so that the
contracts for the various civil engineering works on the line were
placed independently. While Brunel was Engineer-in-Chief he was
given far more scope for his flights of architectural fancy by the
Bristol Committee, so much so that the London members were
sometimes complaining about the extravagance of the works at the
western end of the line. One can be fairly sure that if the London
Committee had had anything to do with it Brunel would never have
been permitted to erect that colossal western façade to the Box

Tunnel, still less the equally grand portals at both ends of the adjoining Middle Hill Tunnel.

Even today Box Tunnel can be a subject of controversy. The gradient is 1 in 100 descending towards Bath, straight throughout, and on one day in the year the rising sun is at the appropriate altitude and azimuth to shine through its two miles from end to end. The fact that this day coincides exactly with Brunel's birthday, April 9th, has suggested to some critics that the immense task of boring the tunnel was done to satisfy the vanity of the engineer, and that a much easier course could have been obtained avoiding the use of a tunnel altogether. A study of the ordnance map, and my own knowledge of the intervening country suggests that this is true. There may have been difficulties in obtaining the necessary land, since the line would have had to pass to the north of two very large estates, and the tunnel may have been the easiest way after all! In any case, the controversy over Box Tunnel is fully in keeping with the mighty legend of Brunel, and necessary or not those lovely tunnel façades are an abiding adornment to a beautiful countryside. The coincidence of the sun shining through the tunnel with Brunel's birthday has always seemed to me to be so strange as *not* to be accidental, and I felt that the facts would be worth checking. The Superintendent of the Nautical Almanac Office of the Royal Greenwich Observatory very kindly had the case examined, and has told me that on April 9th the sun is definitely in the position to make this particular Brunel legend a fact.

With characteristic optimism Brunel had promised to have the line opened from London to Maidenhead in October 1837, but as the Act for the Paddington extension was not obtained until that same year a postponement was inevitable, and the actual opening took place on June 4th, 1838. This in itself was mighty quick work, but so great was the determination of the Directors and so great the zeal of Brunel that wherever the landowners and occupiers were complaisant works were begun in 1836, before the passing of the Act. Today it is strange to realize that from the very platform ends at Paddington the line ran out into open and unspoiled country. One of the provisions of the 1837 Act was that across the railway a new road was to be made to replace the footpath known as Bishop's Walk. That new road is the Bishop's Road of today, and takes its name from the Bishop of London from whom much of the land for the new station and goods depot was purchased. The original passenger station and engine shed were located between the present Bishop's Road and Westbourne Bridges, but long before the permanent engine sheds outside Paddington were ready a temporary depot had been made at West Drayton, and from this the trials of the earliest broad gauge engines were made.

The viaduct over the valley of the Brent, at Hanwell, was one of the largest works at the London end of the line, though the skew bridge over the Uxbridge Road proved the most troublesome. Hence the relatively easy section between West Drayton and the east bank of the Thames at Taplow was finished first, and was a natural testing ground for the earliest engines and rolling stock. The locomotive history of the Great Western did not begin auspiciously. It would seem that all the purveyors of freaks unloaded their ideas on Brunel and he fell for them. But through the bold, revolutionary ideas of Brunel the railway world of Great Britain, small and scattered though it was at that time, was impressed if it was not enamoured by the initial prowess of the Great Western, and though they might not be in agreement with all its precepts, they could not do other than recognize that here indeed was a giant rising in their midst. And one of those who sought to make a career with the giant was young Daniel Gooch.

In July 1837, when he was still a full month short of his 21st birthday Gooch wrote his now famous letter to Brunel:

> Manchester and Leeds Railway Office
> ROCHDALE.
> July 18th, /37

Dear Sir,

I have just been informed it is your intention to erect an Engine Manufactory at or near Bristol and that you wish to engage a person as Manager. I take the earliest opportunity of offering my services for the situation.

I have until the last two months been constantly engaged in engine building and have worked at each branch of the business but principally at Locomotive Engine Work. The first three years of my time I was with Mr Homphry at the Tredegar Iron Works, Monmouthshire. I left him to go to Mr R. Stephenson and was at the Vulcan Foundry 12 months when I obtained leave from Mr Stephenson to go down to Mr Stirling of the Dundee Foundry Co. Dundee, to get a knowledge of steamboat work. I remained with him 12 months and returned to Mr Stephenson's works at Newcastle where I remained until last October when I left, having had an offer from a party in Newcastle to take the Management of a Locomotive Manufactory which they intended erecting but which owing to some unavoidable circumstances they have now given up the idea of proceeding with and we have countermanded the order for machinery. This left me without a situation and I am anxious to engage myself to some Company where I will have the management of the building of engines. At present I am with my brother on the Manchester and Leeds Line, where I have employment until I meet with something more suitable.

I will be glad to refer you to any of the forementioned places for testimonials.

Should you approve of my application I shall be glad to hear from you stating the salary and any other information you may think necessary.

I am, Sir,

Yours Obly.

I. K. Brunel, Esq.   DANL. GOOCH.

Brunel realized, as much as anyone, his need of a locomotive assistant, and having to go north shortly after the receipt of this letter, to check up on the progress of locomotives under construction at Liverpool and Warrington, he secured, before he went, the sanction of the Board to appoint a 'Superintendent of Locomotive Engines'. While he was in the north Brunel interviewed Gooch in Manchester, and engaged him on the spot. No time was wasted on either side, and Gooch entered the service of the Great Western Railway on August 18th, 1837.

For some years he had a terribly uphill fight. Young as he was, he quickly formed some very decided views upon the engines ordered by Brunel. In his diary Gooch wrote:

'None of the engines had then been delivered, though several were ordered. My first work was to prepare plans for the engine-houses at Paddington and Maidenhead, and then I went to inspect the engines then building. I was not much pleased with the design of the engines ordered. They had very small boilers and cylinders, and very large wheels . . . . . . I felt very uneasy about the working of these machines, feeling sure they would have enough to do to drive themselves along the road.'

Early in November the first two locomotives arrived at West Drayton, *Premier* from Mather, Dixon and Co. of Liverpool, and *Vulcan* from Charles Tayleur and Co. of the Vulcan Foundry. Both had travelled by sea from Liverpool to the London Docks, and had been conveyed thence to West Drayton by canal. Both engines were 2-2-2s of diminutive proportions, and at the time they were delivered there was no length of line on which they could be tried. The first record of any actual running comes from the diary of G. H. Gibbs, one of the most active and enthusiastic of the London members of the Board. On January 9th, 1838 Gibbs records the proceedings thus:

'Went down the line to West Drayton. Ealing Station is in a very unfinished state. The Hanwell embankment is not completed on either side, and none of the lines ballasted nor any piles driven; but I did not see anything to induce me to believe that everything might not be completed by the end of March. At West Drayton we were much pleased to find that the two engines were about to be tried. After walking with Brunel as far as the Chequers Bridge admiring the rails exceedingly, we returned to the Engine House. The Engines, after some delay in getting up steam, sallied forth, but the curve in the turn-out proving too sharp for them they got off the rail two or three times, and it was an hour before they could be got on the main line. When there, however, they performed beautifully and we had a very interesting drive.'

Gibbs' reference to the rails leads me on to the subject of Brunel's permanent way – the next item in which the Great Western was at first different from all others. There is no doubt that the most usual way of laying railway track at that time, that is of having a relatively heavy wrought iron rail supported at intervals on massive stone blocks, left a great deal to be desired. It was difficult to maintain, for if some of the blocks sank deeper into the ground than the rest it was next to impossible to correct the levels. Brunel took the older form of rail support, laying a light rail on longitudinal timbers. Although this cost some £500 a mile more than stone blocks and heavier rails Brunel explained his preference thus: 'The excess will be amply repaid, in the first few years of working, in the diminution of the mere cost of repair and maintenance of the way; while the gain in economy, facility and perfection of transport would be cheaply purchased at double the cost.' The really novel feature of Brunel's original road was the piles, though it is fair to say that their purpose has been generally misunderstood.

Nicholas Wood has described their function very clearly in an independent report to the Great Western Board made in 1838, thus:

'The principle of construction is this; the longitudinal timbers and transoms being firmly held down by the piles, gravel or sand is beat or packed underneath the longitudinal timbers for the purpose of obtaining a considerable vertical strain upon the timbers upwards and consequently to effect a corresponding firmness of foundation of packing underneath them. Without piles, the longitudinal timbers could not be packed in this manner, as there would be nothing to resist the pressure of the packing except their own weight, and the piles were therefore introduced to hold down the timbers and to render it practicable to introduce a force of packing underneath.'

The public opening of the line took place on Monday, June 4th, 1838, between Paddington and a temporary station on the east bank of the Thames just opposite Maidenhead. At that time only two intermediate stations were open, at West Drayton and Slough. It is interesting to read from the advertised notices of the opening of the line that although the departure times were given from Paddington and Maidenhead no arrival times were quoted. This perhaps was just as well, seeing what manner of locomotives Gooch had to run the trains! The service opened with eight trains a day in each direction. The advertisements and early notices were signed by the secretaries of both the London and Bristol Committees, namely Charles Saunders and Thomas Osler.

Despite all that Brunel had promised the Great Western Railway got away to a very bad start. The first public train, hauled by the *North Star*, took no less than 80 min. for the 23-mile run, but far more disconcerting than any lack of speed was the bad riding of the carriages, with much jolting and jerking, and obvious deficiencies in the very matters on which Brunel had so enthusiastically extolled the merits of the broad gauge, and of his particular form of permanent way. That most of the locomotives were unreliable was to be expected, from the way in which they had been specified and ordered before the appointment of Daniel Gooch. From its very inception the broad gauge had many opponents; they lost no time in spreading exaggerated reports of the troubles that were being experienced daily between Paddington and Maidenhead, and before the month was out a considerable body of shareholders were expressing its concern in a very open and hostile manner.

The anxiety, even among Brunel's most staunch supporters, was natural. If this unique and costly form of permanent way had begun to give trouble, and become rough after several months it would have been more readily understood; but it was bad from the very first day! Saunders hardly slept at all, so harassed was he with the business side of the railway. Gooch spent most of his nights in the engine house at Paddington, doing what he could in the way of repairs, while G. H. Gibbs, one of the directors, decided to take a trip on the London and Birmingham to compare the standards of travelling. He felt there was a good deal of hostile propaganda in the reports that were circulating, and he was relieved to find that riding over the line from Euston to Denbigh Hall over rails supported by stone blocks, was if anything rougher than their own. This of course was cold comfort to the Great Western, to find they were *no worse* than others, after all that had been promised of being incomparably better. Some of the trouble could certainly be placed on the springing of the carriages. Mechanical engineering was not the strong suit of the G.W.R. in its first days!

Journeying to Maidenhead, and arriving there bumped and jolted despite the slowness of the train, the critics had another point on which to launch a major attack on Brunel and the Board. The beautiful, elliptical arched bridge over the Thames was sufficiently near completion for the onlookers to observe the extraordinarily flat character of the two arches, and of course the wiseacres averred that they would fall down the moment the wooden centerings were removed. There would be no need for them to wait for a train to pass; those arches would not support themselves! Again the rumours were spread abroad, and coupled with the obvious defects of the section of line that was actually opened they served to increase the general anxiety. Gibbs, loyal supporter though he was, does not conceal his own feelings about Brunel:

'Poor fellow', he wrote on July 13, 'I pity him exceedingly, and I know not how he will get through the storm which awaits him. With all his talent he has shown himself deficient, I confess, in general arrangement. There have been too many mistakes; too much of doing and undoing. The draining, I fear, is imperfect, and the carriages made under his directions have not worked well; but I cannot help asking myself whether it is fair to decide on a work of this kind within a few weeks of its opening; and is not the present outcry created in a great measure by Brunel's enemies.'

At Brunel's suggestion the Directors decided to seek the opinion of other engineers on the entire system that had been adopted on the Great Western Railway, namely the gauge, the type of permanent way, the rolling stock and such of the major civil engineering works as were nearing completion. The directors invited James Walker, President of the Institution of Civil Engineers, to preside over the enquiry and to be assisted by Robert Stephenson and Nicholas Wood. All three realized that they would be engaged on highly controversial topics, and Walker and Stephenson declined. Wood, one of the most level-headed of all engineers concerned in the early days of railways agreed to make a report, though on condition that he could not start until September. He had been closely associated with George Stephenson at the time of the promotion of the Stockton and Darlington Railway, and the choice of him by the directors was not to the liking of a strong group of shareholders in Liverpool. At their insistence the Board agreed to ask John Hawkshaw, a young engineer of 27 years of age who was then laying out the Manchester and Leeds Railway, to make an independent report.

Through the autumn of 1838 matters dragged anxiously on. Hawkshaw did not really report on what he had been commissioned to do. He criticized the whole enterprise not on engineering, but on commercial grounds, dismissing it as a sheer waste of money. The only cogent argument he put forward concerned the difficulty of interchanging traffic with other railways due to the break of gauge. True though it was this was hardly a matter of deep concern to the Great Western in 1838, floundering as they were amid the problems of working 23 miles of line between Paddington and Maidenhead. Hawkshaw reported in October 1838, but Wood's report, which was much longer in coming in, was just the kind of sane, well-balanced treatise that would have been expected of him. Unfortunately for the G.W.R. it was, in its very saneness and impartiality, unfavourable to the broad gauge. Wood's opposition was implied rather than outspoken. As Gibbs comments: '. . . not absolutely opposing our gauge but tending to show that we should be better without it.'

Action on Wood's report rested at first with the London Committee. Gibbs, and even Saunders were plainly shaken by it. Brunel was ready to resign. It was even suggested that Joseph Locke should be called in. Such was the strength of feeling that Saunders was forced to admit it might be desirable to have a second engineer as consultant. On December 14th, 1838, there was a meeting of the London Committee, which revealed much confusion of thought, and it was learned that the Chairman had already been to see Brunel, and had put to him the idea of a second engineer. No decision was reached, but after the break-up of the meeting four men met together privately, and argued the matter further. These four were a certain Mr Casson, G. H. Gibbs, Saunders and Charles Russell who was by that time a director. Casson was for sacking Brunel outright, while even Saunders had begun to feel that some definite change was necessary. Gibbs was perplexed, and worried as much by the attitude of the Bristol members, who seemed to have lost all faith in Brunel, as with the actual troubles they were facing every day on the line.

It was at this extremely critical moment that Charles Russell showed his hand, and his great strength of character. He realized, more clearly perhaps than any of the others, that to call in another engineer would bring about the resignation of Brunel. If that happened there was no shadow of doubt that the cause of the broad gauge would be lost, and that the 23 miles of line between Paddington and Maidenhead would be speedily converted. Despite all that had happened, despite the tremendous weight of opinion that was piling up Russell stood absolutely firm: solid in his faith in Brunel, and in the rightness of the original decision to have the broad gauge. At first he was quite alone, and on that critical evening it is no exaggeration to say that Brunel's future depended upon him, and him alone. Gradually however, as the arguments progressed, first Gibbs and then Saunders began to rally, and then all four men went to Duke Street to see Brunel. If any of them had any lingering doubts as to the result of calling in another engineer they were quickly dispelled.

Brunel was most restrained. He had no vanity of any kind, but he expressed to his visitors his view that Wood's report was based upon many fallacies, and Gibbs in particular was deeply impressed with the obvious sincerity of Brunel's confidence in his precepts, and the rightness of the engineering practice the Board had adopted on his recommendation. Calmly and dispassionately he told them he was quite prepared to accept defeat, and it was this very calmness and confidence when everything around him seemed to be falling in ruins that strengthened Russell's determination, and encouraged Gibbs and Saunders to back him up. The full Board met on December 27th, and it was then clear that a large majority of the Board's members favoured concession, with the inevitable loss of Brunel's services. No definite decision was taken, however, and the matter was left to be referred to a Special General Meeting of the Company, to be held on January 9th, 1839, by which time printed copies of the reports of Hawkshaw and Wood, and of Brunel's reply would be in the hands of every shareholder.

One of the points brought out strongly in Wood's report was the very poor performances of the best engine on the line, the *North Star*. Wood had commissioned that supreme purveyor of scientific bunkum, Dr Dionysius Lardner, to carry out some load-hauling and speed trials, and when he found the *North Star* would haul no more than 16 tons at 40 m.p.h. Lardner attributed this to the excessive air-resistance of the wide locomotive and damned the broad gauge on this account. Brunel and Gooch worked night and day on the *North Star*. They found it was not air-resistance but back pressure that was holding her back. An increase in the diameter of the blast-pipe orifice, and an adjustment to bring the orifice exactly concentric with the chimney worked wonders. On December 29th, 1838, a

special test run was made with the directors, from **Paddington to
Maidenhead**, hauling a load of 43 tons. The average speed from
start to stop was 38 m.p.h. and the maximum 45; moreover the
consumption of coke was *one third* of that used when Dr Lardner's
tests were made in the previous September. How much of this vast
improvement was due to Brunel and how much to Gooch we are not
to know, but the results completely changed the attitude of the Board,
and the majority of the directors went to the meeting of January 9th,
with renewed confidence in the broad gauge and in their engineer.
They triumphed, and from that moment the broad gauge went
forward with renewed vigour and enthusiasm.

In securing this result Gooch's work on the *North Star* undoubtedly
played an important part. Brunel was indeed fortunate in this
critical time in his career in the men who supported and helped him,
and it was under the guidance, principally, of four men that the
Great Western went forward from its shaky and uncertain start to
the brilliant high noon of the broad gauge. Before the end of the year
1839 Russell had become Chairman, and with three such men as
Saunders, Brunel, and Gooch in the leading executive posts the
Company and its associates farther west went ahead at such a pace
that those who had scorned and derided now grew thoroughly
alarmed. The Great Western, from being torn and divided within
itself had to face the opposition of every other railway in the land, in
the Battle of the Gauges.

II

Bristol and the Exeter Road

ONCE the critical days of January 1839 were passed, and the Thames was successfully bridged at Maidenhead construction of the rest of the line went rapidly ahead. It was not all as Brunel had originally planned. There were to have been two major tunnels, one on either side of Reading, the first through the high ground near the village of Sonning. The more conciliatory attitude of one of the neighbouring landowners made possible a diversion slightly to the south through the deep cutting so beloved of photographers in our own times. West of Reading, Brunel had planned to go in a direct line for Pangbourne, entering another long tunnel near the present site of Tilehurst station and burrowing under Purley Park. Here, the diversion actually made round the northern flank of the hills has given us one of the prettiest stretches on the London–Bristol main line.

The more spectacular of the scenic beauties of this original main line begin at the western end of Box Tunnel, and it is here also that the more elaborate architectural work authorized by the Bristol Committee is in evidence. The beautiful skew bridge at Bath has long since been replaced, but the succession of tunnels between Bath and Bristol have as fine and diverse a collection of portals as one could wish for. The last one, immediately to the west of St. Anne's Park station was opened out into a vertically walled rock cutting in 1887, when the need arose to enlarge the approach to the Bristol east goods depot. So we have come, somewhat rapidly, to Bristol, which, despite all the drive and enthusiasm that was put into affairs at the other end of the line, was in most ways the spiritual home of the broad gauge. At the very start of things Brunel was a protégé of the Bristol Committee, and following the critical decision of January 1839 it was from Bristol that the first important extension of the broad gauge system sprang.

The Bristol and Exeter Railway was an entirely independent enterprise. Like the Great Western itself it was sponsored in the first place by a group of Bristol merchants, and it is remarkable that not one of the sixteen original directors was a director of the Great Western. Of that sixteen no fewer than twelve were Bristolians. Of the remaining four one hailed from Bridgwater, one from Taunton, and two from Exeter. The Bill had an easy passage through Parliament, and it became law on May 19th, 1836; but having got thus far the Company got into serious trouble before a mile of permanent way had been laid. The earliest contracts for construction of the line progressed very slowly; the general financial depression of the time seemed to put a damper upon all the activities of the company; meantime the directors endeavoured to raise the spirits of their already despondent shareholders by promises of eventual rewards that cannot be described as other than specious. The matter of the gauge had not been settled. Although Brunel was engineer, and the route had been laid out to take the broad gauge, the directors waited for the outcome of the controversy on the Great Western before coming to a decision. Once Brunel's policy had been finally approved, by the special meeting in 1839, the Bristol and Exeter Board was ready enough to adopt the broad gauge.

In view of the obvious advantages to be derived from the closest possible link-up between the two railways at Bristol it is astonishing how little thought seems to have been given at first to the interchange facilities. Indeed, the Bristol and Exeter people were at one time proposing to make their terminus at Pylle Hill, on the south side of the river Avon. Fortunately, however, the provisions of the original Act were eventually carried through by making a junction with the Great Western; but there never seems to have been any suggestion of

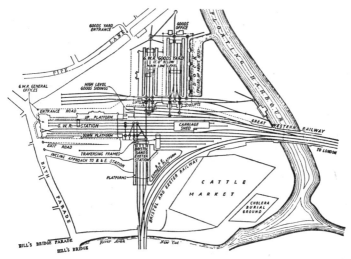

Bristol stations, about 1850.

[*Courtesy* The Railway Gazette

a joint station, and the accompanying plan shows how the Great Western and the Bristol and Exeter stations were distinct and at right angles to each other. The sharply curved connecting spur on the eastern side included the so-called 'Bristol and Exeter Express Platform' – one platform face for all the through traffic, down and up alike. The handsome group of buildings housing the Bristol and Exeter general offices are still in existence today, and form the Bristol Divisional offices.

The Great Western terminus at Temple Meads was a very handsome building. Its fine frontage on to the street exists today, but the interior stretching far into the dark recesses beyond the Midland departure platform is scarcely known to the ordinary traveller. In broad gauge days there were five tracks abreast between the two long platforms, and the entire station was covered in by a magnificent hammer-beam roof of 72 ft span. The original 'Temple Meads' was an example of Brunel at his finest, and the Great Western station presented an astonishing contrast to the makeshift of a 'shack' that was euphemistically called the Bristol and Exeter 'station'. The Bristolians of the day called it the 'cow-shed'! This latter was not opened until 1845. Until then the B & E trains had to run round the connecting spur to Harbour Bridge Junction and then set back into the Great Western station. The B & E Express platform, for the through London–Exeter expresses, was also brought into use in 1845. The line had been opened as far as Bridgwater in June 1841; Taunton was reached just over a year later, and the opening throughout to Exeter took place in May 1844.

The Company had been continually in financial troubles, and grandiosely though the original prospects had been described, the management appeared to be in no state to run a railway as the time for opening grew nearer. A proposal was then made that the line should be leased to the Great Western, and after a period of negotiation this was agreed to by both parties in the summer of 1840. Thus the B. & E. was worked by the Great Western from the outset. Although it was a natural extension of the G.W.R. it was, as we have seen already, far from an integral part of a master plan for development of the broad gauge system. Not long ago a modern critic of Brunel, not knowing the complicated history of railways in the West of England, wrote scathingly of Brunel's choice of a route from London to Exeter, pointing out that the G.W.R. had to spend vast sums in after years setting up what should all the time have been the 'obvious' route. How wise can one become, years after the event, and in complete ignorance of the circumstances existing at the time! It might have caused this particular critic to weigh his words more carefully had someone told him that the Great Western were proposing an 'Exeter Direct' line as early as 1845. To appreciate how this splendid project never came to fruition one must take a look at the railway map of south-west England in the previous year.

The Battle of the Gauges was then working up to full blast, with the Great Western heavily engaged on both flanks. To the south action fluctuated between skirmish and pitched battle with the London and South Western; to the north the Great Western was up against the combined forces of the London and Birmingham and the Grand Junction. At that time, as will be seen from the map, the South Western was then a line of very limited extent, not stretching any further west of the original London and Southampton Railway, other than a branch from Bishopstoke – now Eastleigh – to Salisbury. West of Southampton a new line had been independently promoted, the Southampton and Dorchester Railway, and its management tried to come to terms with the South Western. The latter, hoping by delaying tactics to secure more advantageous terms for a lease, lost their opportunity. Saunders, seeing a magnificent opportunity for heading off the advance of the narrow gauge west of Southampton, secured a lease of the line, and although at the time it was not connected in any way with the Great Western there was just a prospect of a future junction with a line the Bristol and Exeter was then planning from Taunton to Yeovil, Dorchester and Weymouth. This, however, is taking things a little out of strict chronological order. The lease of the Southampton and Dorchester line was obtained in 1845, and we must go back a twelvemonth to trace the events that sparked off more overt rivalry.

Charles Russell, staunch advocate though he was of the broad gauge, was shrewd and far-seeing enough to realize that the Great Western must reap advantages from the interchange of traffic with other companies, and when the South Western began to show interest in promoting a branch line from Basingstoke to serve the town of Newbury, with a future extension to Swindon, Russell suggested a joint line connecting the South Western, at Basingstoke, with the G.W.R. near Reading, with a branch, also under joint ownership, to Newbury. This little system of lines, he proposed, should be laid with mixed gauge. This proposition was made in a letter from Russell to William Chaplin, the L.S.W.R. Chairman, in the autumn of 1844, and it was turned down flat. Both companies thereafter went their own way, and the Parliamentary session of 1845 saw some interesting projects put forward, all of which had some important bearing upon the future direct line to the West of England. The Great Western promoted the so-called Berks and Hants Railway, and a line from Corsham to Salisbury, while the Bristol and Exeter put forward the proposal of a branch from Taunton to Yeovil and Weymouth.

The 'Berks and Hants' was really no more than two branch lines from Reading, one running to Newbury and the other to Basingstoke; but the Corsham–Salisbury line had the makings of a cross-country trunk route, linking up with the South Western at Salisbury and thus providing connection to Southampton, Portsmouth, and the Isle of Wight. It is interesting to see that Trowbridge and Warminster were the only places of any size on this proposed line; as with the Great Western main line from London to Bristol, on which Walling-ford, Wantage, and Faringdon were eventually served by short branches, so the Corsham–Salisbury line project included branches to Devizes, Bradford-on-Avon, and Frome. At this time the 'Railway Mania' was developing, and Parliament, with the idea of saving itself the trouble of having to deal with a plethora of wild-cat and impracticable schemes instructed the Board of Trade to do some preliminary vetting. A committee of five was set up, and although the fact of any scheme being turned down by this committee did not preclude its being presented to Parliament in the form of a Bill, any scheme obviously had a far better chance if it had their approval and backing.

The committee was presided over by Lord Dalhousie, who had recently succeeded Gladstone as President of the Board of Trade; General Pasley, the Inspector-General of Railways; Capt. O'Brien, G. R. Porter, and Samuel Laing. Before the broad gauge schemes were submitted to the 'Five Kings', as the committee was sometimes called, some modifications were necessary because the Bristol and Exeter proved unwilling to carry their proposed branch beyond Yeovil. The Great Western felt it was essential to get to Weymouth to complete the sealing off of the West of England against any narrow gauge advance, and so the Corsham and Salisbury project was greatly enlarged, to extend the Frome 'branch' southwards to Yeovil and Weymouth. This project thereafter became known as the 'Wilts, Somerset and Weymouth Railway'. Various projects were put forward by the South Western, but compared to the carefully-planned strategy of the Great Western they were disjointed and ill-conceived, and it was not surprising that the 'Five Kings' turned them all down, while giving approval to the two major Great Western schemes.

From this resounding success the G.W.R. went on to secure what appeared at the time to be a major diplomatic triumph. In return for the lease of the Southampton and Dorchester, the South Western agreed not to promote any competing lines west of Dorchester, or Salisbury, while the Great Western for their part pledged themselves not to promote any competitive lines from their proposed railhead at Basingstoke. Thus at the cost of surrendering what might well have been an awkward appendage the Great Western had secured, by solemn agreement, the sole right – so far as the South Western was concerned – to develop the railway system west of Salisbury and Dorchester. The South Western thereupon raised no opposition to the broad gauge Bills presented to Parliament in the 1845 session, and in consequence the 'Berks and Hants', the 'Wilts, Somerset and Weymouth', and the B. & E. branch from Taunton to Yeovil had easy passages through Parliament. Thus, as early as 1845, were authorized three sections of what was eventually to become the direct route to Exeter and the West. Today the main line up the Kennet valley is still known as the Berks and Hants line, and many people hearing the name must have wondered where the 'Hants' came in, seeing that it never enters Hampshire and eventually leads into Wiltshire. The 'Hants' refers of course to the Basingstoke branch, which was an important feature of the original 'Berks and Hants' project.

At the time of incorporation, however, it was the Wilts, Somerset and Weymouth, rather than the Berks and Hants, that provided the springboard for further activities, and further trouble! When the Bill for the former railway was under examination by the House of Lords Committee, a pledge was exacted from the promoters that the extension of the line to Weymouth should not be regarded as a bar to the eventual construction of a direct line from London to Falmouth. The making of such a pledge did not appear to the Great Western to conflict in any way with the agreement they had made with the South Western in the January of that year, and so they gave it to the Lords' Committee readily enough. Moreover the Great Western needed no prompting as to the next action they should take. The direct line to the west, urged by the House of Lords, should obviously be part of their own broad gauge system, and Brunel was instructed to prepare plans forthwith to present to Parliament in the very next session.

While the main object of the direct line was to by-pass Bath and Bristol, by using part of the Wilts, Somerset and Weymouth, it was proposed to cut westwards from Yeovil through country hitherto untouched by railways, and passing through Crewkerne and Honiton. At the outset it was realized that such a project would completely short-circuit the Bristol and Exeter Railway, so far as through traffic from London to the west was concerned. The Great Western therefore offered to purchase the line outright. The B. & E. Board agreed, but their shareholders turned it down by a large majority. Thus in striving to redeem their pledge to the Lords' Committee the Great Western had to go on without the collaboration of the B. & E., and the route put forward by Brunel was almost exactly that of the present main line, at any rate as far as Castle Cary. It involved an extension of the 'Berks and Hants' line from Hungerford to Westbury, thence over the Wilts and Somerset, to Yeovil, and thence by Crewkerne, Axminster, Honiton and Stoke Canon to Exeter.

Once this scheme was made public the fat was fairly in the fire. Although the agreement of January 1845 specifically mentioned Basingstoke the South Western now claimed that an extension from *any part* of the Berks and Hants Railway was a breach of the agreement, and that they considered themselves free to promote a direct line from Salisbury to Exeter. Indignant protests followed. Russell accused Chaplin of 'an unexampled breach of faith', and in this stormy atmosphere the Bills for the 'Berks and Hants Extension', and the 'Exeter Great Western' – as the line from Yeovil to Exeter went forward. In the Parliamentary campaign the G.W.R. had to face not only the South Western, but the implacable opposition of the Bristol and Exeter, by the wish of the shareholders and against the wishes of the Board. In the circumstances it was not surprising that the Bills were rejected. In 1847 the Great Western tried again, but with a slightly modified route at the Exeter end. This time, however, the Bristol and Exeter not only continued its opposition, but put up a line of its own from Durston to Castle Cary. This, in conjunction with the Berks and Hants Extension, would provide an even shorter route from London to Exeter than that by the Exeter Great Western. At that time the idea of any railway having a monopoly of any district was becoming repellent to Parliament, and so the most serious consideration was also given to a westward extension of the South Western from Salisbury.

After a Parliamentary struggle of characteristic complexity and bitterness the Commons authorized the Berks and Hants Extension, and the B. & E. branch from Durston to Castle Cary, at the same time authorizing two narrow gauge projects which would give the South Western a clear and independent run to Exeter. Both groups

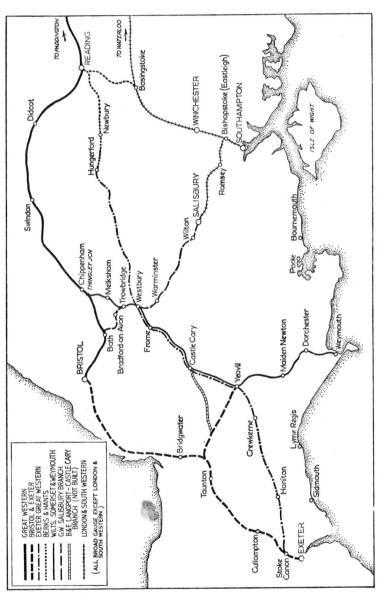

Reading and points west at the time of the Gauge War: lines actually built and proposed.

of Bills passed through the Commons too late in the 1847 session to be
referred to the House of Lords, and so it was not until 1848 that the
Acts authorizing either the broad or the narrow gauge projects
received the Royal Assent. So far as the Great Western was concerned,
however, here, in 1848, was authorized the present West of England
main line, via Savernake, Westbury, Castle Cary and Taunton. All
efforts were nevertheless without avail, for in 1848 the aftermath of
the disastrous period of the Mania made it virtually impossible to
raise funds for any new railway projects, and the Parliamentary
powers obtained at such cost on both sides were allowed to lapse.
So, for another 58 years, the West of England expresses of the Great
Western continued to run through Bristol; but after what I have
written it will be realized that this was not for any want of trying on
the part of the management, nor from any shortsightedness, or
pigheadedness on the part of Brunel!

So we return to the Bristol and Exeter, a splendid road in itself,
and one over which some of the greatest speed records in Great
Western history have been made. Although not one of the most
picturesque of routes there is a fascination about those long, straight
level stretches over the Somersetshire marshlands, so prone to
hindrance in running from adverse winds, when the additional air
resistance seemed to catch the great exposed driving wheels of
Gooch's eight-foot singles, just as boisterous conditions along the
North Wales coast used to impede the progress of Ramsbottom's
7 ft 6 in. singles of the 'Lady of the Lake' class, on the Irish Mails.
There was no great scope for Brunel's genius as a civil engineer to be
manifested, and while he built a shallow arch bridge of extreme
grace over the deepest part of the Uphill cutting a similar style of
bridge carrying the line across the River Parrett, near Bridgwater,
landed him in serious trouble.

Somerset Bridge, as it was called, had a single span of 100 ft with a
rise of only 12 ft – nearly twice as flat, if one may use the expression,
as the brick arch bridge over the Thames at Maidenhead which had
come in for so much criticism. At Bridgwater the foundations
shifted, and although the arch suffered no damage Brunel would not
remove the centering timbers. The obstruction thus caused led to
public protest, which at first Brunel was inclined to ignore. A careful
watch was kept on the foundations in the hope that movement had
ceased. Unfortunately, however, settlement continued, and Brunel
displayed his ingenuity by substituting a timber arch bridge resting
on the same foundations.

At Taunton the station was built in the same style as those at

Reading and Slough with the up and down platforms on the same side. The difference at Taunton was that there were no through lines passing clear of the platforms. Coming in from the west the down station was reached first, and then the up and down lines crossed, scissors wise, so as to bring the up line across to the up station. Then, at the east end the two through lines re-crossed so as to resume the ordinary left-hand running. It was a most awkward arrangement, though it had the point of keeping all passenger business on one side of the line. The second Taunton station, though a great improvement on the original, developed into a bottleneck in later years, and at times of heavy passenger traffic it was quite usual for important non-stopping expresses to be taken over the sharply-curved goods lines while the main line was occupied by another train standing in the station. I have been round the goods lines on no less important a train than the old 3.30 p.m. from Paddington, booked non-stop to Exeter in three hours. It was not until the nineteen-thirties that Taunton got a station worthy of its importance and its traffic.

Beyond Taunton lay the ridge of the Blackdown Hills, and here Brunel could not avoid heavy gradients. White Ball Hill today, marking the county boundary between Somerset and Devon, is a point well known to motorists on account of the long gradients approaching from either side, and although Brunel took the B. & E. through the hill at a maximum depth of 199 ft below the surface of the ground the approach from the Somerset side was very severe. The really hard climbing begins at Wellington station, whence the ascent is at 1 in 90 to the crossing of the Exeter road, at Beam Bridge. This point formed a temporary terminus on the line, from May 1st, 1843, while work was still in progress at Whiteball Tunnel. From Beam Bridge to the tunnel entrance the line makes a gentle zig-zag course slightly to ease the gradients, which are nevertheless as steep as 1 in 85–81, but in the tunnel itself the inclination eases to 1 in 128. This is a fortunate circumstance, as it permits of some easing of the engine on the last stage of the climb, and lessens the chance of slipping in the tunnel.

The actual boring of the tunnel was not an easy job. Before the contracts were let Brunel himself sank one shaft to the full depth of the tunnel so that contractors tendering for the work should know something of what they were in for. General Pasley, who inspected the tunnel for the Board of Trade described it thus: 'The soil was unfavourable, consisting partly of marl and partly of sand, varying from quicksand to sandstone, and partly of gravel and hard conglomerate, so that it was necessary to line it with brickwork throughout its whole extent . . . .' The tunnel, which is 1092 yds long, was finished in February 1844 and the line was opened throughout to Exeter in May of the same year. A large party from London travelled down to Exeter to celebrate the opening, and Gooch drove the special train himself, both ways. He tells the story in his diary thus:

'We had a special train with a large party from London to go down to the opening. A great dinner was given in the Goods Shed at Exeter Station. I worked the train with the *Actaeon* engine, one of our 7 feet class, with six carriages. We left London at 7.30 a.m. and arrived at Exeter at 12.30, having had some detention over the hour fixed. On the return journey we left Exeter at 5.20 p.m. and stopped at Paddington platform at 10. Sir Thomas Acland who was with us, went at once to the House of Commons, and by 10.30 got up and told the House he had been in Exeter at 5.20. It was a very hard day's work for me, as, apart from driving the engine a distance of 387 miles, I had to be out early in the morning to see that all was right for our trip, and while at Exeter was busy with matters connected with the opening, so that my only chance of sitting down was for the hour we were at dinner. Next day my back ached so that I could hardly walk. Mr Brunel wrote me a very handsome letter, thanking me for what I had done, and all were very much pleased.'

The overall time of 4 hr 40 min. on the return journey, with its average speed of 41½ m.p.h. was a wonderful piece of running for that period, and once the line had thoroughly settled down 5 hr became the standard schedule for the down and up mail trains from March 1845 onwards. This was further quickened to 4 hr 25 min. from January 1846. Thereafter the speed of the Exeter expresses varied considerably with the financial state of the G.W.R., with the extent of South Western competition, and with the degree of enterprise displayed with successive managements. At first they were the wonder of the whole country, and a trump card in the hands of those who backed the broad gauge. Such fast schedules were possible only through the Great Western having taken delivery of Gooch's new express locomotives of the 'Firefly' class. These handsome 7 ft 2-2-2 singles were excellent engines in every way. The detailed specification drawn up and supplied to the various manufacturers show a remarkable insight into the finer points of locomotive design on Gooch's part, and were as remarkable as coming from a young man of 24, as they contrasted with the airy-fairy way Brunel had dealt with the supplies of the earlier engines. No fewer than 62 of these locomotives were built for the G.W.R. in 1840–2, though the details of the design and of subsequent broad gauge engines is dealt with more fully in a later chapter.

Despite the glamour attached to the London and Exeter expresses, the proprietors of the B. & E., having shown their independence in vetoing the proposals of their own directors in 1845, and in blocking the project of the Exeter direct line from Yeovil, felt that they would like to be free of the Great Western lease, and in anticipation of its termination orders were placed for locomotives and rolling stock in the summer of 1847. Apart from the through London expresses the B. & E. services had not been particularly distinguished, and the Weston-super-Mare branch train, of three coaches, was hauled by a team of three horses in tandem, each ridden by a boy!

When the Bristol and Exeter went into open opposition to the Great Western extension schemes of 1845–6, Brunel's position as Engineer to the Company became invidious, and in September 1846 he resigned. He was succeeded by Charles Hutton Gregory, formerly engineer of the London and Croydon Railway. There, in 1841, he had installed at New Cross the first semaphore ever to be used in railway signalling, and at Bricklayers Arms Junction, in 1843, he had built what was, in effect, the father of all signal boxes in which the levers for points and signal operation were grouped together in one frame. It so happened that Brunel's resignation from the B. & E. almost exactly coincided with the absorption of the London and Croydon Railway by the Brighton. Gregory certainly walked into a sea of engineering troubles down in the West Country, where the construction and maintenance of the permanent way was not up to the standards of the Great Western itself.

The longitudinals had in many cases not been properly creosoted; the ballast was of inferior material, and badly packed, and there were places where liquid mud was splashed out by the passage of a train. The line was laid with Brunel's bridge rails, and one of Gregory's first acts was to relay some lengths of line with Vignoles flat-bottomed rail. The line as a whole was not in a happy state when the Great Western lease expired in May 1849, and Gregory complained bitterly of the condition in which things were handed back to the owners. His successor, J. J. MacDonnell, attempted to improve the permanent way by dispensing with timbers under Brunel's bridge rails and substituting specially shaped iron plates. This was disliked as much by the drivers for its rough and dangerous riding, as by the plate-layers, who had the greatest difficulty in maintaining a good 'top' and line with it. Some of it nevertheless remained on the main line near Brent Knoll, and between Durston and Taunton until after the line had been fully absorbed by the Great Western in 1876.

III

The Battle of the Gauges

In the previous chapter, in relating how all attempts to provide a direct Great Western line from London to Exeter were thwarted, it was made evident how deep was the antagonism between those who favoured the broad and the narrow gauge. It includes at least one case of a company to whom the Great Western could have looked confidently for support, siding with the enemy and substantially aiding in the defeat of an all-important broad gauge project. The Battle of the Gauges was full of episodes like that. In its constant change of front and shift of tactics it could in some ways be likened to the Wars of the Roses, some four centuries earlier, in which some of the leading protagonists changed sides to suit the jealousies and private feuds of the hour, and in which one-time foes sometimes came surprisingly to the aid of a harassed army.

In the Battle of the Gauges there was never a hint of any defections within the Great Western itself. The harder they were pressed, the more disheartening the news of the day, the closer and more solidly Russell, Saunders, Brunel and Gooch stood together. And by that time the men of the Great Western, right down to the humblest members of the rank and file, were growing to possess a sense of pride in their job and in their railway, and a feeling that in the broad gauge they had that substantial 'extra' that the others had not got. As in the West, so in the Midlands it was among the associates of the Great Western that the doubting Thomases were to be found. Even without the waverers in their midst, however, the most staunch of broad gauge supporters, had they looked many years ahead, must have realized that the mileage of the narrow gauge was already too great for the Great Western to prevail.

Brunel has been stigmatized as pig-headed, and blind in his advocacy of the broad gauge. One feels, however, that he believed in all sincerity that all other railways would change to his gauge once they saw the system in action, and once the public had experienced and enjoyed the pleasure of travelling so smoothly and swiftly in carriages that were so much wider and more spacious than those running elsewhere. By the time the Battle of the Gauges was joined, however, it was becoming crystal clear to everyone that the Great Western was standing alone. Every railway manager, every railway engineer other than those closely associated with the G.W.R. was implacably opposed to it. It is indeed a measure of Russell's force of character and steadfastness that he held so firmly on to his chosen course, and carried the Great Western – Board, shareholders and staff alike – solidly with him. To a man of his clarity of mind it must have been obvious that they would have to yield eventually to the inexorable ring of adverse pressure surrounding them. Only the workings of a democratic society prevented the broad gauge from being killed stone dead in 1846, by the Gauge Act of that year.

The events that led to the setting up of a Royal Commission to enquire into the question of railway gauges make interesting and at times diverting reading. The first direct clash between broad and narrow gauge interests had taken place in 1844 over what eventually became the West of England main line of the Midland, between Bristol and Birmingham. Two separate companies were involved, the Bristol and Gloucester, and the Birmingham and Gloucester, both originally quite independent of each other, and both originally narrow gauge. In 1843 the Great Western purchased the Cheltenham and Great Western Union Railway which cut through the Cotswolds from Swindon, and it would seem that the Bristol and Gloucester people felt they must change to broad gauge seeing that they would be in direct connection with the Great Western at both ends of their line. So they decided to change to the broad gauge, and with their line still unfinished they were able to arrange with the Great Western to use Temple Meads station as their Bristol terminus. This was a great triumph for Paddington, but it soon appeared that the triumph might be a hollow one if it were not followed up by an advance farther north.

The natural flow of traffic at Gloucester was from Birmingham to Bristol, and the decision to change the southern end of the line led to the break of gauge. Brunel made light of the difficulties, but from the very commencement of traffic working in September 1844 the awkwardness and inconvenience of having to tranship every item from one truck to another at Gloucester became obvious. While the Bristol and Gloucester had decided to change over to the broad gauge there had been, up to that time, no suggestion of their incorporation into the Great Western – in fact negotiations with a view to the G.W.R. working the line had broken down, and the job was put out to contract. As their traffic began to develop this company realized that their interests tended to lie more closely with those of the Birmingham and Gloucester, rather than with the Great Western, and an agreement to amalgamate was made between the two companies in January 1845. This was clearly the moment for the Great Western to advance the broad gauge into Birmingham; and the moment the terms of amalgamation were announced Paddington opened negotiations, not only regarding the gauge, but with a view to absorbing the combined Bristol and Gloucester and Birmingham and Gloucester Railways.

There is no doubt Saunders tried to drive a hard bargain, offering £60 of Great Western stock for each £100 of Birmingham and Gloucester. At the prices of the day this did not represent a benefit to the Birmingham and Gloucester shareholders, as the cash values were then £123 against £109. But the Birmingham directors felt they should have had a better offer, and stood out for £65 worth of G.W.R. stock. The first meeting, in Bristol, was adjourned to give Saunders time to consult his Board. Negotiations were to be resumed three days later in London, and in view of the very high stakes for which the Great Western were playing one feels that some attempt to meet the demands of the two West Midland companies would have been wise. The Birmingham and Gloucester constituted a dangerous spearhead of the narrow gauge, and to secure its conversion would have to reverse the strategic position, and point a broad gauge piston into one of the greatest bastions of the narrow gauge – Birmingham.

The Great Western were out of luck in that January! The two Birmingham and Gloucester directors, travelling to London for the resumed meeting with Saunders, happened quite by chance to have as fellow traveller John Ellis, the Deputy Chairman of the Midland Railway. Naturally railways were discussed, and the B. & G. men mentioned the negotiations then in progress with the Great Western, though no details of terms or such like were revealed. Ellis at once realized the danger, not so much from the viewpoint of railway ownership, but that the break of gauge might be shifted to Birmingham, and thus to the very portals of the Midland Railway. The latter company, formed by amalgamation of the North Midland, the Midland Counties, and the Birmingham and Derby was then not a year old. Ellis told the Birmingham and Gloucester men that if they did not get satisfaction from Saunders he would be prepared to negotiate with them. The Great Western stood firm on their previous offer, not advancing in the slightest to meet the combined desires of the Birmingham and Gloucester and the Bristol and Gloucester. With their chance meeting with Ellis freshly in mind the B. & G.

negotiators stood equally firm. Next day they saw **Ellis. He** substantially improved upon the Great Western terms, and within a fortnight agreement had been reached bringing the whole line between Birmingham and Bristol under Midland control.

At the same time as they let this priceless opportunity slip the Great Western had two major broad gauge projects in active preparation. In these days, when travel by cross-country routes can be purgatorial both in slowness and inconvenience it is interesting to note the emphasis placed in pioneer railway days upon the importance of cross-country links. The Great Western already had a southern connection in prospect, through the Berks and Hants project, and a northern extension from Oxford was a thoroughly logical counterpart. The objective of that northern extension, moreover, could not have been more obvious, for a straight line drawn across the map due north from Oxford brings one, in no more than 42 miles, to Rugby. In 1844–5 Rugby was of immense railway importance as the starting point of the only chain of railways leading to Yorkshire and the North. The West Coast route to Scotland was uncompleted, the Great Northern was not even authorized; the Midland 'group', under the Chairmanship of George Hudson, was pre-eminent.

The Oxford and Rugby line was promoted by the Great Western, and at much the same time the company was approached by various trading and manufacturing interests in the West Midlands to build a line from Wolverhampton through Stourbridge, Kidderminster, and Worcester to join the Great Western at Oxford. I need not go into the many vicissitudes these two important schemes passed through before they were presented to Parliament. Naturally they were opposed by all the strength the Midland and the London and Birmingham Railways could muster, and to add to Great Western anxieties in that disheartening month of January 1845, the 'Five Kings' issued a report wholeheartedly in opposition to *any* extension of the broad gauge north of Oxford. They dwelt upon the evils of the break of gauge, and had obviously been unfavourably impressed by what they saw at Gloucester. Not until many years later was it revealed that things had been specially staged for their benefit by the protagonists of the narrow gauge, and that trains that had already been loaded and were ready to leave were unloaded and reloaded amid the scenes of the wildest and most artificial confusion.

When the time came Saunders and Brunel were able to blow the report of the 'Five Kings' sky high, for when they referred to the laying of an additional rail to provide mixed gauge as 'a partial and imperfect palliative of a great evil', they had based most of their objections on the idea that both broad and narrow gauge vehicles might be marshalled *into the same train*. It speaks volumes for the strength and determination of the Great Western management that they decided to go ahead with both the Oxford and Rugby, and the Oxford, Worcester and Wolverhampton projects in defiance of the report of the 'Five Kings'. In the Committee stage in the House of Commons it was indeed a battle royal. The witnesses called included most of the leading railway personalities of the day: Robert Stephenson, Nicholas Wood, John Hawkshaw, William Cubitt, Mark Huish, Saunders, J. E. McConnell, Edward Bury, Daniel Gooch, George Hudson, John Ellis, Charles Russell, and, of course, Brunel.

Astonishing though it may seem, in view of the 'Five Kings' report and of the weight of evidence and opinion against it, the Report of the House of Commons Committee was *in favour* of both Great Western projects. All was not lost yet, so far as the narrow gauge was concerned, and the Midland and the London and Birmingham did everything they knew to beat up opposition to the Committee's report. It was then that the intricacies and intrigues of inter-railway politics came formidably to the aid of the Great Western. Mark Huish, who was then Secretary of the Grand Junction, was having a lot of trouble with his principal associate, the London and Birmingham Railway; and although the object was concealed in the most courtly and diplomatic language he sought to bring the London and Birmingham to heel by solid and unspoken support of the Great Western extension lines to the north. In a notable circular to the Grand Junction shareholders dated June 11th, 1845, he saw 'no inconvenience whatever to arise from the introduction of the Broad Gauge among the Narrow Gauge lines . . . .', and instead stressed the evils that would result from prohibiting the advance of the broad gauge, and allowing the narrow gauge schemes of the London and Birmingham to establish an absolute monopoly in the West Midlands. 'Such extensive powers', he argues, 'would be in the highest degree dangerous to the public, and inconsistent with the fair interests of the Grand Junction Company.' Huish even went so far as to suggest that the Grand Junction might lay down mixed gauges on their main lines from Birmingham to Crewe and Liverpool to facilitate interchange with the Great Western!

Knowing Huish one can be fairly sure all this was merely a move in a game of power politics designed to coerce the London and Birmingham, and not in any way a sincere attempt to further the cause of the broad gauge. Whatever its ultimate object, Huish's circular to the Grand Junction shareholders swung opinion round in complete favour of the two Great Western Bills, and although the opposition was very ably led by Richard Cobden, the arch-priest of Free Trade, both Bills passed through all the stages in both Houses of Parliament, and received the Royal Assent in August 1845. It was a great triumph for the broad gauge, while in Huish's own words uttered eight years later: 'The effect of the circular was undoubtedly to bring about an immediate arrangement between the London and Birmingham and the Grand Junction, and to obtain for the Grand Junction a large sum of money as the price of it.' It is a strange thing to realize that the same document led, on the one hand, to the creation of the L.N.W.R., and on the other to the death warrant of the broad gauge.

The last remark may sound a little odd, as the broad gauge had so recently triumphed despite the report of the 'Five Kings'. The narrow gauge protagonists had, however, found in Richard Cobden a most eloquent Parliamentary spokesman, and following the success of both Great Western Bills in the House of Commons he pleaded for a Royal Commission into the subject of railway gauges; and even before the two Great Western Bills had passed through the House of Lords, the Commission was set up on July 9th, 1845. The members of the Commission were Sir Frederic Smith, formerly Inspector of Railways, George Airy, the Astronomer Royal, and Peter Barlow, Professor of Mathematics in the Royal Military Academy at Woolwich. The Commissioners were not long in getting to work. Robert Stephenson was the first witness to be called, and then there followed Locke, McConnell, Vignoles, J. U. Rastrick, Col. Landmann of the Greenwich Railway, Bruyeres, Bury, both William and Benjamin Cubitt, Capt. Laws of the Manchester and Leeds Railway, Braithwaite of the Eastern Counties, Capt. O'Brien, Buckton of the Brighton, T. C. Mills, Goods Manager of the London and Birmingham, and John Gray, locomotive superintendent of the Brighton. At this stage, having had a strong unanimity of narrow gauge views in no more than eleven days' hearing, the Commission suspended operations, and took a six weeks holiday.

The cross-examination of the more important witnesses such as Robert Stephenson and Locke occupied a whole day, and several of them were recalled afterwards. The Commissioners questioned them on every facet of their professional careers, so that the evidence of men like Stephenson, McConnell, and the Cubitts reads like a complete symposium of their life's work up to that time. Very few of the narrow gauge protagonists argued against the broad gauge on technical grounds at all; they argued against a lack of uniformity in gauge, and as the broad gauge was very much in the minority they argued for it to be constrained from any further advances. Locke, for example, urged that the Oxford and Rugby should be narrow gauge, and that the mixed gauge should be laid in from Oxford to the south so that traffic from the Midland line to Southampton should not be subject to a break of gauge. Like several other leading witnesses he was asked what he would do about the existing broad gauge lines, but on this Locke refused to be drawn, save for giving some rather guarded views about the relative cost of converting the whole of the Great Western to narrow gauge, as against laying in the mixed gauge.

Reading carefully through much of the evidence and the type of question put to the various witnesses, one gains the impression that the Commissioners at first regarded their task as the problem of what to do about the Great Western. There were times when they endeavoured to draw witnesses away from the accomplished fact of the two gauges in general use, and to try and find out what they, as engineers, would have chosen if they had been free to start all over again. Bury as a locomotive manufacturer was non-committal, but hinted at something intermediate; William Cubitt on the other hand went so far as to suggest that *all* existing railways should be changed to 6 ft before it was too late. Asked, in view of this, why he had not made the South Eastern of this gauge he replied that he was committed by the gauges of the railways with which they connected in London. During their holiday the Commissioners must have had many an occasion to reflect upon what these distinguished engineers and railway managers had told them, and on resuming they were immediately confronted with a mass of evidence of a very different kind.

On October 17th, 1845, Daniel Gooch was examined. It is remarkable in a way that he should have been the first of the Great Western witnesses. Not only did he give a most lucid exposition of the technical case for the broad gauge, but he included some extremely interesting details of Great Western operating. These show that in speed, and in general density of traffic the Great Western was ahead of all its rivals, thus:

Railway	Total annual loco. miles	Average weight of trains tons		Average speed of passenger trains
		passenger	goods	
London & Birmingham . .	1,414,941	42·4	162	20
Grand Junction . . .	870,000	43·5	152	20·8
South Western . . .	743,000	36	121	24
Birmingham & Gloucester .	421,000	38·3	152	21
Great Western . . .	1,622,700	67	265	27½

In tractive power the Great Western locomotives designed by Gooch were vastly ahead of anything running on the narrow gauge. A comprehensive table was included in Gooch's evidence, showing that while the Great Western had engines having a calculated tractive effort up to 3,000 lb. at 60 m.p.h., the London and Birmingham and the Grand Junction had nothing larger than 871 lb., and the South Western maximum was 1,398 lb. Gooch submitted indicator diagrams taken off one of his 'Firefly' class 2-2-2s, *Ixion*, showing a tractive power of 2,196 lb. at 60 m.p.h.

Gooch's evidence all served to show that on the Great Western full advantage had been taken of the extra space available with the broad gauge, and that the promises held out by Brunel were now being borne out by the facts of day-to-day operation. In giving evidence before the Commissioners Gooch was followed by Seymour Clarke, then London Divisional Superintendent who afterwards became General Manager of the Great Northern, but throughout Clarke's examination Gooch remained in attendance, and was frequently called upon to answer technical points. Then followed Saunders, and finally, on a Saturday of all days, came Brunel. His examination was one of the briefest of all among the really big men of the railway world, and on that same day the Commissioners had time also to hear G. P. Bidder, the well-known partner of Robert Stephenson, and George Bodmer, the locomotive builder. Seeing that the whole affair has arisen out of Brunel's original recommendation his examination was very brief, and concerned itself with questions as to why he had used other gauges for railways in Wales and Italy, and why he was proposing to use the broad gauge for the Irish Mail line from Oxford to Port Dynllaen.

Following the Great Western witnesses a number of railwaymen of the secretarial and management types were examined; including Richard Creed of the London and Birmingham, Mark Huish, Chaplin of the South Western, John Ellis, and finally the unspeakable George Hudson. The evidence of the latter was the mixture of brag and bounce that might have been expected of him; among other items he told the Commissioners that on the York and North Midland they had carried loads of 700 to 800 tons *with one engine*! Some of the most telling evidence against the broad gauge came from the two military witnesses called, the Quarter-Master General and the Inspector General of Fortifications, both of whom threw an altogether more vivid and unusual light upon the evils of a break of gauge than any of the interested parties had done before them. In view of the remarks of Hudson and other narrow gauge partisans,

Saunders and Brunel asked leave to be heard again. They then challenged the narrow gauge to prove what they had claimed so far as engine power was concerned, by actual test. On December 2nd, 1845, Brunel and G. P. Bidder were called together before the Commissioners and after a long and somewhat acrimonious wrangle the terms of the test were agreed. Of course nothing the narrow gauge could put forward came anywhere near the ordinary performances of Gooch's locomotives, but mere engine tests could not alter the inevitable nature of the Commissioners report.

The broad gauge stood condemned, and recommendations were made for eliminating it forthwith. But first the Board of Trade, and then Parliament so watered down the Report that not only was the existing extent of the broad gauge left unaltered, but many additional lines were laid down in the ensuing years. One of the most interesting and complicated phases of the Gauge War was fought over the proposed northern extensions of the Great Western from Oxford. The line to Rugby was already authorized, and then there came the Birmingham and Oxford Junction. It is extraordinary to recall that this line, which was eventually to become a very important and highly competitive line of the Great Western, owed its origin to the boundless enterprise of the Grand Junction and not to the Great Western at all. Up to that time the 'powers that be' at Paddington seemed to have no thought of attacking such a triply-entrenched narrow gauge stronghold as Birmingham, and were concentrating their energies upon the northward drive to Rugby.

On the other hand the narrow gauge forces in Birmingham were not in the least a happy or united party. The Grand Junction and London and Birmingham were at such continual loggerheads that Capt. Huish of the G.J.R. resolved to have a route from Birmingham to London that should be entirely independent of the Euston route. And so the Grand Junction projected a line to link up with the Oxford branch of the Great Western – broad gauge too! It was at this stage that Huish was talking of laying in the mixed gauge northward over the main line of the Grand Junction. After some initial hesitation, because of some natural suspicion of Huish's motives, the Great Western gave full support to the Birmingham and Oxford Junction, and since by that time the Act had been secured for the Oxford and Rugby the junction of the Birmingham line was fixed at Fenny Compton. The legal proceedings were much complicated by the inclusion in the Bill of clauses relating to the eventual sale of the line to either the Great Western or the Grand Junction, and all the time the London and Birmingham was massing its forces for an all-out attempt to get the Bill thrown out.

The combined strength of the Grand Junction and the Great Western, however, prevailed, and the Act authorizing the construction of the line received the Royal Assent in August 1846. In the meantime, however, the Grand Junction and the London and Birmingham had come to terms, and the previous month had seen the amalgamation that formed the London and North Western Railway. With Huish appointed General Manager of the combined system his interest in the Birmingham and Oxford Junction changed to violent antagonism. The line he had so carefully fostered now appeared as a dangerous rival for the London and Birmingham traffic. The puny little Bury engines of the L. & B. would not have stood an earthly chance in open competition with Gooch's Swindon-built 'flyers'. The danger to North Western interests was accentuated by the authorization of a northward continuation of the broad gauge – the Birmingham, Wolverhampton and Dudley Railway. Even so Huish had much to do in consolidating his great new empire, with headquarters at Euston, and in the meantime Russell and Saunders set to work to effect a full amalgamation between the Great Western, the Birmingham and Oxford, and the Wolverhampton Railway.

Huish was not long in getting wind of these intentions, and he sought to nullify the whole scheme by driving a wedge into the central link. The Birmingham and Oxford Junction included many shareholders with strong North Western interests and sympathies, and Huish worked strenuously through these men and many carefully posted agents to get complete control of the Birmingham and Oxford by buying up all the shares. It was not long before no less than 40,000 out of the total of 50,000 shares were in North Western hands, and to ensure the maximum voting power at his command Huish worked a most audacious 'fiddle' over the ownership of the shares. Providing any individual shareholder did not own more than ten shares, he was entitled to one vote per share, and so Huish parcelled out the Birmingham and Oxford shares to all and sundry on the North Western. There were not nearly enough directors, executives, and senior officers to take all the shares that had been acquired in the maximum holding of ten per person, so they were doled out to many men in the most junior and humble positions. It was said that at one time nearly every porter at Euston was a Birmingham and Oxford shareholder!

Fortunately for the Great Western these tactics failed to dislodge the original directors of the B. & O., and for some months one beheld the strange spectacle of a Board completely at variance with the vast majority of the shareholders. A petition was presented to the House of Lords asking for an independent enquiry; acrimony was piled upon acrimony until Huish and his confederates over-reached themselves. An unscrupulous solicitor was called in to devise plans for a *coup d'état* that would dispense with the old directors, by means of certain legal actions, and to 'legalise' their own actions they actually went to the extent of forging an imitation of the Common Seal of the company. Up till this time the fight, though its outcome was fraught with so many vital consequences, had taken place entirely within the Birmingham and Oxford company. Russell and Saunders had watched 'from the touch line', as it were. Now, however, there seemed a real danger of Huish's wiles pulling off the *coup* so dearly sought by Euston Square. The trend of affairs was so flagrantly opposed to the terms of the Act of Incorporation, and so damaging to the Great Western that Saunders at last intervened, by filing a Bill in Chancery against the B. & O. and against all its eighteen directors by name. The hearing lasted nearly three months, and eventually judgment was given, fully and decisively, for the Great Western. And that was the end of Huish so far as the 'Royal Oxford Route' to Birmingham was concerned.

Having secured possession of the route the Great Western had to fight a new 'battle of the gauges'. One outcome of the Royal Commission on Railway Gauges was that the Board of Trade required mixed gauge to be laid on the Oxford and Rugby, and on the Birmingham and Oxford Junction. The arguments, disputes and protracted procedures that preceded these decisions lasted *years*, with the narrow gauge interests doing all they could to spike the Great Western guns. The North Western engineers, Stephenson, Locke, McConnell, and Trevithick cut a poor figure in the technical quality of the case they put forward against the introduction of a mixed gauge, and in regard to the capabilities of narrow gauge locomotives. One feels that having secured a first class triumph in the Report of the Commissioners, they were sure of the ultimate outcome. On the other hand Brunel and Gooch had to fight every inch of the way, and it was at this time that Gooch built the first Great Western dynamometer car to facilitate the tests on broad gauge locomotives that he was conducting to further his case. It is of historic interest that parts of this original car were included in Churchward's famous car, which, modernized, was used for some of the memorable Western Region trials made from 1948 onwards.

The line between Oxford and Birmingham, laid to the mixed gauge, became part of an important through route to the north, but the complementary project, carrying the line northward from Fenny Compton to Rugby was abandoned, chiefly in face of the implacable opposition of the North Western to any Great Western arrival in Rugby. Fifty years later the Great Western did succeed in getting access to Rugby, and with it a whole series of valuable connections to North Eastern England. This connection came over the newly constructed Great Central Railway, and its most important branch from Culworth Junction to Banbury. It is an interesting thought as to how differently the system of cross-country connections via Banbury might have developed had the Midland and the North Western chosen to collaborate with the Great Western at Rugby instead of driving it away. So far as the Great Central was concerned the line to Banbury was in many ways more important than the London extension itself, and had the traffic from Sheffield, Nottingham and Leicester to the Great Western and the London and South Western lines been developed earlier, over the Midland route to Rugby, there is a strong possibility that the Manchester, Sheffield and Lincolnshire might never have been tempted to embark upon the great adventure of the London Extension.

IV

Swindon

THE Railway Towns of England collectively provide a fascinating study in social history. The Industrial Revolution is often represented as a time of oppression, sweated labour, foul working conditions and all the associated clichés in the repertoire of every tub-thumping, street-corner politician. How different in actual fact was the inception of railway activities in towns like Ashford and Doncaster! How thoroughly does the very origin of Crewe cast the words of the tub-thumper back into his own teeth! In many ways Swindon provides the most remarkable example of them all. Here was no upstart growth, but clustered on the hill to the south of the railway was an ancient town the history of which stretches back far earlier than its mention in Domesday Book.

Old Swindon, as we must now call it, had been a junction of the ways since prehistoric times. Writing of the town in his *Highways and Byways in Wiltshire* Edward Hutton considers that '... the best thing even in Old Swindon remains the unchanging landscape as seen thence, the storied downs with their mysterious entrenchments, camps and castles, where lie the unmemoried dead, across which the ways of our remotest forefathers still wind and hesitate and are lost, and over which the Roman roads still sweep in their arrow flight for Silchester and Winchester. The views are noble, and must explain, I suppose, the affection in which Swindon has always been held by its sons ....'

In the railway age Swindon became a junction as early as 1841, when the first section of the Cheltenham and Great Western Union Railway was opened, from Swindon itself to Kemble and Cirencester. Before even this, however, the decision that was to transform the town and the immediate neighbourhood had already been taken. The circumstances are best told by Daniel Gooch. In his diary he writes:

'1840. During this year further portions of the Great Western were opened and agreements were made for leasing the Bristol and Exeter and the Swindon and Cheltenham Railways, and it became necessary to furnish large works for the repair, etc., of our stock. I was called upon to

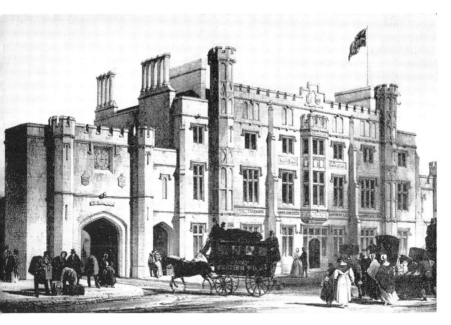

Exterior of Temple Meads Station, Bristol as first opened. From a drawing by
J. C. Bourne.

[*British Railways*

Interior of Bath station. Note posting carriage at rear of train on left. From a
drawing by J. C. Bourne.

[*British Railways*

Sonning cutting, showing occupation overbridge designed in the style afterwards adopted by Brunel for railway viaducts in Cornwall. From a drawing by J. C. Bourne.

[British Railways

Stone arch bridge at Chippenham. From a drawing by J. C. Bourne.

[British Railways

Charles Russell.

Charles A. Saunders.

Isambard K. Brunel.

Sir Daniel Gooch.

[British Railways

2-2-2 Locomotive *Actaeon*, 'Firefly' class, driven from London to Exeter and back
by Daniel Gooch on the day of the opening throughout to Exeter.

[*British Railways*

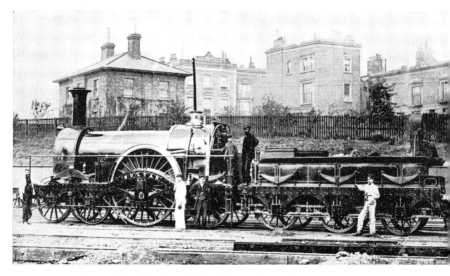

4-2-2 Locomotive *Sultan* in early broad gauge days, with original style of chimney
and no cab.

[*British Railways*

Bridgend Station, from an early print. A view taken soon
after the opening of the line to this point, in 1848.

[Courtesy E. R. Baker

The first train to **arrive at Swan**sea. The inaugural train
drawn by two Gooch **2-2-2 locomo**tives. From a contemporary
woodcut.

[Courtesy E. R. Baker

Pangbourne station, as first opened.

Windsor station, showing a typical Brunel
all-over roof.

Both from drawings by J. C. Bourne.
[*British Railways*

Bristol Temple Meads in the early seventies. The G.W.R. station is to the right: the Bristol and Exeter general offices in the centre, near background, and the B. & E. 'Train shed' on left.

[*British Railways*]

Timber trestle viaduct at St. Germans, Cornwall Railway. Note the timber fenders protecting the main trestles that are fixed in the waterway.

[*British Railways*

Right: A typical signalbox of broad gauge days, Waltham, near Maidenhead.

[*British Railways*]

Left: A standard broad gauge stop signal in the 'all-right' position. The danger aspect showed the disc turned on edge and a crossbar displayed.

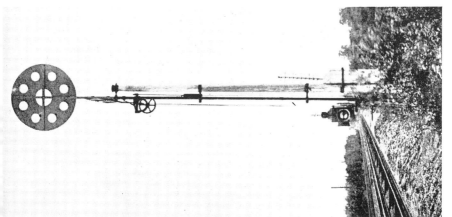

Viaduct over the River Severn at Worcester.
[*British Railways*

The skew bridge over the River Avon, at Bath (note
the crossbar signal.)
[*British Railways*

Brunel's timber viaduct over the River Thames, at Culham.

Tubular Bridge over the River Wye at Chepstow.

Ivybridge station and viaduct, South Devon Railway: an early view showing much interesting detail of construction and permanent way.

[British Railways

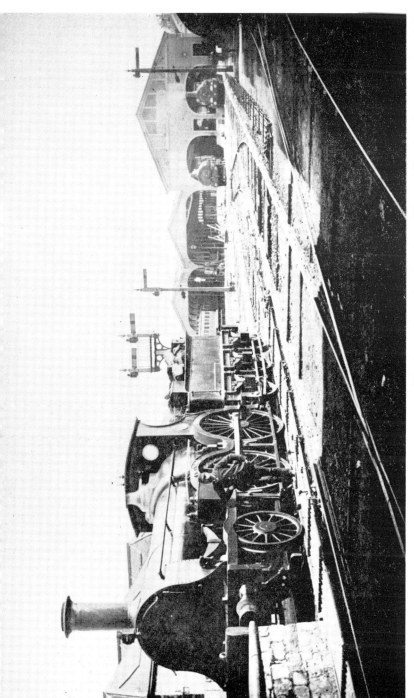

The locomotive yard and station at Newton Abbot, in 1889. 2-4-0 engine *Wood* in foreground.

[The late Rev. A. H. Malan, by courtesy of B.T.C. Archives

4-2-2 express locomotive *Rover*, at Bristol, in 1890.
[*The late Rev. A. H. Malan, by courtesy of B.T.C. Archives*

4-2-2 express locomotive *Iron Duke*, and crew, at Bristol in 1890.
[*The late Rev. A. H. Malan, by courtesy of B.T.C. Archives*

e Devon girder, before raising.

THE ROYAL ALBERT BRIDGE

General view from the Cornish side, before any
preparation for the track had been made.

Up Cornish Express leaving Teignmouth in 1891, hauled by 4-2-2 locomotive *Timour*.

[*The late Rev. A. H. Malan, by courtesy of B.T.C. Archives*

report on the best situation to build these works, and on full consideration I reported in favour of Swindon, it being the junction with the Cheltenham branch and also a convenient division of the Great Western line for engine working. Mr Brunel and I went to look at the ground, then only green fields, and he agreed with me as to its being the best place.'

Gooch's recommendation was accepted by the Board, and in February 1841, the decision was taken to go ahead. Contracts were let for the construction of the workshops, and for the purchase of the necessary plant and machinery, and within two years 'Swindon Works' was in full operation – an astonishing feat of planning and construction that would, if there were nothing else, provide an abiding memory to the genius of Daniel Gooch. When the Works went into full commission on January 2nd, 1843, the Locomotive Superintendent was still no more than 26 years of age. But while the planning of the works was due to Gooch, the Great Western Board realized that a great deal more had to be done than to build a factory amid the green fields that then surrounded the junction of the Cheltenham railway with their own main line; and very wisely and methodically they set out to provide for the welfare of their workpeople in a new town that should be quite independent of Old Swindon.

The works was built in the vee between the Bristol and the Cheltenham lines, and on the south side of the line, and a little to the east of the works were built the houses for the men. In this new town the dwelling houses were originally grouped in six rectangular blocks, and the streets were named in recognition of the extent of the G.W.R. and its broad gauge associates: London Street, Bath Street, Bristol Street, Oxford Street, Exeter Street, and Taunton Street. At a later date Reading Street and Faringdon Street were added. A new church, St. Marks, was built alongside the railway, and adjacent to the houses and the church the Company purchased land which was eventually enclosed and became known as the G.W.R. Park. This splendid example of town planning went considerably further than providing houses, a church and a park. The blocks of workmen's houses were arranged in two groups of three, each group having the blocks abreast of each other, and running parallel to the railway. Between the two groups there was originally a broad open space, but it was quickly filled.

As early as the autumn of 1843 a technical library was formed, and in the following year the Mechanics' Institution was established, 'for the purpose of disseminating useful knowledge and encouraging rational amusement among all classes of people employed by the

Great Western Railway.' A building was erected on part of the space existing between the two groups of dwelling houses, and the activities have grown subsequently to such an extent that the premises now include a full-scale theatre, and a dance hall. The Mechanics' Institution, excellent and extensive though its premises have become, is not greatly different from similar establishments in other railway and industrial towns; but on the other plot of that once-vacant land between the two groups of houses stands the G.W.R. Accident Hospital. This is the present outward and visible sign of the work of the Medical Fund Society established as long ago as 1847, and a very definite prototype of the present National Health Service.

This remarkable piece of early welfare work was set up for the purpose of providing medical and surgical attention and medicine for the members of the society, and their families. In the last days of the Great Western Railway the membership of the Society was some 13,000, while including their wives and families this private health service was available to a total of more than 40,000 persons. The staff consisted of a medical director and consultant physician, a chief surgeon, and no fewer than eight assistant medical officers, while the hospital staff consisted of a matron and nineteen nurses. The dental section was no less comprehensive. When the National Health Service was set up, by Act of Parliament, the G.W.R. Medical Fund Society came to an end, but at the time the National scheme was being planned, senior officials of the Ministry of Health paid many visits to Swindon to study the details and working of the Great Western scheme which had been so successfully launched just one hundred years earlier!

In the meantime Gooch was busy building up his staff. Engine mechanics and boiler makers were not likely to be found in the pastoral Hundreds of Wiltshire, and so it was not surprising that most of the leading men in early Swindon days came from far afield. Gooch himself was a native of Northumberland, having been born at Bedlington in August 1816. While serving his apprenticeship at the East Foundry at Dundee he had met a raw young Scot of almost exactly his own age, named Archibald Sturrock. They worked and studied together, and the story goes that Gooch taught Sturrock to draw. Anyway, to cut the non-essentials out of the story Sturrock was eventually appointed principal assistant to Gooch on the G.W.R., as from 1840, and so he came to share in the anxieties and vicissitudes of the early broad gauge days, working at first with the Paddington engine-shed as his headquarters. When the establishment of a major works at Swindon had been decided upon, Sturrock was made Works Manager; he acted as Resident Engineer during the erection of the various buildings, and so, with the combined ages of Locomotive Superintendent and Works Manager totalling no more than 53 years, the first Swindon Works rose up from the green fields.

Gooch could not have had a finer assistant in those early days. No set-back, no misfortune could damp the fire and enthusiasm of Archibald Sturrock; the broad gauge had no more whole-hearted supporter, and he matched his high spirits and tremendous drive with an engineering skill that made him irresistible. The third member of the early locomotive triumvirate on the Great Western was that somewhat eccentric genius T. R. Crampton, who, strangely enough, was almost exactly the same age as Gooch and Sturrock. Crampton had been employed under Sir Marc Brunel from 1839 onwards, but at some time afterwards he seems to have been transferred to the G.W.R. under Gooch, and took a hand in the designing of the earlier broad gauge express locomotives. Crampton was too much of an individualist to settle in contentedly as a member of a team, and although he was at Swindon in the earliest days he left the G.W.R. in 1844 to take up a job under James Rennie.

While Gooch was officially subordinate to Brunel, the conspicuous failure of the early locomotives led the Directors to deal more and more directly with Gooch. The latter had the difficult task of condemning all that his chief had originally done, though Brunel with his charming loyalty of character made things easy for the Locomotive Superintendent. It could have been an extremely awkward time for Gooch. The Great Western Directors, in asking him to report on the state of the motive power, put him in a position exactly similar to that of Joseph Locke many years earlier, when the latter was asked to report on certain difficulties that were being experienced in the construction of the Liverpool and Manchester Railway. He had either to refuse to make the report, and undoubtedly incur the displeasure of the directors, or report adversely on the work of his chief. The earlier case led to an estrangement between Locke and George Stephenson; but Brunel stepped aside, gave Gooch an absolutely free hand, and both men remained the closest of personal friends.

The directors evidently had the greatest confidence in Gooch, for after the earlier unfortunate experiences they authorized him to place contracts for no fewer than 105 new locomotives of his own designs. These locomotives were of four different classes as follows:

Type	Duty	Driving wheel dia. ft. in.		Number in class
2–2–2	Express passenger	7	0	62
2–2–2	Passenger	6	0	21
2–4–0	Goods	5	0	18
0–6–0	Goods	5	0	4

These were the locomotives with which Swindon had to deal. They had all been received from the various contractors by the time the works was ready to go into operation, and the Great Western Railway did not take delivery of any further new locomotives until Swindon produced its own first.

All the new engines of 1840–2 were examples of good, sound engineering, but it was naturally the 7 ft 2-2-2 singles that captured the limelight. They were big, handsome engines, taking full advantage of the space afforded by the broad gauge, and in their general layout showing clearly their derivation from Stephenson's *North Star*. The boilers were much larger, and included the distinctive feature of the high haystack firebox, which was covered with polished copper. The boiler lagging plates were made of wooden laths, and these, completely exposed, were also polished. The only splasher over the 7 ft driving wheel was a deep brass band. Their four-wheeled tenders also had sandwich frames, and they carried a seat for the so-called 'travelling porter' who rode with his back to the engine, watching over the progress of the carriages and protected from the weather by a shelter sometimes known as the 'iron coffin'.

By later standards the 'Firefly' class, as they were known, were relatively small engines. The cylinders of the earlier batches were 15 in. dia. by 18 in. stroke; the heating surface was 699 sq. ft, and the grate area 13·5 sq. ft. From the outset, however, they were very fast engines for that period. It is recorded that *Firefly* ran a train of three coaches non-stop from Paddington to Reading in 46½ min. no later than a fortnight after Gooch had taken delivery of her from the makers, Messrs Jones, Turner and Evans of Newton-le-Willows. Gooch chose *Actaeon* for the inaugural through run from Paddington to Exeter and back in 1844, and *Ixion* did some excellent work in the comparative trials carried out for the Gauge Commissioners. One of her fastest runs was from Paddington to Didcot in 63 min. 34 sec. with a load of 60 tons, and a maximum speed of 60 m.p.h. On the return journey, with the very slight gradients in her favour, the start-to-stop run of 53·1 miles was made in just under the hour, with a maximum speed of 61 m.p.h. Against this, one of Gooch's 0-6-0 goods engines hauled a load of no less than 400 tons, and attained a maximum speed of 25½ m.p.h.

Although the performance of the broad gauge Great Western locomotives was so much in advance of anything the narrow gauge could then put up in opposition, it had no effect upon the nature of the Gauge Commissioners' Report. The generous tributes made to Brunel and Gooch were wholehearted in every way, but they were not calculated, nor intended to influence the result. The report includes this statement:

'We feel it our duty to observe that the public are indebted for the present rate of speed, and the increased accommodation of railway carriages to the genius of Mr Brunel and the liberality of the Great Western Railway.'

And again concerning the engine tests the Commissioners comment:

'We consider them (i.e. the trials) as confirming the statements and results given by Mr Gooch, in his evidence, proving, as they do, that the broad gauge engines possess greater possibilities for speed with equal loads, and, generally speaking, of propelling greater loads with equal speed; and moreover, that the working of such engines is economical where very high speeds are required, or where loads to be conveyed are such as to require the full power of the engine.'

Although the report had gone so very much against the broad gauge it was not by any means a death warrant, and as I told in the previous chapter Parliament made it still less definite and incisive in its legal implications. The Great Western Board thereupon decided to press home their great advantage in speed with a still more spectacular demonstration of what their locomotives could do. Gooch was instructed to build 'a colossal locomotive working with all speed'. As far as one can judge there was not a line on a sheet of drawing paper when this instruction was received, but Gooch and Sturrock needed no special instigation. From start to finish the job was taken as a major challenge, for the engine was designed, built, and steamed *in thirteen weeks!* Drawing office and shops alike worked night and day, and on April 1st, 1846 the giant 2-2-2 *Great Western* steamed out of the works, appropriately the first engine to be built throughout at Swindon. Only those of us who are concerned with mechanical engineering design and construction today will appreciate to the full the significance of this achievement. To us it is breathtaking. The directors had ordered a colossal locomotive; 'colossal' was the word in every respect!

The *Great Western* was a very much enlarged edition of the 'Firefly' class. Within two months of her completion she had made what was then a phenomenally fast run from Paddington to Swindon, covering that 77·3 miles against the slight gradient at an average speed of 59·4 m.p.h. with a load of 100 tons. This formed part of an astonishing round trip from London to Exeter and back on which the running time was no more than 419 min. for the distance of 388 miles. In her original form she was found to have rather too much weight on the leading pair of wheels, and accordingly Gooch altered her by adding an extra pair of carrying wheels. Although a huge inverted equalizing spring connected the two pairs of carrying wheels under the smokebox the wheel arrangement could not strictly be called 4-2-2, which usually indicates an engine with a leading bogie. Nevertheless the modified *Great Western* was the forerunner in every way of the famous Gooch eight-footers, all of which had the chimney set well ahead of the centre line between the two pairs of carrying wheels. The later engines had larger leading wheels, with polished brass splashers covering that portion of them that came above the running plate.

Regular production of the eight-foot singles at Swindon began in April 1847 with the completion of the *Iron Duke*. None of Gooch's engines on the G.W.R. had numbers; they were distinguished entirely by their names. With the *Iron Duke* a modified form of firebox was introduced. The old hay-cock type, however picturesque and however effective it may have been, was not an easy thing to produce, and Gooch adopted instead a round-topped firebox standing well above the line of the boiler. This was a good feature, providing plenty of space above the water line. The steam was collected in a perforated pipe extending from the front tube plate to the back of the firebox, and through this pipe was carried a rod from the push-and-pull regulator handle on the footplate to the valve itself, which was in the smokebox. It is a matter of history that Sturrock took this arrangement to the Great Northern, where it was used during the Stirling régime. The push-and-pull regulator was used as recently as the Gresley 'K2' class Moguls.

The *Iron Duke* was the first of six 4-2-2 locomotives built in 1847, which had 18 in. by 24 in. cylinders, 1,790 sq. ft of heating surface, and a grate area of 21·66 sq. ft. The boiler pressure was originally 100 lb. per sq. in. but was afterwards increased to 115. The other five engines of the class were named *Lightning*, *Great Britain*, *Emperor*, *Pasha*, and *Sultan*. They differed at first from the more familiar aspect of these famous engines in having the wood lagging of the boiler and firebox exposed, and having a huge bell-mouthed top to the chimney. A beautiful model of the *Iron Duke* in its original condition is now to be seen in the passage leading from the Lawn at Paddington into the Great Western Royal Hotel, opposite to the equally gorgeous model of the Dean 4-2-2 No. 3048 *Majestic*. A very full description of all the technical features of the *Iron Duke* appeared in the *Locomotive Magazine* for November 1901.

Sixteen more 4-2-2 express locomotives of the same general type were completed at Swindon between June 1848 and March 1851. In these engines the lagging on boiler and firebox was covered in, and the chimney, though still remaining bell-mouthed, was approaching a more modern shape. All these engines were originally built without cabs. It is worthwhile recalling their names:

Courier	*Swallow*
Tartar	*Timour*
Dragon	*Prometheus*
Warlock	*Perseus*
Wizard	*Estafette*
Rougemont	*Rover*
Hirondelle	*Amazon*
Tornado	*Lord of the Isles*

The last of the batch was originally named *Charles Russell*, but that great Chairman with characteristic modesty declined the honour Gooch wished to bestow upon him, and the engine was therefore renamed. As *Lord of the Isles* it became perhaps the best known of all broad gauge engines through its presence in a position of great prominence in the Great Exhibition of 1851. Although completed in March of that year it did not commence revenue earning service on the G.W.R. until July 1852. Then the *Lord of the Isles* got to work in earnest and in the next 29 years ran over three-quarters of a million miles, with the original boiler still giving good service at the time of withdrawal of the engine in July 1881.

A great variety of broad gauge locomotives was turned out at Swindon works between 1846 and 1864, including many 0-6-0 goods, though the big 4-4-0s for the South Wales main line put on the road in 1855 were built by Robert Stephenson and Co. As with the 8 ft singles so with the goods and the South Devon 4-4-0 tanks; all were named. Although all of them were obviously from the same school of design none, except the express 4-2-2s, were particularly handsome and some were downright ugly. The South Wales 4-4-0s named after characters in the Waverley Novels were not a success despite their

large size and high nominal tractive power. The leading wheels
were arranged as on the eight-footers, non-bogie, and the long fixed
wheelbase made them very susceptible to derailment. One of them,
the *Rob Roy*, was in a bad accident at Bullo Pill in 1868. The names
of the ten engines of the 'Lalla Rookh' class, as the 4-4-0s were
generally known, were afterwards perpetuated on Churchward's
two-cylinder 'Atlantics' which were eventually converted to 4-6-0s
and included in the 'Saint' class.

One could gossip for whole chapters upon the fascinating lore of
the broad gauge locomotives. Whatever the report of the Gauge
Commissioners may have said there grew up on the Great Western a
tremendous sense of pride, and perhaps superiority-complex in the
possession of the broad gauge. It was a pride that was shared by the
people living in the shires through which the railway ran. More
perhaps than any other railway in the country the Great Western
became an institution in the West; an aristocrat among railways,
often standing in 'splendid isolation', and casting off in its more
mature years the breathless haste of its youth and settling down to
more leisured standards of train running. This was a case of management policy, and not because of any deterioration in the capacity of
Daniel Gooch's locomotives. The deficiencies in overall speed were
sometimes blamed upon the refreshment stop at Swindon, but right
down to the present day the Great Western, and the Western Region
too, has always been inclined to 'make a meal' out of its station stops,
and book even its crack expresses to wait 5, 7 or even 10 min. at
large intermediate stations while the northern lines would schedule
4 min. at the most at places of equivalent importance – even, at
times, if there was engine-changing to be done as well.

The 'refreshment stop' at Swindon remained a sore point for more
than 50 years. While giving every thought to the needs of the
workmen to be employed in the locomotive works the Company had
every reason to try and reduce capital expenditure as much as
possible, and they made an arrangement which they were soon
bitterly to regret. Contracts had been made with the firm of J. & C.
Rigby of Westminster for building all the stations between
Steventon and Corsham; these had been very satisfactorily carried
out, and the builders were approached again in connection with the
erection of the workmen's cottages in New Swindon. Messrs Rigby
were to build the cottages and the station refreshment rooms at their
own expense, and in return the Great Western Railway would stop
all regular passenger trains at Swindon for a period of about 10 min.
to give time for passengers to obtain refreshments. Moreover the

railway company promised that no rival stopping place should be established for refreshments anywhere between London and Bristol. The agreement was finally sealed by the G.W.R. leasing the refreshment rooms to Messrs Rigby for 99 years, from the end of 1841, at a rent of one penny per annum.

One feels that although the Great Western Board made this agreement with the most honourable intentions they were caught napping like a collection of novices. However well the Westminster builders had served the railway in their normal business capacity, one might have questioned how they would react to this entry into the catering business, and, in fact, within a week they had sublet the job to an hotel proprietor in Cheltenham on most advantageous terms to themselves. The service and the food were bad from the very outset; the caterer, who had no interest in Swindon, or the G.W.R., set out to supply the worst he could get away with, and although the terms of the lease to Messrs Rigby reserved to the G.W.R. the right to dictate the quality of food and the price charged, in actual practice it was found very difficult to enforce either. In December 1842 we find Brunel writing to the caterer thus:

Dear Sir,

I assure you Mr Player was wrong in supposing that I thought you purchased inferior coffee. I thought I said to him that I was surprised you should buy such bad roasted corn. I did not believe you had such a thing as coffee in the place; I am certain that I never tasted any. I have long ceased to make complaints at Swindon. I avoid taking anything there when I can help it.

Yours faithfully,

I. K. Brunel

In August 1848 Rigby's sold the lease outright for £20,000!

It cannot be said that the builders skimped things in the actual layout of the refreshment rooms. Two large three-storeyed buildings were erected on either side of the main line. In each of these buildings the basement contained kitchens, offices, and staff rooms; the ground floor provided the refreshment rooms proper, and the top floors of both buildings formed an hotel – the two sections being joined by a covered footbridge across the line. The layout of the refreshment rooms takes some believing today. The apartments were lofty, and decorated in the most elaborate, overpowering style of ornamentation, and were divided by an oval counter in the middle which effectually segregated first and second class passengers. Third class passengers were not allowed in at all! Contemporary drawings show dignified passengers dining in leisured ease, with suave waiters obsequiously attending to their needs; but in the ten-minute halt of the 'Flying Dutchman' the proceedings usually partook of a mad scramble at the counters. It needed a Rowlandson, rather than a Bourne to depict the scene.

Ahrons suggests another reason for the hastiness of that refreshment stop: 'I came to the conclusion, as a result of many observations, that on the London–Swindon run, which is really a steady if very gradual rise, the engines could keep time with six broad gauge eight-wheelers only in the best of weather with no head wind, and when the engines were "thumped". Now the drivers had a good reason for not "extending" their engines as far as Swindon. The Swindon stop existed chiefly on account of buns, sandwiches and liquid refreshments, and as none were offered to the driver, he naturally took very little interest in them. Moreover, the Swindon to Bath run was a downhill performance, which included the Wootton Bassett and Box Tunnel banks of 1 in 100, and as these runs were booked at only 47 miles per hour, there was not the least difficulty in picking up the 2 and 3 minutes dropped between London and Swindon, and reaching Bath to time, and generally I may say this was done.'

The excluding of third class passengers from the refreshment rooms at Swindon may seem extraordinary to us today; but it must be realised that the Great Western was promoted by the wealthy and influential merchants of Bristol and London, to carry their goods and their families. There was little thought of intermediate business, at first, and the line catered primarily for first class traffic. It catered no less for the rich and leisured citizens of Cheltenham and Bath, and stations like Cirencester and Chippenham served the great landed proprietors rather than the isolated rural communities of the country villages. One can smile at the story of the Marchioness of Lansdowne's first railway journey, when she persuaded Brunel to accompany her, and insisted on holding his hand, 'for greater safety'. With the fastest trains the exclusion of third class passengers from the refreshment rooms at Swindon caused no difficulties, as the 'Flying Dutchman', and the 'Zulu' carried no third class passengers at all.

While on the subject of premises a brief digression may be made from the subject of Swindon – twenty miles eastwards in fact, to Steventon. In October 1841, the former London and Bristol Committees were abolished, and the management of the line vested in a General Superintendent, Charles Saunders. Traffic and General Committees were set up, and it was decreed that all meetings of these committees, and of the Board should take place at Steventon, adding that this instruction should take place 'if the requisite offices can be provided there without material expense'. Brunel thereupon set about the alteration of the large house now to be seen beside the station yard, to make it suitable for the Board and the various Committees. So, for a period of six months Steventon was the centre of Great Western administration. Its glory passed almost as soon as it arrived, for in the early months of 1843 headquarters was moved to London, and such administrative work as had previously been done in Bristol transferred. This was naturally a great disappointment in the western city which always claimed it was the birthplace of the Great Western. With the abolition of the original dual control the significance of Swindon as a divisional point vanished, and all attention was thenceforth concentrated on its development as a manufacturing and repairing centre for the rolling stock.

With the expansion of the G.W.R. so the population of Swindon grew by leaps and bounds. In 1831 the Old Town contained no more than 1,742 people; by 1851 the population had risen to 4,876, and by 1871 it was no less than 11,720. From being an entirely rural community Swindon, both 'Old' and 'New', became almost entirely dependent upon the railway, though there has always remained a sharp line of demarcation between those who worked on the railway and those who did not, somewhat analogous to the 'Town and Gown' distinction of the old University towns. In Swindon a man employed in the G.W.R. works is always referred to as 'inside'.

V

South Devon and Cornwall

THE extraordinary character of the Great Western main line west of Exeter is vividly revealed to anyone riding through from London or Bristol on the footplate. In places the curvature is so continuous and so severe as to savour more of a meandering branch than of an important main line, and some of it might, to a casual observer, be attributed to the inconsistencies of policy sometimes displayed by Brunel. The Great Western main line to the west, like much of the entire Western Region network of today, was not the result of a grand strategic plan. There was no central guiding force as there was in the case of the West Coast Route to Scotland, where the Board of the Grand Junction developed the master conception of a single trunk line northwards from Lancashire to Aberdeen; and Joseph Locke's engineering of the Lancaster and Carlisle, of the Caledonian, and of the lines north of Greenhill was all carried out with the single object in view.

Down in the West it was very different. I have already told of the early days of the Bristol and Exeter, and how the efforts of the Great Western to get a more direct line from London were thwarted. The South Devon Railway was another line of entirely independent origin. It was launched in Plymouth, and arose out of the desire of a number of enterprising citizens to have a railway to connect up with the Bristol and Exeter. So little financial backing came forth, however, that the enterprise hung fire for many years. Brunel made a survey as early as 1836, but it was not until the Great Western, the Bristol and Exeter, and the Bristol and Gloucester were induced to subscribe to the project that any progress was made. Apart from Brunel's association with it, the South Devon Railway went its own way without any guiding influence from either Paddington or Bristol, and the whole character of the line seems diametrically opposed to what Brunel had already done between London and Bristol.

The plain fact appears to be that the South Devon was planned as a local railway. There was no intention of building a high speed trunk line between Exeter and Plymouth. The line was intended to serve as many of the intermediate places as possible, and so it was taken round the coast through Starcross, Dawlish and Teignmouth; and then to continue on what might be termed a middle course over the southern slopes of Dartmoor, to pass through Totnes, and to be not too far away from Ashburton on the one hand, and Dartmouth on the other. In the original prospectus, issued in October 1843, it was stated that the line would be double-tracked throughout. A significant passage in the prospectus stated that: 'The length of the line will be about 51½ miles, and in its course combines with the largest amount of local accommodation less engineering difficulties than are found to exist on either of the other Lines that have been projected.' At the time there had been two alternative propositions, one running via Okehampton and following the course eventually followed by the London and South Western line to Plymouth, and a second, proposed by Brunel, running via Torquay and a crossing of the River Dart near Dittisham Ferry.

From the prospectus it is evident that the South Devon Railway was intended to be a line 'on the cheap', and when it came to be constructed further economies were envisaged by building it single-tracked throughout. Though money might be saved thus-wise it was perhaps inevitable that there would be some adventures into the unknown with Brunel as engineer. In view of their strong financial backing the other broad gauge companies were well represented on the original South Devon Board, and the agreed proportions were 5 from the Bristol and Exeter, 4 from the Great Western, 2 from the Bristol and Gloucester, and 10 from the remaining shareholders, though it was stipulated that both the Chairman and the Deputy Chairman should be from the South Devon proprietors, and not from any of the subscribing companies. The first meeting of the new company was held in Plymouth in August 1844, and at the very first meeting there was made what MacDermot refers to as 'a momentous announcement'. In the light of subsequent events it might more correctly be called a bombshell! This announcement was none other than the decision of the directors to adopt the Atmospheric System of traction for the whole line.

In the first place the idea was put up to the South Devon directors not by Brunel but by the inventors and patentees of the system, Messrs Clegg and Samuda. It provided a broad parallel to modern electric traction in that the trains did not have their own self-generating power units, but derived their means of propulsion from stationary power stations along the line. In the case of the 'Atmospheric', a large pipe was laid between the rails, and into this pipe fitted a piston carried on a trolley pole suspended from the

leading carriage of the train. The top of the pipe had a continuous
slit to accommodate the trolley pole, and the slit was sealed by a
leather flap which was pushed aside as the pole advanced and sealed
immediately afterwards. Motive power to propel the train was
provided by exhausting the air from the pipe ahead of the train, the
resulting partial vacuum sucking the piston along the pipe, and
drawing the train with it.

The directors consulted Brunel, who was immediately in favour of
it. A deputation went to Ireland to see an installation at work
between Kingstown and Dalkey, while Sir Frederick Smith,
Professor Barlow and William Cubitt were all staunch advocates of
it. One can understand that from some aspects it was an attractive
proposition, eliminating the use of locomotives, and providing clean
and virtually soundless travel. On the other hand little thought can
have been given to the practical operating of the line as traffic built
up. To maintain the requisite degree of vacuum in the pipe line
pumping stations were needed at intervals of about three miles along
the line. It was typical of Brunel to build these in a strange, yet
distinctive style of architecture, in which the chimney was disguised
as an Italian campanile! At each intermediate station, however, the
train piston was automatically withdrawn from the pipe, and had to
be re-entered on re-starting. This was a thoroughly awkward and
slow process, involving the use of an auxiliary vacuum pipe.

Between the stations some quite high speeds were attained when
the apparatus was in good working order; indeed, Brunel from his
preliminary investigations, and observations on the Kingstown and
Dalkey line, had developed such enthusiasm and confidence in the
Atmospheric system as to persuade the directors that no more than
a single-tracked line would be necessary. The trains would be taken
through the sections so swiftly, and the traffic handled so expedi-
tiously as to obviate any need for a double line. No one seems to have
foreseen the enormous development of South Devon as a holiday
resort. Certainly there was little or no attempt made to foster any
tourist traffic until the very end of the century, and when Foxwell
chided the Great Western, in 1889, for their lack of enterprise in that
direction it was not to South Devon and Cornwall that he pointed as
a potential gold mine but to the Cambrian Coast, from Aberystwyth
northwards to Pwllheli! In the Atmospheric system, in its circuitous
route, its single-track, and its heavy gradients Brunel certainly
bequeathed upon the South Devon a quartet of handicaps to future
development and expansion.

Fortunately for everyone except Brunel and the luckless South

Devon shareholders the Atmospheric proved itself an utter failure long before there was any traffic development. The four Atmospheric trains went into service between Exeter and Teignmouth in September 1847; the working was extended to Newton Abbot in the following January, and to Totnes in May. By that time troubles were coming thick and fast, mainly through the perishing of the leather flap sealing the pipe after a train had passed. This caused such serious leakage that the pumping engines could not maintain sufficient vacuum to draw the train along. As if this were not bad enough the pumping engines were thoroughly unreliable in themselves, and frequently broke down. To cut a long and sorry tale of fiasco short the directors of the South Devon decided to suspend Atmospheric working after the end of August 1848, and to shoulder their grievous loss of nearly half a million pounds, on what the local people came to call 'The Atmospheric Caper'.

Even when the 'Atmospheric' had been abandoned the South Devon were not clear of trouble. The line round the base of the beautiful red cliffs by Dawlish and Teignmouth was a bold project, and here again Brunel's supreme confidence was not borne out by subsequent events. Early in 1845 he reported to the directors thus:

'Considerable delay has been caused by the unusual prevalence during the last four months of easterly winds, which prevented the landing of stone upon the sea shore; nevertheless, a considerable length of the Sea Wall has been completed; and I see no reason to doubt the ability of the Contractors to finish the whole by the period fixed in the Contract, namely – the 1st of June.

'Of the sufficiency of the River Wall to resist anything to which it could be exposed, I believe no fears were really entertained by anybody; but of the Sea Wall doubts have been frequently expressed. The experience of the past winter would have satisfied me, if I had previously shared in those doubts, that they were groundless. Several severe gales have occurred, and if not equal to the worst known they have been amply sufficient to show the manner in which the Sea would act on the work. Wherever the Wall was completed and had time to become solid, it resisted perfectly and no effect whatever was produced; at one point only, near Langstone Cliffs, was any damage done, and here the work was actually in progress when the gale came on, which scoured away the Beach, and the mortar being still soft, the Wall was forced outwards towards the Sea by the pressure from behind. This, of course, could not have occurred had the mortar been set; indeed, the cause itself would not have operated had the groins for stopping the scour of the Beach been constructed. The result of these trials has been highly satisfactory, and I anticipate less trouble with this part of the Line than from the average of contingencies upon inland works.

'In the neighbourhood of Dawlish, the tunnelling through the several projecting points, and the formation of the terrace along the face of the cliffs, requiring very extensive operations by blasting, have proceeded most satisfactorily. Of the principal tunnel, through the headland forming the Parson Rock, 366 yards in length, only about 90 remain to be executed. The greater part of the blasting required at the face of the Cliff has been effected, and the whole of this work from Dawlish to the commencement of the Teignmouth Beach is in a very forward state. The manner and the extent to which these works had have the effect of gathering and increasing the Beach along the Coast are highly satisfactory and fully answer my expectations.

'I think it is highly probable that very little of the line will eventually be reached by the highest tides; leaving the works in perfect security and at the same time, improving very much the shore for all boat service, instead of injuring it, as had been feared by some parties.'

Although the sea wall was substantially built on the most exposed section between the five short tunnels between Dawlish and Teignmouth, certain old photographs show that at the end of the Dawlish sea front the line was carried at a height very little above that of the beach with little in the way of parapet or protection. In the earliest days trouble was experienced with high tide and storm action between the Langstone Cliff and Starcross, where Dawlish Warren station now stands. Here Brunel built a breakwater eastwards from the Langstone Cliff, and this has caused an eastward drift of sand and shingle to form a long and protecting spit across the estuary of the Exe. This has safeguarded the railway effectively at this once troublesome spot. South-west of Dawlish there have been many incidents. There was a serious landslip near the Dawlish end of Parsons Tunnel in January 1853, and a complete breach washed in the line at the Smuggler's Cove, just at the western end of the same tunnel in the terrible winter of 1854–5 – the 'Crimea Winter'. From early statements it would seem that Brunel originally intended to carry the line further out from the base of the cliffs than was eventually done. Had he proceeded according to his first plans the line might have been even more vulnerable than it actually was. The sea wall was vastly strengthened when the line was doubled late in the nineteenth century.

Whatever its early defects, and however one may regard the fiasco of the 'Atmospheric', Brunel bequeathed to us, in the line round the coast from Powderham Park to the estuary of the Teign, one of the most fascinating stretches of railway one could wish to travel over. Today, threading the succession of short tunnels between

Dawlish and the Parsons Rock, one can see clearly how the widening was carried out when the line was doubled. Brunel's original single-line bores were very lofty, and the twentieth century engineers carried out the widening on one side only, and to no more than normal clearance height, with the result that some of the short bores now have a curiously lop-sided appearance. Originally there was yet another tunnel at the extreme south-western end of the sea-wall, where the railway cuts through the line of the cliffs to enter Teignmouth station. This was opened out to a deep cutting when the line was doubled.

At the head of the Teign estuary the line comes to Newton, the engineering headquarters of the South Devon Railway, and always one of the most important divisional locomotive centres on the Great Western Railway. In passing it is interesting to recall that the present name, Newton Abbot, was not used until March 1877. Westwards the railway wriggles its way through a hilly, though not basically difficult country. West of Brent four large viaducts were constructed over the deep valleys of rivers flowing down from the heights of Dartmoor. That over the River Erme at Ivybridge may be taken as typical; it was 252 yd long and 114 ft high, and differed from the better known timber viaducts on the Cornwall Railway, in having the stone piers built more nearly up to rail level. The timber struts supporting the permanent way fanned out from ledges in the piers. All the four South Devon viaducts were constructed in this way. They were completed in 1849, and the successful experience with them no doubt led to Brunel making an even more extensive use of timber in the viaducts he built later for the Cornwall Railway.

So far as the South Devon Railway is concerned, the main line was opened throughout to Plymouth in April 1849. The Torquay branch had been opened in December of the previous year, but it was left to a separate and independent company, 'The Dartmouth and Torbay', to extend the line south of Torquay. It was not until 1864 that the line reached its present terminus in Kingswear. The events leading to the building of this railway provide one of the most fascinating 'might have beens' in the history of the Great Western and its numerous constituents. In 1840 an Admiralty Commission had recommended Dartmouth as an ideal terminus for the West Indian mail traffic, then very much on the increase. Unluckily for the Devon harbour Southampton had got its railway first, and speed of communication with London settled the terminus in favour of Southampton. Some time later a monthly service from Dartmouth to Calcutta was inaugurated, but at that time passengers and goods had to be conveyed between Dartmouth and the nearest railway, at Totnes, by river steamer.

It was then that a prominent landowner, Charles Seale-Hayne, determined that Dartmouth must have its railway. Using all his influence and great wealth, he called in Brunel, and a line was planned on the present course as far as Greenway Tunnel, but then to cross the Dart, and come in to Dartmouth itself. It would have been a splendid project, but again it was the old tale of local, short-sighted opposition. Certain equally influential landowners on the western side of the Dart raised so many objections that the line was kept on the eastern side, with the resulting inconvenience of the terminus at Kingswear, and the ferry connection across the water to Dartmouth.

For many years the train service from London to Plymouth was wretchedly poor. After the abandonment of the 'Atmospheric', and with it the need to stop at all stations, certain 'express' trains were put on, which covered the 52 miles between Exeter and Plymouth at the tremendous overall speed of 25 m.p.h. And when the Great Western and the Bristol and Exeter jointly put on the famous 'Flying Dutchman', in 1862, the South Devon Railway took it to Torquay, and terminated it there. Plymouth passengers had to change at Newton, and go forward by a miserable stopping train! The truth is, of course, that the South Devon, saddled with the 'Atmospheric', got away to a very bad start, and had to continue struggling against the handicap of long sections of single line. As for the gradients, the Dainton, Rattery, and Hemerdon inclines are bad enough with modern motive power. They must have been a perfect nightmare with the old broad gauge saddle-tank 4-4-0s. One can only think that the train loads must have been very light.

Despite its manifold handicaps the South Devon had, at various times, some very able men in its service. The first traffic Superintendent was Herbert Clarke, a brother of Seymour Clarke, who was London Divisional Superintendent of the Great Western, and who afterwards became General Manager of the Great Northern. Herbert Clarke left the South Devon in 1851 to join his brother at Kings Cross, and it is remarkable that his successor at Millbay should, in turn, have become one of the most famous of Great Northern operating officers – none other than Francis P. Cockshott. It is no less remarkable that men whose early railway service had been amid the frustrations of the South Devon line should have taken a leading part in carrying the Great Northern forward to a position pre-eminent in world railway speed, beside which the best contemporary achievements of the broad gauge, if not exactly funereal, were definitely second rate.

The South Devon terminus at Plymouth was at Mill Bay, and Cornwall Junction, just outside this station, became the starting point of the Cornwall Railway. If the South Devon was an individual effort, with little or no co-ordination in conception or planning with the other broad gauge lines east of Exeter, the Cornwall Railway was many times more so. It was promoted in the first place by the business men of Falmouth, who saw their chance of getting better communication with the rest of the country when the South Devon Railway was projected. But instead of getting into touch with the active railway promoters of Plymouth they went to those who they deemed to be the leaders of the broad gauge alliance, namely Russell and Saunders of the Great Western. A meeting was held in Bristol at which Brunel was also present; the men of Falmouth urged the Great Western to use its influence to get the South Devon extended to Falmouth, but as we have seen already the broad gauge association was anything but a strong, united alliance. Russell and Saunders could promise nothing so far as the South Devon was concerned, but they did promise to support the projection of a separate Cornwall Railway.

One cannot help reflecting upon how different things might have been if at that time there had been a Huish, an Allport, or a Moon in command at Paddington: a strong leader who would have imposed a unity of purpose and action into the association of broad gauge companies, and avoided inconveniences like that perpetrated by the independent actions of the South Devon and of the Cornwall Railways in Plymouth. It should surely have been obvious to those who planned the South Devon line that an extension into Cornwall was inevitable, sooner or later. Yet they fixed their passenger station as a terminus, and a terminus so sited that its eventual development into a through station was impossible. Then, when the Cornwall Railway was built its trains also used Millbay, and any through trains from Devon into Cornwall had to reverse direction. The Cornwall Railway, with its promise of Great Western assistance, started in the vaguest manner with a proposal to cross the Hamoaze to Torpoint at a place near to the site of the car ferry which has added to the frustration of many thousands of holiday motorists in recent years. How it was proposed to cross the Hamoaze no one seems to have been quite sure.

The original survey was carried out not by Brunel, but by Capt. Moorsom who afterwards was Chairman of the L.N.W.R. for a short time. Brunel was called in as a consultant, and at one time it was thought that the South Devon might co-operate, and build an extension of their line to the New Passage Ferry to meet the Cornwall Railway. But even though the latter company obtained their Act of Incorporation in August 1846, such difficulty was experienced in raising the money that many years were to pass before anything could be done towards building the line. In the meantime the South Devon went ahead independently and set up their headquarters at Millbay. One gains the impression that whatever may have been the wishes of the merchants and shipowners of Falmouth the people of Cornwall in general just did not want the railway. Shortly after the cutting of the first sod, near Truro, there were anti-railway riots because it was feared that the large influx of navvies would create a shortage of food in the Duchy.

Largely through Great Western influence Brunel was called in as engineer, in preference to Capt. Moorsom, and he altered the proposed route between Plymouth and St. Germans, in order to provide a fixed bridge rather than a ferry across the estuary of the Tamar. As re-surveyed the line ran north from a junction with the South Devon Railway outside Millbay, and the river was crossed at Saltash by the very beautiful Royal Albert Bridge. This superb creation, the most enduring and spectacular of all Brunel's works, is so well known today and has been so fully described on so many occasions that I need not enlarge upon either its principles or its details, except to say this: that the erection of the Tamar suspension bridge alongside has given railway enthusiasts increased opportunities for studying the Royal Albert Bridge at closer quarters, and of photographing the goings and comings of the Western Region diesels on the Cornish trains of today.

Reverting now to the time of the building of the Cornwall Railway, the line immediately beyond Saltash was carried beside and across the tidal creeks of the Lynher river, and one met, in all their distinctive beauty, some of the most interesting of Brunel's timber viaducts. There were no fewer than six of them in the five miles between the Saltash and St. Germans stations. In crossing the creeks no masonry piers were used. Timber piles were driven deep down into the mud, and the appearance of a viaduct like Forder, which looked as though it were carried on wooden stilts, was as extraordinary as it seemed fragile. At St. Germans the railway was carried more than 100 ft above high water mark, and there the towers were tapered from the base upwards; those resting on the saltings above high water mark had masonry foundations, but the river piers were driven down into the mud. Nottar was one of the longest of all the viaducts on the Cornwall Railway; it lay about a mile east of St. Germans, and was 307 ft long and 67 ft above high water mark. The line was diverted further inland on this section in 1908, and these picturesque viaducts across the creeks were then dismantled. Beyond St. Germans there were no fewer than 25 timber viaducts in the ensuing 44½ miles to Truro, and the general design consisted of massive masonry piers built up to about 35 ft below rail level; from the top of these piers four sets of timber legs radiated to support the main bridge girders.

The Cornwall Railway was a long time in the making, and although the Act had been obtained in 1846 it was not until April 1859 that the first train ran through from Plymouth to Truro. Brunel did not live to see the line in full operation, though not long before his death he visited the Royal Albert Bridge, lying on a couch, on an open truck drawn very slowly across by one of Gooch's locomotives. The bridge was opened on May 2nd, 1859, by H.R.H. The Prince Consort, and two days later a public service of trains was inaugurated between Plymouth and Truro. The Royal Albert Bridge was an object of wonder and admiration, but people were scared of the timber viaducts. To increase the apprehension there was an alarming derailment near St. Germans only two days after the opening of the public service. This was due to defective permanent way, but it took place just as the train was approaching the Grove viaduct, and the engine and two coaches fell over the wooden parapet and crashed to the saltings below. Fortunately Grove was one of the less lofty viaducts, and the fall was only 30 ft; but the engine landed completely upside down, and stuck fast in the river mud with its wheels in the air. The driver, fireman and guard were killed, but no passengers were seriously injured.

Although the Cornwall Railway had originally been promoted with the object of providing railway communication to Falmouth, such had been the difficulty in raising funds that construction had stopped short at Truro. Nothing had been done towards building the final portion since 1854, and as yet nothing was completed. In the meantime, as traffic began to flow between Plymouth and Truro considerable difficulties were experienced at the western end; for here, believe it or not, there was a break of gauge! If the chain of railway communication between London and Truro had grown up in a somewhat haphazard way the final stage of the line, between Truro and Penzance, surpassed all. And yet the origins of railway development in West Cornwall were logical enough. Quite early in the nineteenth century the tin mining industry was in a most flourishing state, thanks to the modest degree of mechanization introduced by the pumping engines of Trevithick; and even before the Great Western itself was authorized Parliament passed an Act, in 1834, authorizing the construction of a largely mineral railway from Hayle to Camborne and Redruth, with branches extending to several of the busiest mining districts. Unlike the other components of the present main line to Penzance construction was relatively quick on the Hayle Railway, and the whole line with its branches, totalling 17¼ miles, was open by 1839.

The Hayle Railway was built more on the lines of a colliery railway in County Durham rather than a section of a very popular holiday and tourist route. The gauge was 4 ft 8½ in.; the rails were laid on stone blocks, and to minimize the cost of construction rope worked inclines were included to surmount the hilly country traversed. There was an 'inclined-plane' of 1 in 10 for 30 chains at Angarrack; another at 1 in 22 up into Camborne, and there were two more, on the mining branches. When the pattern of railway communication west of Exeter began to take shape, and both the South Devon and the Cornwall Railways were projected, proposals were made for a 'West Cornwall Railway' which would complete the line through to Penzance by the simple process of extending the Hayle Railway at each end. The original idea was to use the Hayle line exactly as it was, including the two rope-worked inclines on the main line! But Parliament refused to sanction the scheme, and the promoters thereupon called in Brunel to recommend deviations that would avoid the two 'inclined planes'. The broad gauge companies were now definitely interested, and backed the project strongly; and when the Act was obtained in 1846 Charles Russell became one of the original West Cornwall directors.

So far as main line construction was concerned the tale in West Cornwall was the same as it had been in South Devon and with the Cornwall Railway. Money was very slow in forthcoming, and many thousands of shares were forfeited. It had been proposed to build the new extensions, east of Redruth, and west of Hayle, on the broad gauge, and to convert those portions of the original line as would be incorporated in the new through route; but funds were so low that in 1850 relaxation was obtained from a new Act that permitted the continuance of the narrow gauge, to save conversion expenses, providing that the works on the new sections were made wide enough for the eventual accommodation of the broad gauge. Moreover the West Cornwall Railway was required to convert its whole line to broad gauge on six months notice being given from 'a connecting broad gauge company'. As this was the year 1850, and the Cornwall Railway had not yet decided how to cross the Tamar, let alone get to Truro, this must have seemed a safe enough provision to agree to. The chances of being called upon to convert were not likely to occur for some years to come. So it came that the West Cornwall Railway was opened throughout from Truro to Penzance on the narrow gauge, in August 1852.

The West Cornwall line included many fine examples of Brunel's timber viaducts, the finest being one on the Angarrack deviating line with a maximum height of 100 ft. The longest was over the beach at Penzance, where a lengthy viaduct of 347 ft was carried on timber 'stilts' at a maximum height of no more than 12 ft. Brunel evidently underestimated the effects of the sea at this point, for in the very first winter of its use more than half of it was washed away in a great gale, which also demolished part of the sea wall protecting the approach of the railway to the terminus. The viaduct was partly destroyed for the second time in 1868, after which a new, and more substantial structure was built. Before that important alterations had been necessary to some of the larger inland viaducts. Originally these had been built entirely of timber, with timber piers resting on relatively light masonry foundations. It was found necessary to strengthen the foundations, and at the same time masonry piers were built up to the level of the springing of the raking legs, thus making them similar to the inland viaducts east of Truro.

The trouble with the West Cornwall viaducts came mostly after Brunel's death, but he was deeply concerned in another major engineering 'headache' at the time of the construction of the West Cornwall Railway. While Brunel could pursue perfection to the point of extravagance on the Great Western main line he was ready enough to consider means for saving costs where funds were low, and it was this that led him to recommend use of the Barlow type of rail. This can best be described as an inverted V, with the two legs curved outwards, and the point of the V broad enough to provide the running surface. The ballast had to be packed very carefully all round, and hard up underneath the V. No sleepers or other supports were needed, as the splaying out of the V distributed the weight of the passing traffic on to the ballast. But unless the ballasting was very well done and well maintained, the road could be extremely dangerous. Moreover great difficulty was at first experienced in getting the rails themselves rolled to a satisfactory quality. They were used for a time on the South Wales main line, but proved so difficult to maintain that they were replaced in Brunel's lifetime. The West Cornwall Railway had to struggle on with them and make the best of a bad job for many years, because they simply could not afford to scrap them!

So we come back to Truro. The link-up with the broad gauge Cornwall Railway had been made in 1859, and for some five years the two companies put up with all the inconveniences of the break of gauge. Then in 1864 the Cornwall Railway asserted its right, under the Act of 1850, to demand the laying of broad gauge tracks from Truro to Penzance. This caught the West Cornwall people completely 'on the wrong foot', without any funds to carry out the conversion. The outcome was that the Great Western, the Bristol and Exeter and the South Devon jointly took over the line, and the transfer took effect from January 1st, 1866, but it was not until more than 10 months later that the broad gauge was laid through to Penzance, and the line was not authorized for broad gauge passenger trains until the end of February 1867. On March 1st, 1867, through carriages were run for the first time between Paddington and Penzance. Most of the line west of Truro was then laid on cross-sleepered track, with bull-head rails, and the mixed gauge was provided throughout.

Train working in West Cornwall must have provided many an extraordinary spectacle in those far-off days. Most of the freight traffic continued to be handled on the narrow gauge, though of course through consignments travelling east of Truro were loaded into broad gauge wagons. At first these were marshalled into one daily train in each direction, with wagons of perishable stock attached as required to the regular passenger trains. As traffic increased, however, the West Cornwall line began to run freight trains including both narrow and broad gauge wagons. The formation was thus: narrow gauge engine, followed by narrow gauge wagons; then followed a so-called 'match truck', with wide buffers and sliding shackles, and this was followed by the broad gauge trucks containing consignments for east of Truro. These mixed trains were introduced in 1871, and continued until the final abolition of the broad gauge. The various mineral branches all remained narrow gauge. All the through passenger trains were broad gauge, though some purely local traffic was worked with the old West Cornwall narrow gauge. So far as Penzance is concerned, the inauguration of through carriages to and from Paddington brought the journey time down to 12 hr in each direction, though trains stopped at all stations on the West Cornwall line.

In Truro the West Cornwall Railway was first in the field, with a station at 'Higher Town', and, in 1855, an extension to Newham with a wharf on the Truro River. When the Cornwall Railway was opened a tunnel was bored at Penwithers to provide a connecting line to the West Cornwall Railway, and made large enough to accommodate two broad gauge tracks alongside. Actually it was used originally for one narrow gauge line of the West Cornwall Railway, and the broad gauge Falmouth extension of the Cornwall Railway, which was opened in 1863. The Falmouth line was engineered by R. P. Brereton, formerly assistant to Brunel, and no engineer can have had a more devoted friend and follower. The Falmouth line was planned and built entirely in the Brunel tradition of the timber viaducts. Of these latter Ponsanooth, 215 ft long, was the fourth highest of any in the West Country, and had a maximum height of 139 ft. It was exceeded in this respect only by Liskeard, Moorswater, and St. Pinnock, on the main line. The last three to remain in the West Country were on the Falmouth line, and they were not replaced until the mid nineteen-thirties.

I well remember my earliest journeys to Falmouth, in 1924, and the experience of travelling over these lofty viaducts; how there was a faint suspicion of swaying, though in actual fact they were extra-ordinarily sound and safe. The timber viaducts of the West afford a most striking example of the practical engineering skill of Brunel. One tends to remember his adventures with the 'Atmospheric', the earliest broad gauge locomotives, and the pile-supported track between Paddington and Maidenhead, and to reflect that there were no half measures about anything that Brunel did. It was either a colossal success, or an equally colossal failure! In the timber viaducts he produced a design that was not only beautiful to look upon, and economical in first cost; every detail was most carefully thought out for the future inspection and maintenance of the structures, so that timbers could be removed for examination, or be replaced with the minimum interference. The structures bred a magnificent body of skilled bridgemen who became supremely agile and expert in working on these high, very exposed works – men to whom the modern Great Western motto 'pride in the job' was second nature. In no aspect was railway working in the West more completely epitomised, in its unique fascinating appeal, than in the timber viaducts of Brunel.

VI

The Broad Gauge in South Wales

THE Great Western was always a railway of marked contrasts: in the disparity between its best and its worst; in the varying emphasis laid upon different traffics, and in the physical characteristics of its main lines. Wide contrasts developed at a very early stage in the history of its constituents and protegées, and this feature was nowhere more pronounced than in the manner of promotion of its two lengthy main lines, to Penzance on the one hand, and to Fishguard on the other. I have already told of the curious build-up of the famous 'Cornish Riviera' route, and how in most cases it was a group of promoters at the far end, at Plymouth, at Falmouth, in the western mining districts, and even at Dartmouth who made the first steps to obtain railway connection with the slowly advancing metals of the broad gauge. Railway interests in London and Bristol took some persuading to back these projects down in the West Country, and with good reason. Except for tin mining, industry and trade generally were at a low ebb in South Devon and Cornwall, and the prospects of an early remunerative traffic were poor.

In South Wales it was very different. In 1844 when the prospectus of the South Wales Railway Company was issued, great emphasis was laid on the importance of communication with the south of Ireland, and it was as a first class main line through to Fishguard that the project was launched, with strong Great Western backing. Many influential Irishmen were members of the provisional committee, and it was the Great Western Board that announced, in 1845, their support of 'a great national undertaking to connect the South of Ireland as well as South Wales with the Metropolis'. No rival project was put forward, and west of Newport the proposed line followed generally the present route, via Cardiff, Neath, Swansea, Llanelly and Carmarthen. At the eastern end there was considerable dispute as to how the new line should be connected with the existing Great Western system. For many years at the end of the nineteenth century the G.W.R. endured the sarcastic tag of 'Great Way Round', in reference to the circuitous nature of *all* its principal main lines, and this is sometimes laid on the doorstep of

Brunel, as evidence of his 'lack of foresight'. The facts, generally, were very different. I have already told how the high command at Paddington strove to secure a more direct route to Exeter; they were thwarted no less in their attempts to provide a straightforward crossing of the Severn.

The original proposal was to follow the Gloucester line as far as Stroud and Stonehouse, and then to continue west-north-west to a viaduct over the Severn between Fretherne and Awre, and little more than five miles beyond Stonehouse. The line would then have continued down the right bank of the Severn, through Chepstow, to Newport. By this route the mileage from Paddington to Newport would have been about 143½ miles – only 10 miles more than by the present direct line through the Severn Tunnel. Numerous interests combined to block the Fretherne–Awre viaduct scheme. Local opinion urged that east of Newport the line should be taken through Monmouth and Ross, and so through Gloucester, while shipping interests claimed that the proposed bridge would be a serious hindrance to navigation, regardless of the fact that most shipping en route for Gloucester docks used the Gloucester and Berkeley Canal upstream from Sharpness, and thus by-passed that portion of the river that Brunel proposed to bridge. Brunel even proposed to make a new 'cut' for shipping, clean across the Arlingham promontory, which would have avoided the bridge. The Severn Navigation Commissioners accepted the proposal, but in the end it was the Admiralty that forbade the bridge.

In the circumstances there was nothing for it but to go round through Gloucester and add 15 miles to the through journey from London to South and West Wales. In so doing advantage was taken of another project, the Gloucester and Dean Forest Railway, which had been proposed to connect the Monmouth and Hereford Railway with the Great Western at Gloucester. It was eventually arranged that the South Wales Railway would start from a junction with the Gloucester and Dean Forest at Grange Court, 7½ miles from Gloucester itself. The original Act of 1845 authorized construction of the South Wales Railway from Chepstow to Fishguard, with a branch to Pembroke Dock, and a further Act of 1846 authorized the eastward extension from Chepstow to Grange Court. The new railway was planned for the broad gauge; Brunel was engineer, and Charles Russell was the first chairman.

It is significant of the 'through' nature of the line, in striking contrast to railway activities in Devon and Cornwall, that the South Wales main line was taken clear of Swansea. As originally authorized it went no nearer than Landore, and it was only in the supplementary Act of 1846 that a branch into the present High Street station was provided for. The case was thus actually the reverse of that at Plymouth, where a terminus was established in the town by one constituent, and a second came eventually to use it. The direct line, avoiding any reversal of direction, came some years later at Plymouth. Another important branch included in the 1846 Act was that to Haverfordwest, which events combined to promote into a main line for very many years. The contrast with the West of England lines is again in evidence between Kidwelly and Carmarthen. Here Brunel originally intended to go in a straight line between the two towns, tunnelling through the high ground east of the Towy estuary. Later, to save expense, and get better gradients, he took the line round the coast, in a beautiful South Wales counterpart of the Dawlish–Teignmouth section. In recent years I have several times spent an hour or so on the pleasant foreshore at Llanstephen, which in situation and railway outlook is strongly reminiscent of the Devon village of Shaldon, opposite Teignmouth; but while the single-tracked, hopelessly encumbered 'Atmospheric' has developed into a teeming artery of intense holiday traffic, the great trunk route to the South of Ireland seems deserted by contrast, and the up 'Whitland milk' is about the most important train one can see in a summer afternoon.

Today the emphasis in South Wales is in a very different direction, yet it is extraordinary to recall that for some little time after its first opening, in 1850, the South Wales Railway carried no goods traffic! Between the obtaining of the original Act in 1845 and this first opening a great deal had happened to alter the original conception of the line. In a complex situation no one factor affected things more than the terrible Irish potato famine of 1846–7. At that time the great bulk of the Irish peasants were unbelievably poor, not merely by present standards, but in comparison to the English country folk of the day. Potatoes were their staple diet, and when for two years in succession the crops failed the effect was catastrophic. So far as railway development was concerned the grand South Wales project had been put forward in close, though undefined association with various lines in the south-eastern counties of Ireland. But the effects of the famine were to put a complete stop to the majority of Irish railway proposals; and with things at a standstill in Ireland itself, and many Irish supporters of the South Wales Railway forfeiting their shares, the prospects of a prosperous cross-channel traffic receded almost to vanishing point. Although works had been commenced over almost the entire line from Grange Court to Fishguard in 1847 operations were entirely suspended on the sections west of Swansea, and it was between Chepstow and Swansea only that the line was opened in 1850.

The difficulties of the situation led to friction between the South Wales Railway and the Great Western. The latter company had taken a lease of the line at a guaranteed rent of 5 per cent. on a capital of three million in shares, and one million in loans; but this payment did not commence until the line was completed from Grange Court right through to Fishguard. In their dilemma the South Wales people approached the Great Western with a view to bringing the lease agreement into operation when the line was opened to Swansea; the Great Western refused, and Russell, who could do nothing to bring the two sides together, resigned his chairmanship of the South Wales Railway. Directors and shareholders of the latter company grew bitter against the Great Western; it was felt strongly that Paddington and Bristol knew as well as they did that it was hopeless to press on to Fishguard in the prevailing circumstances, and that they were standing out for the strict fulfilment of the terms of the lease simply because they felt the South Wales Railway would be bankrupt long before they reached Fishguard, and the Great Western would not have to pay the rent due on the lease anyway!

In South Wales there are several examples of the way Brunel carried out his activities far beyond that of engineer. When the South Wales Railway was first promoted he and Saunders personally did nearly all the canvassing for subscribers, and now, at this critical time of dispute between the two companies Brunel took it upon himself to act as mediator, and he went on to the extent of drawing up a draft settlement that was accepted by both Boards. The sequel set a precedent that was followed some years later when the Great Western and Bristol and Exeter Boards had agreed terms for the amalgamation of the two companies: the shareholders of the smaller company refused to ratify the decision of their directors. In the South Wales case the directors were urged to proceed with the line to Fishguard. Work was therefore recommenced west of Swansea, but negotiations were soon reopened with the Great Western, and a settlement was reached in March 1851 that pleased everyone. Instead of Fishguard it was agreed to establish the western terminus at Neyland Point, on Milford Haven, which was to be reached by extending the branch already authorized to Haverfordwest. Work on the line beyond the projected junction – near the present Clarbeston Road station – was now finally stopped.

Even though it had been opened as far as Swansea in 1850 the South Wales Railway was still completely isolated from the Great Western. Brunel's remarkable viaduct over the Wye at Chepstow was not yet completed, and all the locomotives and rolling stock for working the line between Chepstow and Swansea had to be shipped across the Severn from Bristol. From Bristol also came the third of the celebrated Clarke brothers, Frederick, to be Superintendent of the Line. Until then he had been Superintendent of the Bristol Division of the Great Western, so that from 1850 one had the interesting position of Seymour Clarke being on the G.W.R. in London; Herbert Clarke, Superintendent of the South Devon Railway; and Frederick Clarke, Superintendent of the South Wales. Except for Clarke himself and many of the locomotive enginemen all the staff of the South Wales Railway were recruited locally. So far as engineering was concerned, except for the Chepstow viaduct which I shall discuss in detail later there were large timber viaducts across the Usk at Newport and across Swansea valley at Landore. Both of these had wrought-iron bowstring girders for the large central spans across the rivers, and the remaining girders were timber, supported entirely on timber legs.

At Chepstow the river Wye and the requirements of navigation set Brunel a rare problem. On the left bank there is a limestone cliff rising almost sheer from the water to a height of some 70 ft above high water mark, while the right bank is flanked by muddy flats and ground rising gradually towards the town. A clear head-way of 50 ft had to be provided beneath the projected viaduct, and a clear span of at least 300 ft demanded to satisfy the needs of navigation. Brunel's solution of the problem is of great interest and importance, as his use of tubular main girders, from which the rail carrying girders were suspended, formed the prototype of the Royal Albert Bridge at Saltash. Another puzzle, that of getting a good foundation for the western pier of the main span in the mud of the right bank, was also neatly solved by Brunel. He constructed large cast iron cylinders, forced them down into the mud by loading more and more weight on to them, and then filled them with concrete. The eastern end of the main girders rested on the solid rock of the left bank escarpment of the river. One line over the bridge was opened for traffic in July 1852, and thus completed the line of railway communication between London and Swansea. The second line was opened in April 1853.

Thus despite the Battle of the Gauges, and despite the findings of the Gauge Commissioners, the broad gauge continued to extend. In

Cardiff, however, there was already an important narrow gauge line in the Taff Vale, and the fact that it was built by Brunel himself does appear to throw some light upon the great engineer's conception of what the railway network of the country might have been if the broad gauge had won the day, and the existing main lines been converted. The Gauge Commissioners, detecting some inconsistency in his practice, questioned Brunel on this point. Although the Taff Vale was not authorized until a year after the Great Western, the first section of it was not opened until two years after the first section of the Great Western was opened. In answer to the Commissioners Brunel said: 'One of the reasons, I remember, was one which would not influence me now; but at that time I certainly assumed that the effect of curves was such, that the radius of the curve might be measured in units of the gauge, in which I have since found myself to be mistaken. Then I expected to have to lay out that line with a succession of curves of small radius, which is the case as the line is laid out; and I assumed that the narrow gauge was better than the wide gauge as regards curves. I do not remember whether connexion with any other railway there, or likely to be there, influenced me.'

This is, in many ways, a most curious statement. The main lines of the Taff Vale, despite what Brunel said, are remarkably straight, but he was perhaps alluding to the many steeply graded branches leading into the colliery districts. One feels that he was 'hedging' when he said he could not remember if the thought of connections with existing railways influenced him. Brunel was always on the most intimate terms with Russell and Saunders, and one can well imagine that their ideas of penetrating into South Wales had been discussed long before the prospectus for the South Wales Railway was issued. Equally one feels that the folks at Paddington would have had a good deal to say to Brunel about his proposed gauge on the Taff Vale if it had not fitted into their general strategy. No; it seems clear that Brunel himself saw no difficulties in a break of gauge, and engineered the Taff Vale in much the same way as later engineers built sub-standard gauge feeder lines to the main systems in India, Ireland, and elsewhere. His ideas on curvature had evidently undergone a remarkable change by the time he laid out the South Devon line between Newton Abbot and Totnes!

Apart from the financial disputes with the Great Western affairs on the eastern end of the South Wales Railway went along smoothly enough, though the company found it necessary to come to terms with the Taff Vale very early in its life. No sooner had the broad gauge line arrived in Cardiff than a connection with the Taff was felt desirable. Parliamentary powers were obtained for a short connecting line, broad gauge of course, and then there came the question of the actual junction. The South Wales people seemed to expect the Taff to welcome them with open arms, and lay down mixed gauge for their convenience; but the Taff Vale was really quite indifferent to the whole business. Their coal traffic to Cardiff docks was working up to very large and profitable proportions, and to use a modernism they could not have cared less whether or not they had a connection to the South Wales Railway. The latter company was told in no uncertain terms that if they wanted interchange facilities it was they, and not the Taff Vale, that must lay down the mixed gauge. So they did, not only on the connecting line from Bute Street, but through their own principal station, and for half a mile westward to some exchange sidings.

We must now pass on to the interesting section of line west of Swansea. In crossing the neck of the Gower peninsular some tremendous gradients were involved, climbing for nearly 2 miles at 1 in 50 from Landore up to the eastern end of Cockett Tunnel, and then descending for $2\frac{1}{4}$ miles at 1 in 50–53 to Gowerton. The tunnel itself was only a short one, on a rising gradient of 1 in 71 against west bound trains. Once past Gowerton the line follows the coast, and apart from short inclines which hardly affect the speed the gradients are not worth mentioning in the ensuing 25 miles on to Myrtle Hill Junction, Carmarthen. On this section there were originally two timber viaducts of considerable size, both with the central spans opening for shipping; one had a wrought iron swing portion of 30 ft opening, and the second, with a lifting span, was at Kidwelly. At Carmarthen the original station was on the main line, some distance from the town and near the site of the present Myrtle Hill Junction. The line was opened to this point in 1852, and it was not until eight years later that the connection to Carmarthen Town was brought into service, and then not by the South Wales Railway but by the so-called Carmarthen and Cardigan, which never reached Cardigan but stopped short at Convil.

From Carmarthen westward the main line of the South Wales Railway was carried through eastern Pembrokeshire as a fast-running, well-designed trunk route, though this was largely in hopeful anticipation of developments rather than in any response to immediate needs. In reporting to the South Wales Board in 1856 concerning the terminus at Neyland Brunel was unusually modest and cautious – quite unlike his usual buoyant, optimistic self:

'A temporary Passenger Station was erected, and provision has been made for carrying on a certain amount of Goods Traffic across the Harbour by lighters.

'A fixed Pier, extending a certain distance into deep water, and the deepening of the shore where the Coal Shipping Staithes are to be placed, have been commenced and are now nearly completed.

'The designing and constructing of the Terminus of a Railway upon the shores of a Haven, at a point where no trade of any sort at present exists, although there is every prospect of a very large trade being created, must necessarily be progressive and must mainly consist of expedients contrived from time to time to keep pace with each requirement as it may grow. Such has been our commencement at Milford Haven and such must, for some time to come, be the character of our proceeding. The Wharf accommodation provided for the lighter trade is already found insufficient and is about to be extended, while the success of the Steam Boat communication with Ireland has shown that a portion, if not the whole, of the Floating Pier, as originally designed, is not only desirable but essential for carrying on the trade, particularly in cattle, which promises to be considerable. Accordingly a portion has been ordered and will be immediately proceeded with.'

In concentrating upon Neyland the company got themselves into serious trouble. It was one thing to abandon the original idea of going on to Fishguard; nobody really minded that. But it was quite another thing to try and allow the Parliamentary powers granted for the Pembroke branch to lie unfulfilled. At that period the so-called 'Cardwell clause' was included in all railway Acts to enforce the construction of all lines for which powers had been granted. This was to ensure that all railways promoted were bona-fide concerns, and not the dream of speculators; it was a result of the Mania days, and provided for all dividend payments to be stopped until all lines authorized by Parliament had actually been built. A certain aggrieved party in the Pembroke district obtained an injunction against the South Wales Railway, suspending payment of the dividend. Further litigation ensued, the eventual result of which was that the House of Lords Committee decided there was no case for a separate branch to Pembroke. In their opinion the public need was small, and that the presence of the new railhead at Neyland, conveniently reached by ferry from Pembroke Dock, was quite adequate. Thus the South Wales Railway was able to resume paying its dividend, while the furious landowners of Pembroke decided to have a railway of their own. Thus the Pembroke and Tenby Railway was promoted, and as if to underline its antagonism to the defaulting South Wales Railway the new line proposed was to be narrow gauge!

In 1864 this little line was authorized to extend northwards to a junction with the South Wales main line at Whitland. It was a junction only in the broadest sense, for there was originally no physical connection with the broad gauge line, and indeed the Pembroke and Tenby had a separate station. As if this were not enough Parliamentary powers were obtained for an extension eastwards to Carmarthen, so that a junction could be made there with the narrow gauge Llanelly Railway, which would eventually connect with the Central Wales line of the London and North Western coming down from Llandrindod and Builth to Llandovery. This was twisting the tail of the broad gauge lion with a vengeance, and the Pembroke and Tenby people cunningly secured the inclusion of a clause in their Act whereby they would forego their powers to extend from Whitland to Carmarthen if the South Wales Railway would provide narrow gauge access for them to Carmarthen. The broad-gaugers fell for this piece of strategy, and instead of laying down mixed gauge decided to convert one of their existing tracks to the narrow gauge. Their own traffic, as yet, scarcely justified a double line. Thus the Pembroke and Tenby got to Carmarthen merely by making the physical junction at Whitland and by making the western spur of the present Carmarthen triangle so that their trains could run straight into Carmarthen Town, without the necessity of reversal at the South Wales station – Carmarthen Junction.

Today when nearly all through trains for West Wales travel into Carmarthen and reverse direction there, it is interesting to recall that both the spur lines they traverse were originally no part of the main conception of the South Wales Railway, and that one indeed was built by an out-and-out rebel. The Pembroke and Tenby people were in no way placated by the South Wales gesture of converting one of their lines to narrow gauge and granting them running powers; they rubbed salt into the wounds by arranging with the L.N.W.R. for through carriages to be run from Manchester and Liverpool to Tenby, from 1869 onwards. This working did not last for very long. The year 1872 saw the abolition of the broad gauge in West Wales, and from that time onwards the Pembroke and Tenby trains did not run east of Whitland, and the through L.N.W.R. carriages were conveyed by Great Western trains from Carmarthen westward to Whitland. By mention of the abolition of the broad gauge in these regions I am however carrying the story forward several years, and the events leading up to it must next be related.

In the mining districts it was the local, narrow gauge railways that were carrying the coal traffic. The South Wales Railway itself took very little, and in any case the coal owners would have been reluctant to admit broad gauge wagons to their premises. Compared with the handy little narrow gauge trucks, which carried a surprising amount of coal in relation to their size and tare weight, the broad gauge vehicles of the day were massive and cumbersome. The handicap of the break of gauge was felt more severely in South Wales than anywhere else. There was an economic side to it also, from the private traders' point of view. Many of them found it convenient to provide their own wagons, and with cost of equipment to be considered they naturally preferred to have the lighter and cheaper narrow gauge vehicles. The break of gauge was bad enough where it was a case of transferring packed or parcelled consignments; with coal it was a wretchedly slow and inefficient process.

From the outset the South Wales Railway had been worked by Great Western engines and rolling stock under the general supervision of Daniel Gooch. This was a matter of constant dispute, with the local people saying that the operating expenses were much too high because Gooch had fixed the load limits for each class of engine at much too low a figure. In consequence more locomotives were in use than were warranted by the traffic. There were many other complaints of Great Western 'incompetence', and the South Wales Board was seriously proposing to raise additional capital to enable them to work the line themselves. Allegations led to open dispute, and eventually to arbitration; but the ultimate result, instead of complete separation, was amalgamation of the two companies, in 1863. To the Great Western directors, however, the trouble in South Wales must have been no more than a mild diversion in comparison with the prolonged and exhausting struggle they had only recently ended in the West Midlands. Before this latter campaign was over Charles Russell had retired, worn out with anxieties of his office. Illness affected his brain, and he died by his own hand in 1856. When the South Wales Railway became a part of the Great Western Lord Shelburne was Chairman.

VII

Oxford, Worcester and Wolverhampton

A PASSENGER of the nineteen-twenties, or thirties, travelling by a train like the 1.45 p.m. from Paddington and seeing the legend PADDINGTON, WORCESTER, KIDDERMINSTER AND STOURBRIDGE on the roof boards of spacious chocolate and cream coaches would never guess, and if told scarcely believe the story that lies beneath that delightful railway that makes its way into the high Cotswolds by the Evenlode valley; that descends so abruptly to the Vale of Evesham, and turns northwards into the most westerly regions of the Black Country. With its westward extension to Malvern and Hereford, its connections with the Midland at Abbots Wood and Stoke Works and its penetration to Wolverhampton and a group of farther-north connections, it seems today so obvious and natural an artery of railway traffic. It was all that, and construction of it was authorized as early as 1845; yet such were the legal, financial and strategic battles fought with the Great Western, that it was not until seven years later that the company was able to declare as much as 36 miles open for traffic. And then they had not a penny left with which to purchase any locomotives or rolling stock!

The factors that led up to this absurd situation would have been farcical were it not for the distress caused to many unfortunate shareholders, and for the great anxiety it caused continually to the Great Western management, frequently diverting a great deal more of their attention than could really be spared from the affairs of their own line. Brunel was the first engineer, and the first cause of dispute arose over his estimate for the cost of the line. This was made prior to the Act of 1845, and was based on the costs of materials and labour then prevailing – namely £1,500,000. By the time the O.W.W. was ready to get going the Mania was at its height; materials and labour for railway making were so much in demand that the prices had risen enormously, and it was evident that Brunel's figure of £1½ million would not be nearly enough. The difficulty and subsequent disputes arose over the Great Western guarantee of 3½ per cent on the authorized capital. It was then that the O.W.W. Chairman approached the Great Western for an upward adjustment of the guarantee.

Now the O.W.W. Chairman, Francis Rufford, was a Stourbridge banker, and moreover one who was not held in very high esteem locally. Unluckily the remaining O.W.W. directors placed implicit trust in him, so that for a time he assumed the part of a virtual dictator. In 1845 Russell readily agreed to the reasonable nature of Rufford's application, and the Great Western agreed to guarantee a sum of £2,500,000, and to pay a minimum interest of 4 per cent. In February 1846 a General Meeting of G.W.R. shareholders empowered their Board to enter into negotiations with the O.W.W., with a view to extending the guarantee. The rate of interest was definitely stipulated as 4 per cent but the actual amount was not mentioned. The wording of the resolution ran: 'by extending the guarantee to such sum as shall appear to them necessary for the completion of the said railway and works . . . .' In the negotiations between the two Boards the sum of £2,500,000 was stipulated as a maximum; why it was left out in the resolution passed at the Great Western shareholders meeting is not clear, but its omission proved disastrous. Rufford carefully omitted to tell his own shareholders of the maximum figure, and they were led to believe that the Great Western were prepared to pay 4 per cent upon whatever sum was incurred in the construction of the line.

From this shocking start, with the subsequent bombshell when the truth eventually came out, relations between the two companies degenerated into those of a cat and dog order. It would be tedious to follow, point by point, the phaeton course of the wrangles, accusations and counter-accusations, swearing of affidavits, and goodness what else, that went on *for nine years*, till the momentous events of 1854, which at the time might have been taken as the consummation of all Russell's patient, straightforward and patently honest negotiations, in the face of some extraordinary manoeuvres by the other side. But no! Russell was to retire from the scene, and the injunction he obtained against the O.W.W., and the new Parliamentary powers obtained were to be flouted as brazenly as earlier 'agreements'. And so events went on, sometimes more violently than ever, for another nine years which ended with complete amalgamation with the Great Western.

At this distance in time, seeing how closely the interests of the two companies would seem to have been allied, one can well question what the persistent rows were about. A great deal hinged upon the fact that throughout this 18 years of railway warfare the O.W.W. was in the hands, successively, of two very strong, resolute, and entirely self-seeking men, who thought from first to last of the financial gains to be derived from each successive transaction, and little or nothing about the job of running a railway. The first of these two characters, Francis Rufford, has already been mentioned. He was well-known in the Stourbridge district as 'a man of straw', and on this account the public locally had no confidence in the railway. In November 1850 the O.W.W. gathered into their midst an even stronger and more dictatorial personality in John Parson, a London solicitor who became legal adviser to the company. Rufford retired from the chair at the same time as Parson entered upon the scene, and no one of any standing in Stourbridge was surprised when six months later Rufford went bankrupt, and his bank stopped payment. The O.W.W. lost £24,000 over this affair.

The next factor was the vexed one of the gauge. The original Act of 1845, which was obtained, (as told in Chapter Three) when the Grand Junction came so unexpectedly to the aid of the Great Western, and in flat opposition to the London and Birmingham and other narrow gauge parties, provided for the O.W.W. to be a broad gauge line. The company was also required to lay in the mixed gauge between Abbots Wood Junction, on the Midland main line to Bristol, and Wolverhampton, and also on the branch to the Midland at Stoke Prior, just souht of Bromsgrove. This was to permit of Midland trains between Bristol and Birmingham being diverted via Worcester, and of interchange between the Midland, from the Bristol direction, and the Grand Junction at Wolverhampton. To men like Rufford and Parson the gauge of the railway meant nothing. It might perhaps have been thought that they would have become the tools of narrow gauge protagonists who might use the existence of the mixed gauge line from Wolverhampton to Worcester as a means of weaving a wily way through the West Midlands to take the Great Western in the flank. In actual fact the gauge appears to have been a mere bone of legal contention: just one of many items to quarrel over with the Great Western!

The whole business of constructing the line was hopelessly mismanaged, and by the summer of 1849 practically all the company's money had been spent and not a mile of line was opened to traffic. Worse than this, construction had not proceeded on any orderly plan. Capital had been frittered away on works distributed throughout the whole length of the railway, instead of concentrating on one section, getting that open, and earning some revenue. Complaints poured in, from the corporations of the towns that had been looking forward to railway communication; from landlords whose property had been cut up, and the works thereon left unfinished; and above all from the unfortunate shareholders. Things got to the stage of the Railway Commissioners ordering the Great Western to take possession and finish the job, as they had promised to do if the need arose. It was at this stage that John Parson entered upon the scene. At once new energy was infused into the O.W.W. by getting rid of directors with Great Western sympathies, by promoting a Bill to enable more capital to be raised, and then, to the consternation of Russell and Saunders, opening negotiations with the North Western and the Midland with a view to those companies working the line when completed.

Then followed a scramble in which the Great Western offered terms for working the line which it was hoped would be preferred to those arranged with the North Western and the Midland. The O.W.W. Chairman, Lord Ward, had already made it clear to Parson that any arrangement with Euston and Derby was illegal; but such matters as legality didn't worry Parson, and he went ahead in defiance of his Chairman. When he carried the rest of the Board with him Lord Ward resigned in protest. Then the legal battles began in earnest. The proposed alliance between the North Western and the O.W.W. was defeated, but the North Western was proposing to make a branch from their Bletchley and Oxford line that would make a direct connection with the O.W.W. Then the Great Western discovered that the portions of the Worcester line that were nearing completion were being laid with only the narrow gauge. Brunel, thoroughly disgusted with the whole business, resigned his office as engineer in 1852, though for the year previous to this he had played little part. One of the greatest difficulties in the acid relations between the O.W.W. and the Great Western was that the original agreements of 1845 were so loosely worded that neither side could be held bound to them in the event of litigation. The difference was that Russell and Saunders were men of their word, and did their best to honour their pledges in the spirit in which they were originally given, whereas John Parson was quite without scruples.

Then out of this whirlpool of railway politics and jumbled finance came comedy, light and hearty. In October 1850 a section of line had actually been opened, 3·9 miles of it between Worcester and Abbots Wood Junction; and in February 1852 another 9·7 miles was opened, between Worcester and Stoke Works Junction. So far as motive power was concerned these caused no embarrassment to the O.W.W., for they were used entirely by Midland trains running between Bristol and Birmingham, and making the detour via Worcester. As May 1st, 1852, approached it was another matter; the main line was to be opened, northwards to Stourbridge and southwards to Evesham, a total length of 36 miles. The improvident and penniless O.W.W. had not got a single engine, carriage, or wagon of its own, and not a man in prospect to drive or fire. John Fowler had succeeded Brunel as engineer, and he recommended that the work be let out to contract; C. C. Williams, of London, got the job, and on the recommendation of E. B. Wilson, the locomotive builder of Leeds, David Joy was appointed as resident locomotive superintendent to Williams, on the O.W.W.

The comedy was only just beginning. Joy was appointed on April 18th. Williams could supply carriages and wagons, but Joy had just a fortnight in which to find engines and men with which to open the line on May 1st. The next few days are best described in Joy's diary:

'Went to Welwyn – Great Northern Railway – and got "Mudlark", a contractor's engine, to Offord – got a big six-coupled long boiler, by Stephenson, in very good condition. Then next day to Shrewsbury to hire Shrewsbury and Hereford engines; had to see Jeffrey before breakfast, but he could spare none. On to Leeds and Pontefract after a four-coupled "Jenny" a contractor's engine, just put in fine order at Railway Foundry, with the cheque (£1,250) in my pocket to pay for it. Then to Leeds to see a little engine in the shops at Railway Foundry – called "Canary"; she was a little mite. Arranged for all these to go to Worcester.'

Then came the inaugural run. Again to quote Joy:

'I got the first four engines to Worcester, and on Saturday (April 29th.) we had a trip with about 10 carriages and engine "A", with Jas. Greenham (driver) to Kidderminster for an opening dinner. All the directors, John Fowler, Williams etc., were present. About 7 p.m. half the party wanted to get back to Droitwich, to catch a Midland train. I could not find Greenham, so took the engine myself, and did splendidly till I had delivered my passengers at Droitwich. Then in running back round my carriages the station master himself turned the wrong points, and shot me off the road on the bridge over the canal – tender first. Somehow I had not a thought of my own personal danger, though the whole lot of us might have gone over into the canal. My only idea was my engine, for the train was fast – she was badly off the road, so I at once got hold of the contractor's engine, "Jack of Newbury" – an old "White Horse of Kent" type – and got to Kidderminster as fast as I could, to fetch my directors, etc. Utterly done up, I got to Worcester, and to bed.'

There is no doubt that Joy took the difficult conditions on the O.W.W. as a challenge, and fairly revelled in it. Devoted to his work with locomotives, long hours and hard toil meant nothing to him, and he took intense pride in the gradually improving standards of engine performance and speed. While so much that was sordid and disagreeable was happening at management level the O.W.W. was very fortunate in having a contractor's engineer in residence who was such a thorough-going enthusiast. One entry in his diary is illuminating:

'Of course we began without shops or tools, and a most shabby shed (running) at Worcester, for two engines. I could only get repairs at a little smith's place which had a lathe that could turn a valve spindle. Meanwhile I did my own valve setting.'

The line from Evesham to the junction with the Great Western at Wolvercot was opened in June 1853, single line only. Not all of the line had been completed as double track when Williams' contract ended and Joy left at the end of 1855. The last section, that between Charlbury and Campden, was not doubled until August 1858. In the meantime efforts had been made to try and make the O.W.W. comply with the provisions of its Acts, so far as the broad gauge was concerned, and by the summer of 1855 mixed gauge had been laid throughout from Wolvercot to Wolverhampton. There were, however, no broad gauge trains at all – indeed MacDermot records that the only occasion of a broad gauge train running over the line at all was on the Board of Trade inspection from Wolvercot to Evesham and back in 1853!

One must give John Parson every credit for his drive and energy, no less than for his adroitness in evading legislation. He openly admitted that he ran the whole show; that he was responsible for the legal and other expenses, and although the Board were strangely complaisant to all his activities he did not think they were a very satisfactory body. The Chairman, he averred, could not keep order. His antagonism to the Great Western showed itself frequently in various attempts to organize traffic arrangements with that 'intriguing, web-weaving protocoller', Captain Huish of the L.N.W.R. – as Richard Moon once called him. But Parson was no match for Huish, and never brought off anything worth while for the O.W.W. Towards the end of its independent career, however, the O.W.W. became the senior partner in a new alliance that soon blossomed into the amalgamation that formed the short-lived West Midland Railway. This partnership arose out of a common interest in a railway that had been authorized in 1853 but had never been constructed, the Worcester and Hereford.

At the western end of this line was the northern extremity of the

Newport, Abergavenny and Hereford Railway; this concern was anxious to secure an eastern outlet other than that of the broad gauge Monmouthshire Railway, with its connection to the South Wales main line at Grange Court. The N.A. & H. had not the means of subscribing all the outstanding capital that was required to build the Worcester and Hereford, so they approached the O.W.W. The latter agreed to help, and the associations thus formed led to the full amalgamation of all three companies in 1860, under the name of the West Midland Railway. This step might have been extremely serious for the Great Western in view of the apparently friendly relations between Parson and the North Western, and particularly as the West Midland gathered into their fold that stormy petrel of the railway world, Edward Watkin. Practically all London traffic from the West Midland was passing on to the North Western line at Yarnton, and travelling via Bletchley. It was then that Parson and the newly constituted West Midland Board over-reached themselves, and a supreme act of diplomacy at Paddington completely altered the whole complexion of railways west of Oxford.

For some years there had been some talk of an entirely new main line to London from the West Midlands. The two alternatives, via Oxford and Didcot on the one hand, and via Bletchley on the other were both roundabout, and it had been felt desirable to have a direct route opening up the country between the two. Proposals in this direction had already been made, but had come to nothing, and a general agreement had been concluded between the Great Western and the O.W.W., in 1858, that neither railway would back any line likely to compete with the other. In 1861 following a series of manoeuvres of a highly questionable character, of which Parson was undoubtedly though covertly the architect, the West Midland found themselves backing a new project, the London, Buckinghamshire and West Midland Junction Railway, which would run from a terminus near Knightsbridge via Uxbridge, Beaconsfield, Risborough and Thame to join the West Midland line near Wolvercot Junction. The fact that it would compete with both existing lines from Oxford to London brought the North Western and the Great Western together in strong and united opposition, and there was every prospect of a Parliamentary fight of the first magnitude. Then, when everyone was ready to start, it was suddenly announced that the Great Western and the West Midland were to amalgamate. There were no hitches this time, and within a week of the first breaking of the news full agreement as to terms was reached.

How this step was approached and finally concluded has never been fully revealed, but one can be fairly sure that Saunders and Lord Sherburne had made contact with the more reasonable and honourable of the West Midland Board, and that they in turn had acted behind the back of Parson. It savours something of the kind of railway diplomacy in which Edward Watkin used to be involved; but however it was accomplished it was a great triumph for the Great Western, for it secured to them a large tract of country which might quite easily have fallen into the hands of the North Western. From now onwards the West of England main line of the Midland, running from Birmingham to Bristol, became an interloper in territory that was now solidly Great Western, and its great one-time danger was greatly reduced. Six West Midland directors joined the the Great Western Board, among them Edward Watkin and Parson himself; but however the latter individual may have been able to cut his capers in the past, it was another thing in the Board Room at Paddington. A libel action in which he was involved brought so much scathing criticism upon his conduct that he took an early opportunity of getting out, and with his going, in March 1864, the twenty-year saga of the O.W.W. and the West Midland comes to an end.

Moving now to the operational and engineering aspects of railway activity, it is time to bring Wolverhampton fully into the picture, and the year 1864 marked the beginning of a great change in Great Western locomotive affairs that led up to the eventual integration of the once wholly-independent practices of the broad and narrow gauge locomotive headquarters of the line – Swindon on the one hand, and Wolverhampton on the other. To trace the gradual rise in importance of Wolverhampton we must go back more than 10 years. Unlike Swindon it was a thriving industrial centre long before the first railway came within its boundaries. So closely knit were its industries, indeed, and so well served in transport by canal that the town turned the cold shoulder to the Grand Junction Railway. Thus it passed no nearer than a country station at Heath Town, 1¼ miles from Wolverhampton town centre. That was in 1837, and curiously enough the next line to arrive came in from the north, the Shrewsbury and Birmingham in 1849. The Oxford, Worcester and Wolverhampton line was opened in July 1854, and before the end of the year the broad gauge Great Western line from Birmingham was completed, finishing over the tracks of the O.W.W. from Priestfield which was laid with mixed gauge. It was from the north, however, that the influence came that was to guide the railway engineering fortunes of Wolverhampton for nearly fifty years.

The Shrewsbury and Birmingham Railway was closely associated with the Shrewsbury and Chester. The Great Western made strenuous efforts to envelope them both within the broad gauge fold; they would have constituted a natural extension to the northern main line from Oxford and Birmingham, and a valuable connection to the O.W.W. had that line been built as originally intended on the broad gauge. But both these lines north of Wolverhampton had been planned by Robert Stephenson, and other influences were strong. Curiously enough, however, Huish seemed favourably inclined to an extension of the broad gauge north of Wolverhampton, and as told in Chapter III, was talking about laying down mixed tracks from Wolverhampton over the Grand Junction, to Liverpool and Manchester. What Locke would have thought about this we are not to know, for the cost in widening works would have been tremendous; but it was actually no more than a move in the game of railway politics. This happened in days prior to the formation of the L.N.W.R., and Huish acting on behalf of the Grand Junction used this threat to send all their London traffic by Great Western in order to coerce the London and Birmingham. In this he was completely successful. The L.N.W.R. was formed in 1847, and after that he resumed warfare with the broad gauge! The Shrewsbury and Chester and the Shrewsbury and Birmingham Railways were amalgamated with the Great Western in 1854, but on the definite condition that the broad gauge should not be extended north of Wolverhampton.

With this amalgamation of 1854 there came into Great Western service a man destined to be one of its most distinguished officers – Joseph Armstrong. He had previously been locomotive superintendent of the Shrewsbury and Chester Railway. The southern associate, the S. & B., had been worked by contract until 1853, but when the contract expired the entire working was placed under Armstrong and he moved his headquarters from Chester to Wolverhampton. The almost simultaneous arrival in Wolverhampton of the broad gauge with the absorbtion of the two northern lines demanded some co-ordination of Great Western locomotive activities, and Daniel Gooch appointed Armstrong to the job. Unlike some of those who assumed great engineering responsibilities in the early days of the Great Western, Armstrong at 38 was bordering upon middle age; but if he had not been born among locomotives, he certainly grew up among the atmosphere of the pioneer railways. His home from the age of eight was at Newburn-on-Tyne, where George Stephenson and Timothy Hackworth were close friends of the family. The story goes that he learned to drive locomotives on the Stockton and

Darlington; certainly at the age of 20 he was a fully-fledged driver on the Liverpool and Manchester Railway.

With Joseph Armstrong into the Great Western service came his redoubtable younger brother, George, who, after an early life full of exciting adventures had joined the Shrewsbury and Chester Railway as a driver. But George Armstrong, like his brother, was no mere mechanic; he was a tremendously strong personality and leader of men, and when his brother was chosen to succeed Gooch, George Armstrong took his place at Wolverhampton, and reigned in virtual independence for 33 years! The Armstrong régime at Stafford Road Works thus lasted for 44 years, for one must include the year Joseph spent there in charge of the S. & B. shops before the line was absorbed into the Great Western. The virtual autonomy that came to be enjoyed by Wolverhampton did not come immediately. On taking over the S. & C. and the S. & B. the Great Western decided that the policy of designing their own locomotives and building as many of them as possible in their own works should be extended to Wolverhampton. This was a decision not to be taken lightly, for the line north of Wolverhampton was the first piece of narrow gauge for which the G.W.R. had taken full responsibility. New shops had to be built at Stafford Road, while provision had to be made for stabling the broad gauge engines working northwards through Birmingham.

It was a time of evolution that required the greatest skill in management by Joseph Armstrong. Gooch himself designed the first Northern Division narrow gauge engines – 0-6-0 goods and 2-2-2 express – very much on the lines of the famous Swindon broad-gaugers, with sandwich frames, domeless boilers, and a raised firebox. They also had the huge bell-mouthed tops to their chimneys. A significant point of difference was that all these narrow-gauge engines were unnamed. Swindon built the first batch of narrow-gauge 0-6-0 goods engines. Two or three pits in the works were adapted for narrow gauge construction, but there was no track outside, and thus the engines could not be steamed or tested in any way. Some special wagons had to be built to transport them to Wolverhampton, and the entire job of breaking them in and incidentally nursing them through their teething troubles rested with Armstrong and his men. These twelve goods engines had all been delivered by 1856.

Swindon Works could not cope with the construction of a second narrow gauge design at that time, and so the order for the 2-2-2 express locomotives was placed with Beyer, Peacock and Co. Apart from being a handsome and workmanlike example of Gooch's designing style the first four of these locomotives are historic in being the first turned out at Beyer's famous works at Gorton; 'The Tank', as the style has become so well known. It is pleasing to think that the progenitors of the century-long tradition of locomotive building that culminated in the gigantic Beyer-Garratts that are doing yeoman service in so many far-away and remote places, were designed by Daniel Gooch, and were run by a man who learned to drive engines on the Stockton and Darlington under the guidance of Timothy Hackworth. So far as personalities go I must also record the entry to Stafford Road Works, as an apprentice, in 1855 of a young man named William Dean. Thus were congregated in Wolverhampton, in the 'fifties of last century, three men who were to pay a very big part in Great Western locomotive affairs before that century was out.

In the meantime important alterations and additions were made to the Stafford Road Works, and reluctant though the powers-that-were at Paddington must have been to authorize the step, the decision was taken gradually to withdraw the broad gauge southwards from Wolverhampton. Through working to Shrewsbury and Chester was envisaged, and unless the Great Western was to have within its own system the inconveniences of a break of gauge at Wolverhampton the through trains must inevitably be narrow gauge. More locomotives and stock would be required, and with an ever-increasing demand upon Swindon for broad gauge power, for South Wales, and for Devon and Cornwall, the Stafford Road Works would clearly be called upon to take an increased share of the responsibility. From the very start Gooch seems to have given Armstrong a pretty free hand, and the latter designed his narrow gauge engines to the dictates of his own heart and experience rather than from any promptings from Swindon. His first express passenger engines, designed and built throughout at Stafford Road, appeared in 1858, and at once struck a new note, so far as Great Western practice was concerned.

It immediately recalled Armstrong's earlier experience, before he joined the Shrewsbury and Chester Railway, and the story is well worth retelling. After four years on the Liverpool and Manchester Railway Armstrong had gone to the Hull and Selby Railway, in 1840. Compared to the Liverpool and Manchester this might have seemed a retrograde step; but Armstrong had been influenced not so much by the status of the railway as by the type of locomotive he would have to drive. At the time the locomotive superintendent of the Hull and Selby Railway was George Gray, who was generally considered to be one of the most advanced designers of the day. His express engines were of the 2-2-2 type, with inside bearings for the driving wheels and outside bearings for the leading and trailing wheels. They were much larger, more powerful and more economical than anything running on the Liverpool and Manchester, and when Gray was appointed locomotive superintendent of the Brighton Railway Armstrong went with him. It was from contacts at Brighton that David Joy developed Gray's 2-2-2 into the very famous *Jenny Lind*, and it can be said that Armstrong's first 2-2-2 for the Great Western, built at Stafford Road in 1858, was in every way of the 'Jenny Lind' type. But although several more of the type were built at Wolverhampton, Armstrong had plenty of opportunity to compare their overall performance with that of Gooch's sandwich-framed Swindon engines, with the result that he eventually adopted as standard practice a blend of the two, using double plate frames throughout.

Then to increase the responsibilities of Joseph Armstrong came the absorption of the West Midland Railway, in 1863, and with it the acquisition of a heterogeneous collection of locomotives of all shapes and sizes, the majority of very doubtful value. A separate locomotive division of the G.W.R. was formed at Worcester, but Stafford Road had to take responsibility for repair of the locomotives. The Northern Division, based on Wolverhampton, was extended down the old O.W.W. line to Stourbridge, but shortened on the London main line by moving the boundary point from Oxford to Leamington. Also, in connection with the joint ownership of the Shrewsbury and Hereford line with the North Western, the boundary, so far as G.W.R. locomotive working was concerned, was fixed at Ludlow. All this additional work Joseph Armstrong absorbed with conspicuous success, and a very strong and virile tradition grew up at Wolverhampton. There was every need of it, for profound changes were to come over the Great Western during the next few years.

VIII

Adversity and Resurgence

ALTHOUGH the year 1863 had seen the triumphant, yet unexpected end of the long drawn-out West Midland dispute and the full incorporation of the South Wales Railway within the Great Western fold, it was a time of great anxiety and financial stress for the company, and to set against his diplomatic successes farther afield Charles Saunders had to endure the effects of a humiliating rebuff at the very portals of Paddington from the newly constructed Metropolitan Railway. This was originally planned as a railway to provide an underground connection between Paddington and Kings Cross. Later, the eastern terminus was located at Farringdon Street, and the Great Western, realizing that the situation of Paddington on the western fringe of London put them at a disadvantage for business travellers, subscribed substantially to the new project. Moreover the Great Western agreed to work the line – broad gauge of course! – and Gooch designed some engines which would consume their own smoke, in accordance with the requirements of the Metropolitan Railway Act.

The line was laid throughout with mixed gauge, and at Kings Cross there were from the outset connections with the Great Northern main line. From York Road, indeed, there was originally a westward connection on to what is now the westbound Inner Circle line so that Great Northern trains could, if necessary, run to Paddington. Anyway the Metropolitan manager, Myles Fenton, was much too energetic and go-ahead for the rather conservative Great Western, and when he sought to intensify the service and run more than four trains an hour in each direction Saunders was horrified. Fenton persisted in his demands, whereupon the Great Western replied that they would cease to work the service as from the end of September 1863. After this Fenton told Saunders that the Metropolitan would work its own service as from October 1st. The Great Western announcement had come on July 18th, and there is little doubt that all concerned at Paddington thought Fenton was bluffing; the Metropolitan had no locomotives of their own, and no carriages, and no one else had any condensing engines at that time.

The Great Western management then decided to intensify its bullying tactics to the point of issuing what could well have been thought an impossible ultimatum. Not content with their threat to cease working from the end of September, Saunders next wrote to say that they would withdraw all their engines and carriages at the end of the day's working *on August 9th*. This threat was obviously intended to bring Fenton to his knees. Unfortunately for Saunders it had just the opposite effect. Arrangements had already been concluded for the Great Northern to work into Farringdon Street, with its own engines as from September 1st, and to do this Gooch's former right-hand man, Archibald Sturrock, was in process of adapting some old Sharp 2-2-2s into condensing tank engines. After he had received the Great Western ultimatum Fenton went to Kings Cross and asked whether Sturrock's engines could be ready for August 9th. Sturrock was not the man to refuse such a challenge; he set all Doncaster on to the conversions, and by working night and day enough of them were ready to take over the service on August 10th.

One can imagine with what apprehension Paddington waited for some reply from the Metropolitan; but none came, and on the evening of August 9th all the broad gauge engines were withdrawn. Next morning Paddington had the mortification of seeing the Metropolitan running, not merely 'as usual', but to the intensified service Fenton had asked for, and with a swarm of Great Northern engines under their very noses at Bishops Road. The fact that an ex-Great Western man had been mainly responsible for the defeat of their ultimatum did not make the defeat any sweeter! Some sardonic amusement may have been derived from the troubles that were experienced with Sturrock's hasty improvisations. Some nine months later another Sturrock engine created a terrific sensation by blowing its dome off in Bishops Road station. Engine troubles or not, the Great Western passenger trains, and with it the broad gauge, were out of the Metropolitan tunnels for many a long day. Sixty-five years later, when I used to travel daily from Ealing to Kings Cross by a through Great Western train, I would often recall the details of the Saunders–Fenton affair of 1863.

At the time of the Metropolitan dispute Saunders was nearing his end. For nearly 30 years he had carried unparalleled burdens. Staunch upholder of the broad gauge though he was, he must have realized that he was fighting a losing battle. He had seen Russell go, and then take his own life; Brunel had died in 1859 still a relatively young man, yet utterly broken, and at the end of the Parliamentary session of 1863 Saunders himself resigned. He was then 67 years of age, and was feeling the strain of things severely. Thus, at the close of that momentous year only Gooch remained, of the four men who had literally built and sustained the broad gauge. Their unity of purpose, and the adversities they had so constantly faced, drew them all together in the closest personal friendship. In his diary Gooch wrote of Brunel:

'By his death the greatest of England's engineers was lost, the man of the greatest originality of thought and power of execution, bold in his plans but right. The commercial world thought him extravagant, but although he was so, great things are not done by those who sit down and count the cost of every thought and act. He was a true and sincere friend, a man of the highest honour, and his loss was deplored by all who had the pleasure to know him.'

At the end of September 1864 Gooch himself retired, not through ill-health, but because the opportunity came to him to lay the Atlantic Cable, using Brunel's leviathan of a steamship, the *Great Eastern*, for the purpose. Almost at the moment of his own resignation came the death of Saunders, and with his passing it could be said the last links with the original conception of the Great Western Railway had been broken. Perhaps one of the most telling tributes to Saunders came from his old adversary in so many railway battles, Captain Mark Huish. It was not a direct personal tribute to the man as to the company he served; but it was nevertheless made at a time when Saunders and the G.W.R. were synonymous: 'I do not know of any company so difficult to come to an agreement with as the Great Western, or one which keeps so honourably to an agreement when once made'. With Russell, Saunders, Brunel, and Gooch all gone, and with many miles of purely narrow gauge line now incorporated the Great Western from 1864 onwards was in many ways a new company.

The unique position held by Charles Saunders was not filled by any one individual. His nephew F. G. Saunders was appointed Secretary, but two other posts of top-ranking importance were created to do parts of the work that Charles Saunders had previously shouldered single-handed. James Grierson was made General Manager, but his duties were much less than that of officers with the same title in later years, in that he dealt only with Parliamentary work and the general responsibility for traffic. The engineering chiefs reported direct to the Board. The third new office was that of Superintendent of the Line, to which G. N. Tyrrell was appointed. It is no disparagement to successive holders of the office of Engineer

to say that they are mere names beside the mighty Brunel. T. H.
Bertram and then Michael Lane were followed by W. G. Owen, who
carried through the first large-scale conversion of the gauge. Owen,
indeed, held office from 1868 to 1885, and it was the experience
gained in South Wales during the early conversions that enabled the
final change in May 1892 to be made so swiftly.

The resignation of Daniel Gooch in 1864 did not lead to the same
hiatus in outstanding personalities that had followed the death of
Brunel. For Joseph Armstrong was selected to succeed Gooch as
Locomotive and Carriage Superintendent, and his brother George
Armstrong was appointed Divisional Superintendent at Wolverhampton. It has been said that the arrival of Joseph Armstrong at
Swindon ushered in a new era, in which north-countrymen took
command of an essentially west-country works; but actually all
Swindon's greatest men had hitherto been northerners – Gooch
himself, and Archibald Sturrock. It was not indeed until the year
1941 that a Swindonian born and bred assumed the chieftainship of
the locomotive department of the G.W.R. In another way, however,
the coming of Armstrong in 1864 did start a new tradition. He was
the father of a very large family, having five sons and three daughters,
and the company built a new house for him, which afterwards
became the official residence of the Locomotive and Carriage
Superintendent.

This large and commodious dwelling was built alongside the main
line, opposite to the works and a little to the west of St. Mark's
Church, and Armstrong, who was very proud of his descent from the
great Border clan and of his connections with Tyneside and the
early railways there, named the new house 'Newburn'. To become
the occupant of Newburn thenceforward became the ambition of all
the keenest men of the G.W.R. locomotive department, though as it
turned out there were only two others after Armstrong. But it is
significant of the spirit of tradition that developed among Great
Western men that when Sir William Stanier moved to the L.M.S.R.
and took up residence in Chorley Wood he named his new house
'Newburn'; not only this, but when in later years he moved from
Chorley Wood to Rickmansworth he transferred the name to his
new home. As a former colleague of his once remarked to me: 'He
was determined to live in Newburn!'

Houses apart, Armstrong had a tremendous task ahead of him at
Swindon. The ultimate conversion of all the broad gauge lines was
clearly foreseen, and plans had to be made for a large increase in
works capacity for building and repairing narrow gauge

locomotives. Further, the Board decided that the time had come when henceforth the G.W.R. would build its own carriages and wagons. It is amusing to recall that the original proposal to establish a works at Oxford was abandoned because of the outcry raised against the industrialization of the ancient city of learning. Shades of Joseph Armstrong! They must have chuckled when the day came for an American tourist to remark to his wife: 'This is Oxford, the English Detroit!' Be that as it may, the opposition in the eighteen-sixties led to the Great Western carriage and wagon works being set up at Swindon. To assist in the work at Swindon Armstrong brought in two new men, both from the Northern Division, and both destined to be locomotive chiefs in after years. James Holden, previously at Chester, was appointed manager of the carriage and wagon works, while William Dean was transferred from Wolverhampton, and became Principal Assistant to Armstrong in 1868.

But while Armstrong was building up a strong team in the locomotive and carriage department the company in general was in a very bad way. The year 1865 saw three bad accidents in rapid succession; finances were bordering upon bankruptcy, and with the resignation of Richard Potter from the chairmanship no one among the existing directors appeared either equal or willing to take on the onerous task. In their extremity the Board turned to Gooch. His first attempt to lay the Atlantic Cable had been unsuccessful, but he had recently been elected as Member of Parliament for the Cricklade Division of Wiltshire, and had thus renewed his interest in Swindon in another way. Arrangements were made for a seat to be found for him on the Board, and he was duly elected Chairman in November 1865. In the following summer he made a second and successful attempt to lay the Atlantic Cable, and for this pioneer work he was created a baronet. With his increased status, prestige, and national fame he literally came to the rescue of the impoverished Great Western Railway.

In the critical year of 1866 it was not perhaps surprising that an improvident and badly managed concern like the London, Chatham and Dover Railway should fall into the hands of receivers; but it is surprising to recall that for several months the Great Western itself was tottering upon the selfsame brink. There was a general recession of confidence in railways at that time. A large banking house that had financed several large contractors had failed; contractors failed with them, and rumours began to circulate on the London Stock Exchange that the Great Western could not meet its debenture obligations. Normal attempts to raise new capital failed completely.

An application to the Bank of England for a loan was turned down flat, and things had got to such a pitch that Sir Daniel Gooch sought help in a personal interview with the Chancellor of the Exchequer. It is strange indeed to think of the man who, as a mere youth, had pulled the early broad gauge chestnuts out of the fire, going cap-in-hand to Downing Street to try and raise funds for the G.W.R.

How the storm was eventually weathered, by financial operations and rigid economy in every department, is a long story. There were no half measures about Sir Daniel's 'axe'. The most spectacular cut was the taking off of the company's crack train 'The Flying Dutchman', while the finances were further embarrassed by the conceding of a wage claim by the locomotive men in face of a threatened strike in 1867. Much as Sir Daniel himself must have deplored it the end of the broad gauge was foreseen, and little or no money was spent on the repair and maintenance of broad gauge carriages. As a result the stock got into a sadly dilapidated condition which increased the ill-will displayed towards the company by the travelling public. As there was then no money available for the conversion of the gauge, it can be well imagined how chaotic things began to get. Gooch's steadfastness of character was never displayed to finer effect than during this exceedingly critical time. He never panicked even when things were at their worst, and was at all times a rallying point for directors and officers alike.

Strangely enough it was at this very time that the broad gauge was extending to its maximum mileage. The map at the end of the book shows broad and mixed gauge lines of the G.W.R. as they existed in 1868, from which it will be seen that apart from the lines of the Great Western and its associates in Devon and Cornwall, two important connecting lines, the Bristol and Gloucester, and the London and South Western between Exeter, Barnstaple and Bideford were also laid with the mixed gauge. Even this was not the final extent of the broad gauge, for as late as the year 1877 a new branch was constructed in Cornwall, from St. Erth to St. Ives. The West Cornwall Railway was never wholly broad gauge, and as previously related the branches of the old mineral line remained narrow gauge throughout. The construction of the St. Ives branch as a broad gauge line was presumably to enable through coaches to be run from Paddington. The last piece of through route built to the broad gauge was that between Taunton and Barnstaple in 1873. This was quite an independent concern, the Devon and Somerset Railway, promoted by local landowners. It joined the Bristol and Exeter main line at Watchet Junction, a point 2 miles west of Taunton. It was also the point of divergence of the West Somerset Railway – hence the name of the junction. Watchet Junction in due course became Norton Fitzwarren.

The Devon and Somerset Railway had something of a history. Apparently the financing of it was done entirely by local subscription, and the greatest difficulty was experienced in making any progress. Although it was authorized in 1864 it took nine years in all to get the 43 miles of single-line constructed. It was agreed that the Bristol and Exeter would maintain and work it, for half the gross receipts, and in anticipation of its arrival at Barnstaple, an extension line to Ilfracombe was projected and authorized under the auspices of the London and South Western. The Devon and Somerset was offered a half-share in the ownership of this line, with the opportunity of laying mixed gauge track throughout. Unfortunately for the cause of the broad gauge the Devon and Somerset was so hopelessly embarrassed financially with its own line that the joint ownership of anything else was out of the question. The South Western was not prepared to go it alone at that time, and so the Ilfracombe line lapsed for the time being. The Devon and Somerset remained outside the general amalgamations of 1875–6 in the west country, and was not absorbed by the Great Western until 1901.

The elimination of the broad gauge between Oxford and Wolverhampton was followed by the conversion of the whole of the South Wales lines, in 1872. The work involved in this is described in some detail in a later chapter, but its effect was to cause some serious changes of heart farther west. The Bristol and Exeter, the South Devon, and the Cornwall Railways had always been among the purest and unalloyed adherents of the broad gauge; but their directors and shareholders could not fail to observe the trend of things north of the Bristol Channel, and with the advance of the South Western to Exeter and beyond they were faced for the first time with severe competition. The Great Western had recently had its hands full enough with the aftermath of the absorption of the West Midland and the South Wales lines, and with the great expense of converting the gauge in South Wales; otherwise they might have been increasingly aware of the danger that was developing in the west, where the proprietors of the Bristol and Exeter felt that they had been isolated long enough and that the time had come to amalgamate with a larger railway. When the line was originally built it was not so very much smaller a concern than the Great Western itself; but in the year 1875, although the Bristol and Exeter had extended by various branches, and had the impoverished associates that branched off at Norton Fitzwarren, the Great Western by its Welsh and Northern extensions had become a very big railway.

In Bristol, however, it was perhaps inevitable that there should be a large body of shareholders whose sympathies lay with the Midland rather than with the Great Western. In Bristol resentment over the broad gauge and the financial troubles it had brought ran very deep, and as late as 1887 one finds John Latimer writing in the *Annals of Bristol*: 'The time has long passed away since there was any difference of opinion as to the deplorable error of the original Board in neglecting the sober-minded, practical and economical engineers of the North, already deservedly famous, and in preferring to them an inexperienced theorist, enamoured of novelty, prone to seek for difficulties rather than to evade them, and utterly indifferent as to the outlay which his recklessness entailed upon his employers. The evil consequences of his pet crotchet, the "broad gauge" system, on the commerce of Bristol will have to be noticed hereafter . . . .' In 1875 the great danger to Great Western interests was that the Bristol and Exeter in looking forward to the time of gauge conversion might team up with the Midland, rather than with the Great Western. Had not the Midland been considerably embarrassed itself at that time its enterprising and opportunist management might have cashed in on the Bristol disaffection, and ultimately extended its own main line to Penzance!

It so happened, however, that Derby was then committed, much against its better judgment, to the very costly Settle and Carlisle line to Scotland. Originally launched as no more than a threat to the North Western, its bluff had been called by Euston; when the Midland wished to retire gracefully from the position its tactics had created, the North British and the Lancashire and Yorkshire, who were both interested in the Settle and Carlisle, said 'no'; and so that magnificent line was built, and probably saved a battle-royal over the Bristol and Exeter. By the autumn of 1875 things were boiling up in Bristol, and a dangerous situation was averted by the action of the Bristol and Exeter General Traffic Manager, J. C. Wall. A letter from him to James Grierson speaks for itself:

BRISTOL,
September 23rd, 1875.

My Dear Sir,

At our Board Meeting yesterday there was a long discussion as to our present and future prospects, one section of our Board having strong

Midland proclivities, another section, and, I am happy to say, the largest, having Great Western proclivities.

The matter was put to an end by my saying that if the question was postponed until after our conference at Paddington on the 5th proximo I believed that I should be enabled to place before them something like a tangible proposition. Now you must be prepared to do something, and I have a scheme in my mind that I believe will enable you to hold your present position in the West at a very small risk, and under the worst circumstances entailing only a comparatively trifling loss. I will meet you on Monday, 4th of October to discuss this question if convenient and you think it desirable, and I am sure it is needless for me to assure you that next to the interests of my own Company, I desire to act in a friendly and loyal spirit to yours.

If you think right, pray show this letter to your Chairman.

I must add that I am now sure a change in our position is inevitable and that it will take place at this or any short period.

I am,

Very truly yours,

J. C. WALL.

J. Grierson Esq.,
Paddington.

Grierson acted at once, and within a month the terms of the amalgamation were agreed by both Boards. Now the Great Western and the Bristol had got to this stage before, in 1845, only to have the proposal vetoed by the Bristol and Exeter shareholders; and having regard to the undoubted strength of the Midland faction there must have been many on both sides who waited in anxiety for the result of the Company meetings on December 17th, 1875. This time however there was no mistake; the proposals were ratified by the shareholders of both companies. Full amalgamation took place as from August 1st, 1876. This merger brought about the retirement of the B. & E. locomotive and carriage superintendent James Pearson, who will always be remembered by students of locomotive history for his extraordinary 4-2-4 express tank engines with driving wheels of no less than 9 ft diameter. Henceforth the Bristol and Exeter locomotive stock came under the jurisdiction of Swindon, and it was not before Gooch's eight-footers were the regular passenger engines of the line.

The South Devon Railway, in 1875, took its cue from the Bristol and Exeter and arrangements were made to amalgamate with the Great Western even more rapidly. Although a working arrangement existed from February 1st, 1876, it was not until 1878 that the amalgamation was finally authorized by Parliament. Following this one would have thought that absorption of the Cornwall Railway would have followed, almost automatically. The Great Western became sole lessees, and had virtually complete control of the line. But the Cornish folk seemed to resent this state of affairs from people east of the Tamar, and some distinctly difficult years followed. There were agitations against the so-called bad management of the G.W.R.; attempts to make financial arrangements with the Cornwall Railway shareholders were turned down flat, and the fact that in 1882 the railway made a profit for the first time in its history seemed to stiffen resistance. The Joint Committee of management, which prior to 1876 also included a representative of the Bristol and Exeter, now had a preponderance of Great Western strength, though things continued fairly smoothly until the question came up of renewing two of the famous timber viaducts in 1883.

P. J. Margary was engineer to the Joint Committee and in 1883 he reported thus, concerning the timber viaducts:

'All the viaducts are maintained in the same general state of repair as far as the soundness of timber is concerned, the practice being to send gangs of men to each viaduct in turn to examine and change every piece of defective timber that may be discovered. Although some pieces may escape detection, I do not apprehend that any viaduct will be found to have defective timbers sufficient to cause any alarm. There are, however, some of them which offer considerable difficulties in the way of keeping them perfectly fit for fast running and heavy trains.

'On some of the viaducts the line is so straight as to offer no special difficulty, but on others there is either a curve or an inherent weakness in the original construction, and in these there has been distortion in the shape of the timber superstructure, necessitating the introduction of numerous shores, which formed no part of the original design, in order to check the lateral movement. And this becomes increasingly the case as the original timbers are removed and others substituted, for these renewals are made piece by piece under circumstances of considerable difficulty with the traffic going over the viaducts while the renewals are taking place, and the frames are necessarily weaker than when put together at one time and under very different circumstances in the original construction of the viaducts.

'For this reason and in any case timber is so liable to decay internally before any signs are manifested upon the surface, I would strongly recommend the advisability of reconstructing the whole of the timber viaducts in more durable materials.'

Some of the viaducts had by then been replaced by stone arched structures, and as a result of Margary's report the Committee ordered the replacement of two more. It was then that the Cornwall Railway directors suddenly declared that such a decision was one for the Board, and not for the Joint Committee. Dispute was followed by deadlock, and on this seemingly simple issue the Great Western and the Cornwall Railways actually went to arbitration. It would appear that the Cornwall people went out deliberately to pick a quarrel with the Great Western, and they fastened on to a point in the lease that the Cornwall Railway should be 'kept and maintained exclusively as a railway upon the broad gauge'. The Great Western, looking at things in a more practical light, proposed to build stone viaducts of a width sufficient to take a double line on the narrow gauge. Absurd though it may sound, the Arbitrator ruled virtually in favour of the Cornwall Railway, by deciding that the Joint Committee might renew the viaducts in wood, stone, iron or any other material, but *not* for a double narrow gauge line unless the permission of the Cornwall Railway was obtained. In other words, although the broad gauge was dying out everywhere, he ruled strictly in terms of the lease. Six years later the Cornwall Railway was amalgamated with the Great Western, and the latter were then freed to continue with the renewal of the viaducts as it became necessary.

The Cornwall Railway was the last section of the West of England main line to be fully absorbed. It is one of the curiosities of the Great Western build-up that the West Cornwall should have been absorbed some years earlier. The latter company was jointly owned by the Great Western, the Bristol and Exeter, and the South Devon. The Cornwall Railway had no part in this particular association, and when the former three companies were amalgamated in 1876 the West Cornwall Railway became a part of the enlarged Great Western. The absorption of the Cornwall Railway in 1889 saw the virtual completion of the main line network as we know it today. The cut-off lines had yet to come, though the Severn Tunnel had been completed in 1885. But the year 1889 was signalized and saddened for all Great Western men by the death of its oldest and greatest servant, Sir Daniel Gooch.

IX

On the Line: A Chapter of Anecdote and Reminiscence

IT IS easy to become nostalgic over the old railways; to recall the sheer beauty of their colouring, to delight in the quaintness of their detail. Much of that is happily preserved for us in old drawings and photographs, and in the vivid memories of the older ones amongst us today. I am old enough to have seen the Dean 'singles' in much of their original glory, and to have heard my own father's recollections of the broad gauge. But in my own boyhood the transition from the spacious, unhurried atmosphere of Gooch's last years to the fire-eating prowess of Churchward's new locomotives was practically complete so far as the main line expresses were concerned, and it is to a much earlier period that I am now looking back. The Great Western was a concern that inspired great affection and loyalty among its men, and they were pleased and proud to write about their early life on the line. It is from some of these first-hand stories together with those of certain other enthusiasts that the present chapter has been compiled.

Before proceeding to the tale itself I feel that a few notes on the men who have indirectly contributed to it would be welcome, as they were all undoubtedly 'characters', and their own careers throw much light upon the conditions of the railway service in mid-Victorian times. First of all there is G. Grant, who joined the Great Western as a lad of sixteen in 1864, at Bridport, and who eventually rose to the responsible position of Divisional Superintendent, first at Chester and then at Plymouth. Then there is T. Houghton Wright who commenced his railway career as early as August 1851, at Swindon, as an articled pupil to Daniel Gooch. After a most varied career Wright eventually became Divisional Locomotive Carriage and Wagon Superintendent at Neath. Prior to that, however, he was at Gloucester for many years and was intimately connected with the changing of the gauge throughout the former South Wales Railway. For reminiscences of early days in the West Midlands one turns naturally to the diaries of David Joy, while the personal friendship of Mr. H. Holcroft with members of the Armstrong family has enabled him to present a very comprehensive story of the early days at Wolverhampton.

Among non-railwaymen the records and photographs of the Rev. A. H. Malan are outstanding. For many years this gentleman was living at Teignmouth, and so far as the broad gauge was concerned he seems to have been the Bishop Treacy of the day. Judging from the scores of superb 'portraits' of broad gauge engines and their crews that are now in the possession of the Archivist of the British Transport Commission, Malan was obviously something of an 'honorary member' of the shed staff at Newton Abbot, and when he was out on the line photographing trains at speed, whether at Exminster, Stoke Canon, Brent Knoll or in the deep cutting between Uphill Junction and Bleadon, his enginemen friends from Newton Abbot would recognize him and salute from the footplate. He seems to have had the firemen well trained in the technique of giving good smoke effects at the right moment. Lastly of course there is Ahrons, and I have taken the liberty of quoting in full a 'pheasant story' from the Wilts and Somerset Line that he told in the inimitable series of articles he contributed to *The Railway Magazine* in 1915–6.

The Great Western of broad gauge days, so picturesque in many original ways, was no less picturesque in its early signals. The array of discs, cross-bars and fantails might well, in their apparent complexity, out-vie some of the French railways in pre-nationalization days with their chessboards, discs, and palettes! Brunel's original design of signal was simple enough in its function. It was an 'absolute stop' signal, erected at every station, at the entrance to the long tunnels, and at the level crossings with the principal public roads. A disc displayed flat-on to the oncoming train indicated 'all right', and if the train was required to stop the vertical shaft was rotated so as to turn the disc edge-on and to display instead a cross-bar. The night indications were white for 'all right' and red for danger. Although the masts were very tall, usually between 40 and 60 ft from ground level to disc, the whole post was revolved – all sixty feet of it! – by a lever mechanism at the base. There were no such things as ladders in early broad gauge days; the posts themselves were notched alternately on either side to provide footholds for a man climbing up to attend to the lamps. Brunel was the only engineer of the early days to give a positive 'all right' signal to the drivers. On other railways, as in France until quite recent times, the *absence* of any positive indication was taken as the 'all right'.

At a very early stage in Great Western working the need for a third indication was found desirable, namely 'caution', and Brunel introduced an extraordinary device that opened and closed like a lady's fan, and displayed, when opened, a green or red flag as the case may be. These did not last long as the first strong wind on the exposed stretches of the Bristol and Exeter line tore the 'flags' to shreds. The 'fantail' caution boards were adopted in substitution for the Brunel 'flags' and lasted almost until the 'seventies'. The combination of a fantail caution signal with the standard disc and crossbar on the same post contributed a direct prototype of the more modern home and distant semaphore arm, also on the same post. The earlier combination dates back to 1842, and at that time, of course, there was no interlocking or slotting between the operating mechanisms of the two different signals. So far as the main signals were concerned, both disc and crossbar were painted the colour now well known as 'signal red', though at the time of its introduction it is interesting to find it referred to as 'sealing wax red'!

For a long time after the establishment of the broad gauge there was no interlocking between points and signals. For a time Grant was at Westbury, and even in the sixties it was a busy place as junction of the Salisbury branch with the Wilts and Somerset main line. It was really more than this, because the line from Bath and Bradford-on-Avon joined in at Trowbridge, not far to the north, and Westbury was the focal point of four different routes, not to mention traffic from the Berks and Hants line via Devizes. The Westbury iron works was by then in full production, so that taken all round the traffic was as diverse as it was heavy. To quote Grant:

'Signalmen were termed pointsmen. Some of the points in shunting yards were worked from a capstan by a horizontal lever, and the disc on the capstan indicated the position of the points. They were on duty twelve hours. Their work involved running from one end of a shunting yard to the other, across sidings, over rough ballast, through pools of water. This had to be done day and night. There was no overhead illuminant; a man had only his handlamp to guide his footsteps. When a shunter had uncoupled trucks, the pointsmen had to turn the points of the siding into which they were going. Shunting operations might be going on in contiguous sidings or engines blowing off steam.

'While thus engaged he had to think of trains on the main line, the signals for which he had to work, and to satisfy himself that all points were set in the right position. There were no telephones then, and the telegraph instrument was in an office some distance away. Time was his guide or the whistle of an approaching train. His instructions were that no second train might follow an express under a margin of five minutes; an ordinary passenger train must have a start of ten, and a goods train fifteen.'

It is amazing to think nowadays of the responsibilities these men carried. The only shelter they had from the weather was a crude little hut like a sentry box. Night and day they had to keep their wits about them, and a constant source of anxiety was that someone, perhaps an over-zealous shunter, might have moved the points after they had set them. The hearts of those of us who are concerned with the design of modern electric control panels and illuminated diagrams go out to the men who had to keep the whole picture in their mind's eye: how each pair of points were set, what trains were expected, with no telegraph to warn them, and only an engine's whistle in the dark to herald the approach of a train. At night there was no such thing as lighting in the yards. Pointsmen and shunters alone had to rely solely upon their oil-lighted hand lamps. And these worthies then worked a 72-hour week!

The shunters shared in the trials and anxieties of the pointsmen, with many others added. All this was long before the days of shunters' poles, and the men had to go between the wagons and heave up the heavy chain couplings. Moreover the shunters could not take their hand lamps between the wagons, so that at night the coupling and uncoupling had to be done in the darkness. From the point of view of yard working there was one great disadvantage of Brunel's broad gauge permanent way – the 'baulk road' as it became known. In wet weather the water used to lie in pools between the longitudinal timbers; it had no means of draining away as with transverse sleepered road, and the hapless shunter was splashing about up to his ankles, as often as not. The only modest recognition of the severe conditions in which shunters had to work was the free issue of an overcoat once every two years. Some of them might have preferred a pair of stout boots, or leggings!

In the mid-sixties the electric telegraph was installed over no more than the merest fraction of the whole line, and there was no means of discovering where trains were in the event of late running. The progress of goods trains was incredibly slow by modern standards, and Grant recalls the case of the old 4 a.m. daily goods from Swindon to Weymouth, which called and did shunting at nearly every station en route. This train was regularly worked on alternate days by two brothers, and they were often 16, 17 or even 18 hours on the trip of 90 miles. What 'lodging' at Weymouth then entailed Grant does not reveal, but he does record that however late

their over-night arrival it was a point of honour with both the
brothers never to be a minute late in starting away on the return trip
at 4 a.m. from Weymouth. The measures taken when passenger
trains were overdue brings me to the reminiscences of T. Houghton
Wright, and for a time the scene moves from the actual running of
the trains to the interior of Swindon Works.

Wright joined the G.W.R. in 1851, and at that time it is interesting
to learn how many north-countrymen and Scots occupied
responsible positions in Swindon Works. Gooch and Sturrock had
obviously brought 'their ain folk' with them, though the Locomotive
Works Manager, Minard Christian Rea, was an Irishman. The
running shed foreman at Swindon was a real 'Geordie' who had
come south with the *North Star* from Stephenson's works in Newcastle,
and had stayed ever since. Engines were changed at Swindon in
early days, and as the electric telegraph did not then extend west of
Slough there was no means of knowing where a train was if it did not
arrive on time. Then old Henry Appleby would sit outside the shed
until he could bear the suspense no longer. Then he would shout for
the pilotman and tell him to 'gang and look for it'. So out the pilot
used to go, feeling his way down the line in search of the overdue
train.

It would be strange amid the broad Wiltshire accents of modern
Swindon to hear some of the conversations between the locomotive
men of Gooch's day. There was Robert Patterson, for example, who
regularly had the *Lord of the Isles:* one day the big eight-footer was
stopped for a defect, and Patterson had *Cerberus*, a 7 ft 2-2-2 instead.
They made a poor run, so much so that when he eventually did turn
up at Swindon the relieving driver, on *Castor*, asked him where the
blue pencil he had been! Patterson replied, more in sorrow than in
anger: 'Man, she winna dee it.' Engines were seemingly unaccount-
able things in those days. Regulators had a way of flying open, and
one of them broke away while it was being turned at Didcot –
without its tender. The turntable was too small to take both engine
and tender, and the sudden jerk when the regulator opened threw
the driver off the footplate, and the engine careered away on its own
towards Reading but on the *down* line! The driver of an eight-footer,
seeing what had happened, started off in chase, without any orders
or signals, running on the up line. He overtook the runaway, and
reached Goring in time to get the pointsman to reverse the cross-over
road, so that the runaway passed on to the up line. Running ahead
of it this fearless and resourceful driver let the runaway gradually
close in on him, and once contact was established it could be stopped.

Wright tells of another weirdly complicated affair:

'On Saturday, June 17th, 1854, the engine *Hirondelle* (Robert Harle) was standing in the usual siding, the men being away in the cabin having their food. From some unforeseen cause the regulator flew open, and away she went towards the station. The Carriage Department men were engaged in rolling a pair of wheels for a carriage, and seeing the engine coming signalled to stop, but no notice was taken, and the engine pushed the wheels aside, and continued her course. A ballast engine, *Ajax*, David Gibb, seeing what had happened, followed and overtook the runaway at Faringdon Road, now Challow. Mr Appleby and Mr Andrewes, the District Superintendent, followed on the *Great Western* but before their arrival the engine was put in the siding, and my mate took the train up to Faringdon Road, and Harle and his mate came up and went on with their engine to London.'

When trains were being signalled according to the ten-minute rule there was no means of warning drivers of an obstruction ahead, if, for example, a train broke down in mid-section. An express train might be running at full speed when suddenly it would come round a curve or emerge from a tunnel to find the preceding train immediately ahead – stuck! With the primitive brakes then in use there was no hope of stopping. Such were the circumstances that befell the up Milford mail at Bullo Pill in November 1868. A cattle train from Carmarthen had stopped with engine trouble, and then up came the mail, hauled by the big broad gauge 4-4-0 engine *Rob Roy*. The rear van of the cattle train was demolished and six of the eight men inside killed, while the engine ploughed on into the cattle trucks, and 36 beasts were killed. Although the mail train was brought to such a precipitate stop no one on it was so much as injured, in itself a tribute to the robustness of the broad gauge carriage stock of the day.

As might be imagined David Joy has some good stories of running on the 'Old Worse and Worse', as the Oxford, Worcester and Wolverhampton was known. Whatever the tactics and policies of its management may have been there was always plenty of enthusiasm in the locomotive department, and plenty of incidents on the road. Writing of Campden Tunnel, and of a curious swelling of the formation that took place on the line, Joy continues:

'It was down this Honeybourne bank that one of my very best men got into a bother – the first time of our being forced into the use of coal alone, owing to a big strike at the collieries. Joe Burt was alright, as long as he was pulling, but we used to sweep down Honeybourne at 60 m.p.h. (it was always in magnificent order) with the least whiff of steam on – just to keep the cylinder moist, and the tail end brake on, just to steady the train. It was just lovely to go down like that. With an inch of snow on the rails, you could hardly hear the train run. But this time Joe had come down like this, and at the bottom found himself without steam (we had not steam gauges then), you could only feel the spring balance. The fact was, with no blast on, and the dampers close shut, nearly air tight, the smoke from the coal had backed into the firebox, and choked the fire dead. Joe pulled along quietly, and soon whipped up his fire. Those engines, 23 class, were so sensitive to any coaxing. He was soon on the way again. Still, it was something to remember.'

The 'Crimean Winter' of 1854–5, when the weather was exceptionally hard and severe, gave Joy many anxieties in keeping things going:

'One piece of smart action by J. Ludham, to wit. He was bringing down a coal train from Dudley with No. 25, and slipping down the long bank into Droitwich, with the white light in front of him, and be sure not slowly, when suddenly the white popped into red just in front of him, but too late, on the bank and with the speed, to stop at the signal box, and to his dismay he saw the mail sweeping round the curve with the signal in his favour. To attempt to check speed would be just to meet the mail at the junction and smash up. He took the other chance, caught the attention of the mail driver, and hypnotised him to check up, and himself with (engine No.) 25 and his string of coal wagons rushed through the junction in safety to both trains.

'The thought of a moment carried out in a moment; but did not that signalman get it! – Joe got "Kudos".'

Joy liked nothing better than to get on the footplate himself, and an experience of October 31st, 1855 is worth quoting:

'This evening I had a big spin with No. 31 – J. Burt. I had stripped this engine and made her into a single "Jenny" 5 ft 6 in. wheels, but I could get any pressure into her I liked.

'This evening she was on the 5.0 p.m. train for London, the last day of the Worcester Races, and all our directors and Williams going by the train to catch the London and North-Western Railway train at Handboro', so there was a good train on – 13, with horse boxes.

'Adcock, traffic manager, sent for me to know if I was aware of the train, and that "my little engine" was on (they knew I was petting the thing). I answered in a wax, "I'll eat her if she does not do it", told Joe Burt, sent for my coat, and we went off 14 sec. late with 150 lb. steam. By the time we got to Honeybourne we had 175 lb. and went up the bank in fourth notch, crashing like guns at the chimney. Lost a few minutes to Moreton, but the guard winked at us, and said, "You'll do it, sir." We had to catch the North-Western at Handboro'. Then we ran (slightly down) as

hard as the engine would run, she rolled in those elastic horn plates like
a ship at sea; with 150 lb. I guess she went, and arrived at Handboro'
2 min. before time.

'This trip was run in 1 hour 14 min. deducting 14 sec. late, and 2 min.
inside time, including the bank, the Birdcage crossing at Campden, and
stopping at Moreton.'

This must have been a grand run, for the distance from Worcester
to Handborough is exactly 50 miles, and to run it in 74 min. with
thirteen on with a little 5 ft 6 in. 'Jenny Lind' 2-2-2 was a pretty
marvellous feat, even considering that Joy himself was on the
footplate.

For some first-hand impressions of footplate work on the broad
gauge in its later days we can turn to the notes taken by the Rev.
A. H. Malan on the Bristol and Exeter road. Malan evidently had
little in the way of engineering knowledge, but in describing things
exactly as he found them he includes details that a professional
locomotive man or a hardened footplate rider would probably not
think worth mentioning. He was an out-and-out broad gauge
enthusiast, and had no time at all for William Dean's 7 ft 8 in.
singles which were in evidence at Bristol before the actual conversion
of the gauge on the West of England line. He compared their top-
heaviness with the massive stability of the broad gauge 4-2-2s. It
would seem that Brunel's 'baulk-road' gave a very harsh ride,
having nothing of the 'spring' of a transverse sleepered road. Indeed
the older enginemen always said that locomotives were one or two
coaches stronger on a sleepered track. But, nevertheless, let Malan
tell his own story of a trip on the *Iron Duke*, hauling the up 'Dutchman'
from Newton Abbot to Bristol, and stopping only at Teignmouth
and Taunton.

'This trip', he wrote, 'served indeed to correct several wrong impressions. Someone has written somewhere, that in going round sharp curves
the feeling is frightful, as though the engine were actually off the line. But
nothing of the sort was experienced; the engine then, on the contrary,
seemed unusually steady; in consequence, no doubt, of the flanges a-
pressing against that rail which bore the centrifugal force; and moreover
the lines are hidden for some distance ahead, on account of the length of
the boiler; a long stretch of straight line was infinitely worse; for a bad
length of rail here and there would cause the wheels to bang against the
metals, first on one side and then on the other, with a series of jerks, and
deafening crashes, like the united blows of many hammers breaking up
iron plates in a foundry yard. It seemed, on these occasions, as if the tyres
of the wheels, especially the big driving wheels, were bound to snap, or

the spokes to break off at the axles. Let the metal be of the very best, it is well known that constant vibration quite alters its character, rendering it crystalline instead of fibrous, and surely such tremendous strains must influence its nature, if anything in the world can. The sensation at these times was indescribable – "terrific" being the only word suggesting itself. If this be "steadiness of motion", one thinks, is it possible for any one to conceive the state of unstable equilibrium in which a narrow gauge engine must find itself under the circumstances?'

He returned on the down 'Dutchman', leaving Bristol at 2.2 p.m. with engine *Rover*:

'It was a fine sunny afternoon. The ground rises the first six miles to Bourton, and this has to be done in nine minutes, to keep time. The regulator was full open, and the lever in four-and-a-half notch to the top of the bank. Posted at the left hand glass, it was the fireman's turn this time to have his observations interfered with. The most dangerous part seemed as before, crashing past the platforms; there was just time in many cases, but not in all, to spell out the names of the stations; one's whole attention was concentrated once more on the signals. And here an unforeseen difficulty presented itself. The sun was getting low (3 p.m. November) and shone full in our faces right up to sunset; the farther we proceeded the worse the dazzle; it was utterly impossible for one unused to the work to see whether many of the signals were on or off, right in the glare and against the sun, and this must be a great strain on the men's eyes. When questioned about it, the driver confessed it was "bad enough", but remarked that after all it was not half so trying as snowstorms when the snow would darken the glass so that scarcely anything at all could be seen. . . . After Norton, the pace soon began to be less violent, and the panting of the engine showed that the resistance on the pistons was increasing. As Wellington was neared another notch was given to the lever, and still another. Then began an anxious time. Having read in a certain work that "to climb a long bank, instead of the engine blowing off, it should rather be inclined to be short of steam, so that the steam can be allowed to push the pistons to the end of the stroke, following it up with an even pressure", I thought that with a boiler full of steam, as ours was, some steps would be taken to partially close the regulator, or notch up the lever. But here, again, doctors obviously differ. The regulator was wide open, the lever in the second or third notch, and the intention evidently was to mount the bank as quickly as possible by the sheer force of high pressure steam.

'The driver and fireman "stood by" eagerly listening, and at the least suspicion of slipping, worked the sand-gear quickly. A little rain was falling and the rails were moist, and the sand-lever had to be worked more than once.

'"Then you don't put down the damper, or check your steam in any way, up the bank?" I remarked.

'"No, let her have it: the *Iron Duke* stuck in the tunnel last week," answered Sansom.

'I noticed as we laboured on how the fireman kept tending his fire with extreme care, selecting nothing but clean lumps without any small stuff and constantly feeding the furnace, keeping the needle well up to 140. There must be a tremendous blast in the furnace when the lever is well over. A great lump of coal does not get dull red first round the edges, as in a grate, but disintegrates uniformly and at once; fiery smoke comes between the strata of the block; it seems all in a simmer and grows white hot almost in a moment.

'And now the pace was at last really slow, but then here we were entering the tunnel, and our troubles were over. The lever was put back in the seventh notch, and away we started for Tiverton, Collumpton, and Silverton – here speed is always great on down trains – and so on, in the waning light through Stoke Canon, right into St David's, without a single check from Bristol, and only one adverse distant signal, which, being observed far ahead, was "blown down" by the whistle without altering the speed.

'Many trains had been passed, some broad, some narrow gauge, these did not look at all as if they would run into us, as one saw a long way off that the coming train was on its own line; and in every case the din and turmoil of our own engine entirely drowned all noise from the other; even as an express rushed past, no increase of sound whatever was perceived: it might have been a phantom train; or standing still.

'At Exeter we went down under the engine, but there was no need to oil anything as the *Rover* proved to be in tip-top trim; cranks of the driving wheels quite cool, bands of eccentrics just luke-warm. Between St Thomas's and Exminster attention was drawn to the "new road", which was pronounced much better than the old, being "more springy"; this, like many other things, had to be taken on trust by one who could not detect the slightest difference in the vibration; anyway I am sorry to see the old longitudinals thus disappearing, which have always proved so safe, when an engine has gone off the rails. We flashed through Starcross at great speed; a nasty, risky piece of line, where it looked as if the engine would bump against the wall of the Hotel, and *ricochet* on to the pier; and so on in the gloaming, through the warm red cuttings and tunnels of Dawlish, by the sea-wall of Holcombe, and on into Teignmouth, where the trip ended.'

For the lighter side of life on the G.W.R. in Victorian times one turns inevitably to Ahrons. He was trained at Swindon, and did a lot of footplate work on the line; but the two following anecdotes have nothing to do with regulator openings, cut-offs, drawbar horsepower, or any of the more serious sides of locomotive performance. The first more strictly concerns natural history.

'The pheasant', Ahrons begins, 'is a very different sort of bird from a crow, not only in outward appearance, but also in his mental outlook. He hasn't the same adaptability for railway matters, and being somewhat of a fool he generally manages to get in the way, when he ought to be somewhere else. For this reason he sometimes flies into telegraph wires or gets hit by the front of an express engine, but as the Board of Trade inspectors do not hold enquiries into this sort of accident, he goes on doing it. Moreover, his easy-going habits make him so easily poached that he leads people astray who would otherwise be good citizens. There was once a pheasant on the "Wilts and Somerset" line that did this to a friend of mine, whom I will call K——, who was at the time firing on the engine of a slow goods train. Between two certain stations, which I will call A and Z, there is a very stiff bank, up which, when approaching the summit, a fully loaded goods train can only proceed at a crawl of some 4 or 5 miles an hour. I have not named the exact locality, but many Great Western Railway men will probably recognize it, for at the particular spot the railway passes through a thick wood, which in the late "eighties" was full of pheasants of an exceeding tameness. I very much doubt whether guns ever shot over it at that time, with the result that all the pheasants in the county made it a rendezvous, and the population increased so rapidly that they appeared to average a density of some four or five to the square yard. If one of them turned round he generally hit the bird behind him in the eye with his tail.

'One fine afternoon one of the crowd found that he had not sufficient "elbow-room", and decided to climb the fence and explore the railway, just as the slow goods was approaching up the bank. He was evidently so accustomed to trains that he hardly budged, and I regret to have to add that when the engine came alongside, a well-planted shot with a lump of Welsh coal hit him in the abdomen, a portion of his anatomy which the driver termed his "firebox". To quote Bret Harte under somewhat similar circumstances, "the subsequent proceedings interested him no more", for it took but a moment at the slow speed at which the train was moving, for K—— to descend from the engine and fetch the bird on to the footplate, where the driver executed a "danse macabre" by performing on him with the fire-shovel, and he was promptly stowed away inside the tool-box.

'Then the trouble started. As K—— afterwards phrased it in telling the story, "Have you ever had a conscience that thumped like a bad big-end brass? You see my father is a J.P., with decided views as to the ownership of pheasants. I began to feel so uncomfortable that I completely missed the firehole with the next shovelful of coal, and when I scattered it all over the footplate, the driver made some very pungent observations. It was too late to put the bird back, so I offered it to the driver, who declined it with thanks. I believe that after the first excitement was over, he too began to feel uncertain as to the merits of our performance. But he excused his refusal by stating that his missus positively turned sick at the smell of game, and it was as much as he was worth to take it home with him. Had it only been a turkey the case would have been different." But it wasn't, and so eventually the bird arrived at Swindon, where it was smuggled out of the shed to K——'s rooms. K—— had been a public schoolboy, and certain of the history of the Middle Ages occurred to him, chiefly, as he put it, that part where the ancient barons used to go crusading or marauding or doing something they ought not to have done, and then presenting the proceeds – when they departed this life – to the Church. It was a happy thought and provided a means of "taking up the brasses" of his conscience, so he packed up the bird and sent it round with a polite note to one of the curates, without any unnecessary comments as to its origin. K—— said, "All's well that ends well, but I don't mean to have any further truck with railway pheasants." '

The section of the line where this affair took place was on the Bruton bank, on the last stage of the climb from Castle Cary to the summit now marked by Brewham signal box.

Lastly we may let Ahrons retell the story of the Golden Jubilee, and how it was celebrated at Swindon:

'In the year 1887 Her late Majesty Queen Victoria had a Jubilee, and as the Great Western Railway is nothing if not exceedingly loyal, it was forthwith decided to commemorate the event in suitable fashion. The participation of Swindon took the form of a fete and tea in New Swindon park. Great as were the rejoicings, greater still was the quantity of tea to be provided for perhaps 15,000 people, and the locomotive department was called upon to decide the problem. Finally, after much cogitation, some genius, whose name ought to be immortalized with that of George Stephenson, suggested that the tea should be boiled in the tenders of a number of locomotives set apart for the purpose. I believe the original idea was to empty cases of tea into the tenders filled with cold water and then turn live steam from the engine loose into the mixture. The drawback was that the resultant tea might have left something to be desired as a cheering beverage, and moreover if someone had turned the wrong handle and started the injectors to work, the cones of the latter would have become blocked with tea leaves, so that the fete might have to be temporarily stopped whilst a new engine was being sent for. However, a modification of the original idea was actually adopted. There were a number of older tenders which were regularly used as water tanks, and travelled between Swindon and Kemble Junction, where the water was obtained. What the water was actually used for I do not at this moment remember, but the first thing to be done was to have the tenders cleaned out. They were in a pretty bad state too, for the man who got inside to do the job came out in about ten seconds with the remark that if tea was to be made in those tanks he would turn over a new leaf and drink beer for the rest of his natural existence. However, they were finally got into a fair state of internal order, so that the resulting beverage in the end had only a moderate "twang". Taps were fixed in the sides of the tenders and on the festive day three or four tenders were placed in the siding at Rodbourne Lane Crossing, the nearest point to the park, with a goods engine duly connected to them by means of a steam pipe. Steam was then blown into the tenders, one by one, and the revellers filled their tea urns from the taps. Never had Swindon imbibed so much tea in the course of its existence, and I am glad to be able to add that the doctors, in spite of the "twang", had no more cases than usual to deal with during the following week. The whole scheme was a veritable locomotive triumph for the cause of temperance – the man who cleaned the tenders alone excepted.'

X

Narrow Gauge in the Ascendant

By the time Joseph Armstrong was well established at Swindon the days of the broad gauge had passed their zenith, and his organization had to be delicately balanced between keeping the broad gauge locomotives and rolling stock fit for their work, and preparations for the eventual complete changeover. However badly the broad gauge carriages were allowed to deteriorate, and thus lose something of that public goodwill that had been built up so carefully by Charles Saunders, and which has always been so cherished a tradition of the Great Western, there was was no such deterioration in the standards of maintenance of the broad gauge engines. The photographs of eight-foot singles taken by the Rev. A. H. Malan in the last years before final conversion show the locomotives in immaculate condition, with the great brass bands that served as driving wheel splashers polished till they shone like gold.

Although the design of the eight-footers dated back to 1847 they were to last till the final conversion of the gauge. The first 24 of them were built at Swindon, and then a further seven, with names associated with the Crimean War, were built by Rothwell and Co. in 1854–5. By the time of Queen Victoria's Golden Jubilee, in 1887, their numbers had been reduced to 21, and all the survivors had been almost completely renewed. With the putting on of additional broad gauge expresses, the 'Jubilees', more locomotives were required, and as late in broad gauge history as the year 1888 three new eight-footers were built at Swindon. One's pen almost runs on to add that these engines were built to the original drawings, but this is not so, for the simple reason that no such drawings existed. The three engines of 1888, *Great Western*, *Prometheus*, and *Tornado*, must have had the shortest lives of any express locomotives that had a 'peaceful' end.

At the outset there had been drawings of the original *Great Western* and *Iron Duke*, but since the days of 1847–51 the day-to-day experience with these engines had suggested one change here, another one there, and so on, until the engines actually in traffic bore little resemblance to the original drawings so far as detailed dimensions were concerned. The eight-footers were all maintained under the care of Bill Cave, the leading hand in 'C' shed at Swindon. No drawings were needed. Cave and his men knew all they wanted to know by heart, and the rest they made up to suit any individual case that came along. The three new engines of 1888 were built in 'C' shed without any drawings whatever! The result was, of course, that no two of the eight-footers were exactly alike. The extraordinary thing was that at the very end of broad gauge existence someone in authority decided that it was about time they had drawings of these famous engines. Then Bill Cave had to be consulted over every point of importance. Heaven knows where the drawing office would have been without his aid.

The eight-footers were stationed at no more than two running sheds, Westbourne Park and Bristol. Engines at the latter depot did all the express working between Bristol and Newton Abbot, and had one turn to London in addition. The London engines did not work beyond Bristol. In 1888 the allocation was 13 to Westbourne Park, and 11 to Bristol, though the latter shed had the two unnamed engines 2i001 and 2002 which were rebuilds of the Pearson 9 ft 4-2-4 tank engnes of the Bristol and Exeter Railway. As rebuilt these engines had inside frames throughout, and leading bogies. The Gooch engines, although of the same wheel arrangements, were non-bogie. Both the B. & E. rebuilds and the standard G.W.R. 4-2-2s looked very large and massive, though in actual fact they were not powerful engines, by the standards of the 'eighties of last century. The cylinders were 18 in. diameter by 24 in. stroke, and the boiler pressure was 140 lb. per sq. in. The heating surface was varied in different batches from a total of 1,728 sq. ft up to 2,064 sq. ft in the new engines of 1888, but in actual running they never appear to have been pushed very hard.

On two runs with the down 'Dutchman', booked to reach Swindon in 87 min. from Paddington, the actual times were 90 min. 52 sec. with engine *Rover* and seven bogie coaches, 90 min. 50 sec. with *Eupatoria* and the same load. Speed barely exceeded 60 m.p.h. at any point on either run, and both engines unblushingly lost $3\frac{3}{4}$ min. in running. Things were usually a little brighter on the eastbound run with the help of the very slight descending gradient, and of the prevailing wind. The accompanying log with the engine *Alma* shows steady, but not very sensational running, and a start-to-stop average speed of 55·2 m.p.h. with a load of 180 tons. There was a slight slack through Didcot, costing less than a minute, and inclusive of this the average speed over the 71 miles between mileposts 73 and 2 was 57·7 m.p.h.

G.W.R.: SWINDON – PADDINGTON
Load: 180 tons
Engine: Broad gauge 4-2-2 *Alma*

Distance miles		Actual min. sec.	Av. speed m.p.h.
0·0	SWINDON	0 00	—
4·3	Milepost 73	7 24	—
7·3	,, 70	10 44	54·2
12·3	,, 65	16 02	56·6
17·3	,, 60	20 59	60·6
22·3	,, 55	25 57	60·4
27·3	,, 50	31 48	51·5 *
32·3	,, 45	37 04	57·0
37·3	,, 40	42 05	59·8
42·3	,, 35	47 07	59·6
47·3	,, 30	52 12	59·0
52·3	,, 25	57 09	60·6
57·3	,, 20	62 12	59·4
75·3	,, 2	81 10	57·0
77·3	PADDINGTON	84 08	

* Slack through Didcot

In the very last year of the broad gauge four eight-footers were stationed at Newton Abbot, and this was the prelude to the allocation of several Dean 7 ft 8 in. singles to that shed after the conversion of the gauge. The broad gauge engines had some hard work to do in climbing the Whiteball bank, and assistance was frequently taken from Taunton. Unfortunately I have not been able to find any detailed records of express running over this section. In the course of his training on the G.W.R. Ahrons was on the footplate of *Lightning* one afternoon on the up 'Zulu' when a deliberate attempt was made to attain a record speed down the bank towards Wellington. Clocking with the second hand of an ordinary watch, and recording every milepost, a maximum speed of 81 m.p.h. was noted, though on account of the method of timing this speed would be subject to slight adjustment either way. In any case it is clear that a speed of at least 80 m.p.h. was attained. Special efforts apart, however, the section between Taunton and Exeter saw the fastest daily running made on the broad gauge. On the London road the booked times of the down expresses were so liberal between Swindon and Bath that there was rarely any occasion to go hard down the Dauntsey bank and through Box Tunnel. On the other hand there was no time to spare on the ordinary bookings west of Taunton and maximum speeds of 70 m.p.h. and over were of daily occurrence.

Even though the ultimate disappearance of the broad gauge was inevitable, and definitely in sight by the seventies of the last century, it is extraordinary how the higher management of the G.W.R. clung to the rapidly dwindling services that remained broad gauge, and continued to invest them with an air of immeasurable superiority over anything that was worked on the narrow gauge. After the conversion of the South Wales Railway, for example, the New Milford boat expresses were narrow gauge, and like the broad gauge 'Dutchman', 'Zulu' and 'Jubilee' ran non-stop between Paddington and Swindon. But the 5.45 p.m. was allowed no less than 97 min. for the 77·3 miles – ten minutes more than the crack broad gauge timings. The difference, of course, was that the narrow gauge trains kept time easily, even when the loads were nearly 200 tons, whereas the broad gauge celebrities were nearly always late in arriving at Swindon.

The preferential treatment given to the broad gauge expresses probably arose from their conveying only first and second class passengers. Although it was done in a more gentlemanly and subtle way managerial antipathy to the third class passenger was as strong at Paddington in the seventies and eighties as it was at London Bridge and Victoria. Towards the end of the broad gauge era the management would probably have liked to admit third class passengers to the 'Dutchman' and the 'Zulu', but could not do so for two very good reasons: first, that they had no third class carriages to spare that were fit to run on such celebrated expresses, and secondly, if they had, the old 4-2-2 locomotives would have been quite incapable of hauling the increased loads. The 'Jubilee' conveyed all three classes, but it was a new train in 1887 and had not the well-established clientèle of the older broad gauge expresses to the West of England.

At times of the heaviest traffic it became customary to run narrow gauge reliefs to the broad gauge expresses. Then, the broad gauge trains conveyed their normal rake of coaches, and all the additional traffic was piled into the reliefs. Carrying all three classes, these trains loaded up to such tonnages that there was no chance of keeping the normal schedules. The narrow gauge relief trains could not be run beyond Exeter, and on some occasions they were diverted via Weston-super-Mare to serve that resort directly. In the ordinary way passengers travelling by the crack broad gauge expresses from London had to change at Bristol for Weston-super-Mare. Whatever the high authorities at Paddington might have thought about the relative merits, in running, of broad and narrow gauge trains, there were no delusions about the matter in the Locomotive Department, either at Swindon or Wolverhampton, and the narrow gauge express drivers never let an opportunity slip of having a real 'go' at the broad gauge schedules, to try and bring them down from their pinnacle of untouchability. Unfortunately, the occasions were usually accompanied by such heavy loading as to make timekeeping impracticable.

One such occasion, just before the Easter holidays, may be specially mentioned. The train concerned was the down 'Zulu', leaving Paddington at 3 p.m., and booked to reach Swindon in the standard broad gauge timing of 87 min. How the regular train was loaded does not appear in this particular record, but the second part, narrow gauge and not running beyond Exeter, had no less than 195 tons behind the tender. The normal broad gauge load would be about 120 tons. To haul this heavy train an Armstrong 2-2-2 of the 'Queen' class was provided, No. 1123 *Salisbury*, and her driver made an all-out attempt to keep the broad gauge timing. One feels that the attempt would have been foredoomed to failure from the outset, because the broad gauge first part would not keep time itself. So indeed it turned out! *Salisbury* made a grand start, covering the 18½ miles out to Slough in 23¼ min. Reading was passed in 42½ min., but then they caught up the first part and suffered a succession of signal checks. But for these they would have been very near to the 87 min. schedule, as from Didcot splendid work was done up the rising grades to Swindon, covering the last 24¼ miles in 27½ min. pass to stop. The net time was between 88 and 89 min. – a splendid effort, with a load some 50 per cent greater than that of the 'Dutchman'.

Having reached Swindon it is now time to look at the narrow gauge express engines in a little more detail. Between the years 1866 and 1879 sixty 2-2-2 locomotives were built at Swindon, and although the last ten came out after Joseph Armstrong's death they can be considered together. From time to time there were innumerable varieties of these engines, due to various boiler renewals, fitting of cabs, closing in of splashers and so on; but they were originally of three distinct classes, all with 7 ft driving wheels.

G.W.R. NARROW GAUGE 2-2-2s

Class	Date	Number in class	Cylinders dia. stroke (in.)	Total heating surface sq. ft.
'Sir Daniel' .	1866–9	30	17 × 24	1269
'Queen' .	1873–5	20	18 × 24	1278½
157–166 .	1878–9	10	18 × 24	1214¼

Originally the first engine of the 1873 series, No. 55 *Queen*, differed from the rest of the class in having a polished brass dome; the others had 'straight-back' domeless boilers, with a polished safety valve column over the firebox something after the Patrick Stirling style. Because of this difference from the first engine to be built the class were more usually known as the 'Sir Alexanders', after the name bestowed upon engine No. 999. Both this class and the 'Sir Daniels' had outside plate frames like Joseph Armstrong's first Wolverhampton engines, but in the 157–166 class turned out under Dean a reversion was made to the sandwich frames used by Daniel Gooch on the broad gauge express locomotives. Those who had a good deal of footplate experience considered that the sandwich frames enabled the engines to ride more smoothly on the old 'baulk' road, laid with the longitudinal timbers of Brunel's design. This track was exceedingly stiff and engines rode 'dead' over it. All three classes of 2-2-2 originally had completely open splashers, but these, picturesque as they were, proved a continual source of danger through drivers putting their arms through the spokes when oiling round.

Both the 'Sir Alexanders' and the '157' class were excellent engines on the road. In their prime the allocation of these 18 inch 2-2-2s was as follows:

Westbourne Park	Wolverhampton	Gloucester
13 'Sir Alexanders' 6 '157' class	5 'Sir Alexanders' 4 '157' class	2 'Sir Alexanders'

The two Gloucester engines ran the Milford boat trains to and from London, the working of which was entrusted to the 'Sir Daniel' class in South Wales itself. The London engines were maintained at Swindon, while Wolverhampton works looked after the nine 18 inch 2-2-2s that were stationed at Stafford Road shed. From this hangs a long and exceedingly vigorous tale. I have told in a previous chapter how Joseph Armstrong placed his younger brother, George, in charge of the Wolverhampton Division when he left for Swindon, and if ever there was a tough character it was George Armstrong. He openly asserted that he took orders from no man. If he had been no more than a fire-eating autocrat things might have become very awkward, but he was in fact an extremely able locomotive engineer. His brother gave him complete freedom of action and Dean did the same.

Through the whole of his brother's chieftainship at Swindon, and for no less than 20 years of Dean's, George Armstrong reigned as undisputed 'King' of the Wolverhampton Division. During that time the locomotives had a livery of their own, quite distinct from that of Swindon in the bluish tone of the basic green, and in the much darker shade of the underframes. The copper caps to the chimneys were also of a shape quite different from those of Swindon. But the Wolverhampton of George Armstrong's day did not display its individuality in superficial details alone. Its practice differed from that of Swindon in the very important respect of valve setting. It has always been a common practice, not only on the G.W.R. but generally, to set the valves with equal 'lead' at each end of the cylinder. This provided for equal admission at the very commencement of the piston stroke, but inequality in port openings which meant that one end of the cylinder was doing more work than the other. Valve setting is always something of a compromise, and at Wolverhampton the valve setter made adjustments to provide equal port openings. As a result the engines were consistently stronger in pulling than others of the same class which had the valves set at Swindon.

There was every significance in this difference, for the Wolverhampton engines had to do some of the hardest express work on the G.W.R. By that time the Oxford, Worcester and Wolverhampton line had been fully integrated with the purely Great Western line via Birmingham, and the express locomotive diagrams of Stafford Road shed included many 'round trip' workings: for example, Wolverhampton to Paddington direct via Birmingham and Banbury, and returning from London with a Worcester express, continuing up the O.W.W. to Wolverhampton. There were similar workings from South Wales after the final conversion of the gauge, in which locomotives ran from Newport to Paddington, and returned via Bath and Bristol. So far as the London workings from Wolverhampton were concerned, leaving out the slow-running section between Birmingham and Wolverhampton, there were three inclines which would severely tax the capacity of a single-wheeler and its crew: the ascent from Honeybourne to Campden Tunnel on the O.W.W.; what used to be called the Harbury bank, climbing southbound from Leamington to Southam Road; and, of course, Hatton bank.

There is no doubt that a magnificent tradition was built up at Wolverhampton under George Armstrong. The locomotives were superbly maintained, and the express drivers at Stafford Road shed acquired consummate skill in handling their 7 ft single-wheelers with quite heavy trains, making brisk starts, and climbing banks like Campden and Hatton with a surefootedness that would make many a modern engineman rub his eyes in wonder. The logs detailed in Chapter Fourteen will bear this out. While George Armstrong was at Wolverhampton, and ruling the roost without the slightest regard for what was happening at Swindon, there is no doubt that a very healthy rivalry grew up between the two establishments – both works being a closed shop to any representatives from the 'rival' establishment. The difference in practice over valve setting was an interesting and important case in point.

Some years ago I was in conversation with a veteran locomotive engineer who had held high office on the Great Western, and I mentioned this point to him, asking which practice prevailed over the other when full standardization took place under Churchward. He looked extremely blank, and said it was the first time he had ever heard that there had been a difference. Certainly there had been no change at Swindon; and he would know! Armstrong had to provide locomotives for the north main line to Chester and Birkenhead, and also for the north-to-west route from Shrewsbury, via Hereford and the Severn Tunnel to Bristol. From the inception of the through express service from Manchester and Liverpool to the West of England over this route in 1888, the locomotive workings over the 'joint' part of the line, between Shrewsbury and Hereford, were shared between the G.W.R. and the L.N.W.R., and stories are told – one by Sir William Stanier – that rather suggest that the working was not always as harmonious as it might have been, and that the North Western repeatedly blocked any Great Western ideas of using their latest or most powerful four-coupled engines. In later years, it was to meet the continuing restrictions upon locomotive power that Churchward designed his 4-4-0 'County' class. From 1888 until the abolition of the broad gauge the service to the West of England was provided by connections at Bristol. The through carriages to Torquay and Plymouth date from 1892.

In 1888 some of the best trains over this route were worked throughout by Great Western engines of the 2-4-0 type. Those from the Bristol end were a typical Dean production of the period, rebuilt from an early class originally used on the Berks and Hants line; the Shrewsbury engines had 6 ft 6 in., against 6 ft coupled wheels, but had double sandwich frames, and were most distinctive and handsome little things. Engines of various 2-4-0 types worked on the north main line between Wolverhampton, Chester and Birkenhead, where most of the service was of a very 'intermediate' nature, and appropriately very slow. The curious thing about the two crack expresses over this route was that they by-passed Chester

– no more than narrowly it is true – as they took the west curve, almost within sight of the General station, and this arrangement made it possible to run through with one engine between Wolverhampton and Birkenhead.

These trains began running in 1880, on the same day, in fact, as the broad gauge 'Zulu' was inaugurated. The down Birkenhead train left Paddington at 4.45 p.m. and to distinguish it from its broad gauge contemporary, it became known as the 'Afghan' in the London division in recognition of another remote fastness of Empire where Great Britain had recently been involved with the native tribes. But whatever Paddington may have thought or decreed, Wolverhampton went its own way, and to everyone north of Oxford the 4.45 p.m. down was the 'Zulu'! The corresponding up express left Birkenhead at 11.50 p.m.; it was likewise known as the 'Zulu', and thereby hangs one of those tales of railway tradition that have survived to the present day. The lineage of the old 11.50 a.m. can be traced through the reigns of six British monarchs, two world wars, nationalization, and the early stages of the Modernization Plan to the train that has for many years left Birmingham at 3 p.m. And today, as surely as it was eighty years ago, that train is still known by railwaymen as the 'Zulu', when the lineage of the *real* 'Zulu' has long since been lost and forgotten!

To work the 'Northern Zulu', as it should be more correctly called, George Armstrong had three of the 'Sir Daniel' class 2-2-2s stationed at Birkenhead. These included *Sir Daniel* itself, No. 378, and additionally Nos. 473 and 578. Originally on the run northward from Wolverhampton the train stopped at Wellington, Shrewsbury and Gobowen, thereafter running non-stop from Wrexham to Birkenhead. The Chester coach was detached at Wrexham. The next step was to omit the stops at Wellington, Gobowen and Wrexham, and to go into Chester General station. The fastest working was from 1888, when the Wellington stop was restored and no passenger stop was made at all between Shrewsbury and Birkenhead, a working stop was made at Chester Cutting Box to detach the Chester through carriage, and the booked speed from Shrewsbury to this stop was the excellent one of 50·6 m.p.h. The route includes much sharp, switchback grading, and it was certainly a test of capacity for the old 'Sir Daniel' class 2-2-2s.

At that time engines and men made a return trip to Wolverhampton, outward on the 11.50 a.m. and returning by the 7.52 p.m. from Wolverhampton due in Birkenhead at 9.53 p.m. The 'link' included only one other duty, and a most curious one at that, from Birkenhead

2-4-0 passenger locomotive *Brindley*, built at Swindon 1864.

[*F. Moore*

Above: A former Bristol and Exeter 4-2-4 tank engine rebuilt at Swindon
as an 8 ft. 4-2-2; No. 2001 at Dawlish in 1883.

[*The late Rev. A. H. Malan*

Below: One of the four South Devon saddle tanks remaining in 1891:
Gorgon photographed at Newton Abbot.

[*The late Rev. A. H. Malan, by courtesy of B.T.C. Archives*

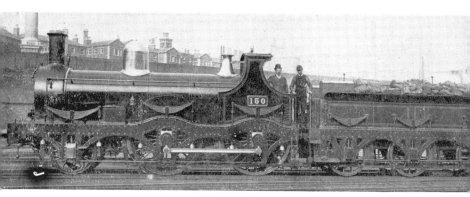

2-4-0 No. 150 of the 'Chancellor' class. Originally built by Geo. England and Co. in 1862. Rebuilt at Wolverhampton in 1878, and used on West to North expresses.

NARROW GAUGE 2-4-0s

[F. Moore

2-4-0 No. 69 *Avon*, originally built as a 2-2-2 single (69-76 class) in 1872. Rebuilt at Swindon as 2-4-0 in 1895.

Below: 2-4-0 No. 444 ('Bicycle' class) originally built at Swindon 1868. Shown as rebuilt Wolverhampton in 1885.

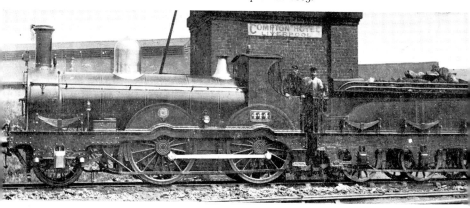

The Severn Bridge, opened in 1890: a group taken during constructional work.

[*British Railways*]

The down 'Cornishman', passing Uphill Junction, hauled by 4-2-2 locomotive *Emperor*, while a narrow gauge goods from Weston-super-Mare waits on the loop.

[*The late Rev. A. H. Malan, by courtesy of B.T.C. Archives*

The 'North Mail' near Exminster, running over transverse sleepered track. Engine *Warlock*, with T.P.O. van second from front of train.

[*The late Rev. A. H. Malan, by courtesy of B.T.C. Archives*

The conversion train at Grange Court in 1869, after completion of the work on the Hereford, Ross, Grange Court line. Note the signals and 0-6-0 locomotive *Nelson* (built Swindon 1853).

CONVERSION OF THE GAUGE

The 'graveyard' at Swindon, in 1892, with broad gauge engines awaiting conversion or scrapping.

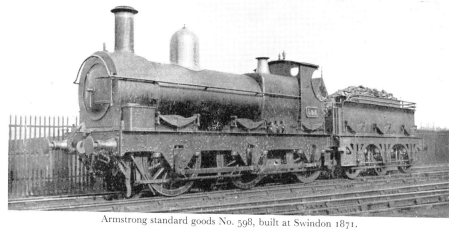

Armstrong standard goods No. 598, built at Swindon 1871.

[*Courtesy P. J. Garland*

NARROW GAUGE 0-6-0s

Beyer type double-framed goods No. 336; originally built 1864, here shown with Wolverhampton boiler, and mountings as rebuilt at Stafford Rd. in 1880.

[*F. Moore*

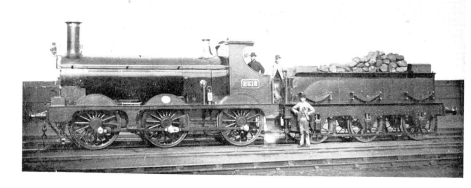

Below: Dean standard goods No. 2318; one of the first batch of these famous engines which were built at Swindon in 1883 with domeless boilers.

[*F. Moore*

Left: Wednesbury station.
[*Courtesy P. J. Garland*

: Worcester,
b Hill, showing
No. 835 (built
don 1874) and
strong 0-6-0
s No. 427
vindon 1868).
[*F. Moore*

Left: Llanybyther station,
'Manchester and Milford Railway', showing Alexander Allan
type 2-4-0 locomotive, 5 ft. 6 in.
coupled wheels, built 1866.
[*British Railways*

Work in progress at Plymouth Millbay, in May 1892.

CONVERSION OF THE GAUGE

Slewing the rails near St. Germans, Cornwall, during the great weekend conversion.

18 in. 2-2-2 No. 584, 'Sir Daniel' class, built originally at Swindon in 1869. Here shown as rebuilt 1888–90.

NARROW GAUGE 2-2-2s
[F. Moore

'Sir Alexander' class 2-2-2 No. 1126, as rebuilt at Wolverhampton with raised firebox and Wolverhampton type chimney top.

Below: A Dean 7 ft. 8 in. single in 2-2-2 days: No. 3024 *Storm King.*

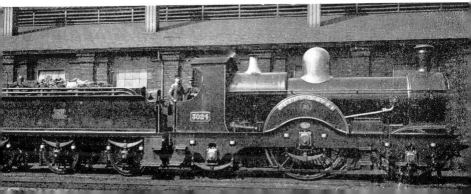

Viscount Emlyn (afterwards Earl
Cawdor), Chairman 1895–1905.

Sir James Inglis, Chief Engineer
1892–1904, later General Manager.

Joseph Armstrong, Locomotive Carriage
and Wagon Superintendent, 1864–1877.

William Dean, Locomotive Carriage and
Wagon Superintendent, 1877–1902.

One of the flat arches of Maidenhead Bridge during widening works.

IMPROVING THE LINE
[*British Railways*

Bristol No. 1. Tunnel, in course of opening out into a deep cutting prior
to widening the line in 1887.

The Maidenhead-Twyford Widening. Slinging a girder of a new occupation bridge into position.

Paddington arrival side in mixed gauge days. 2-2-2 locomotive No. 1122
Beaconsfield propelling empty stock.

[*L.G.R.P. No.* 21785]

A scene at Rattery summit, South Devon line. A 'Duke' class 4-4-0 returning light
engine to Newton Abbot after having assisted a heavy express to Brent. Note one
line 'baulk road', and the other transverse sleepered.

[*Courtesy P. J. Garland*

A down broad gauge express approaching the station, showing new signals and works in progress.

MAIDENHEAD WIDENING

[*British Railways*

A narrow gauge express, hauled by a Dean 7 ft. 8 in. 2-2-2, passing the widening works.

Brick arch bridge being demolished by explosive.

WIDENING IN SHOTTESBROOK CUTTING

[*British Railways*

Girders of new bridge, arrived on site in work train.

Above: Queen Victoria's train of 1890, drawn by 2-2-2 engine No. 55 *Queen*.

ROYAL TRAINS

Right: The Diamond Jubilee train of 1897, drawn by 4-2-2 engine No. 3041 *The Queen*.

[*British Railways*]

via Chester and Warrington to Manchester Exchange. One can well imagine what a magnificent sight a 'Sir Daniel' made, in the grimy precincts of Manchester, in all its glory of Brunswick green, light red underframes, polished brass dome, and copper capped chimney. Expert handling of the 'Sir Daniels' and other singles was not confined to the Wolverhampton Division, and an interesting reminiscence of another engine of the class, No. 579, was told some years ago by one of the Bristol men, Mr J. Robson. It relates to an incident of 1888, some two months after the North to West service had been inaugurated, when rivalry for north traffic with the Midland was intense at Bristol.

'The two companies', writes Mr Robson, 'had each decided to run a fast special express, from Bristol to Leeds, to convey back to the latter place the Yorkshire people who had visited the annual wool fair, held at Bristol, in the month of September. It was to be nothing more or less than a race.

'My father was selected to drive the Great Western train from Bristol to Shrewsbury, the London and North Western taking the train from there to Leeds. Both trains started from the same platform, one on each side, and left Bristol at the same moment, 1 p.m. I may state that my father, although he was given a schedule time to run to, was instructed by the traffic and locomotive departments at Bristol to do his best to beat the Midland, but they refused to withdraw the running instructions in force.

'The Midland put on an engine of the 2-4-0 type, but she was no match for No. 579, which got ahead of her from the commencement, in spite of the Midland road being straight at the platform and the Great Western curved. My father, when backing on to the train at Bristol, opened the valves of the sand-boxes thereby coating the rails with sand for two or three hundred yards, which enabled him to get the single-wheeler away without any slipping. The Great Western train, which was composed of four 8-wheelers, passed under the bridge that carries the Midland Railway near Stapleton, before the Midland train passed over, and cleared Severn Tunnel Junction – 17 miles from Bristol – at 1.20 p.m., which latter information was telegraphed back to Bristol, when the train passed through.'

In telling of narrow gauge prowess and the development of new train services I have not yet referred to the construction of the Severn Tunnel itself. Although the story has been told many times before, no account of the Great Western Railway in the nineteenth century would be complete without some details of this great work. Today, it seems to me that the story has a deeper significance. The Severn Tunnel was constructed when a great amount of experience in railway tunnelling had been accumulated; yet the work was constantly fraught with hazards and terrifying difficulties greater than anything encountered before. The fact that tunnels exist does not necessarily mean that another one can be driven nearby, and parallel without difficulty. The troubles that were experienced in the building of the new Woodhead Tunnel will come freshly to mind. And yet at this very time plans are actively in hand for the boring of a tunnel more than 20 miles long under the English Channel! Today we may well ponder upon the epic of the Severn Tunnel, driven by one of the most experienced tunnelling engineers of the day under a mere 4 miles of comparatively sheltered estuary.

XI

The Severn Tunnel

By the year 1872 the Great Western Railway had recovered from its financial embarrassments to such an extent that plans could be made for improving and integrating more closely the lines previously owned by the various independent companies that had been absorbed. One obvious need was to improve the means of communication between Bristol and South Wales. At this time a service was provided by the Bristol and South Wales Union Railway, crossing the River Severn by steam ferry between Passage Pier on the Gloucestershire side, and Portskewett. This was known as the New Passage Ferry, to distinguish it from the Old Passage, which is still maintained today between Aust and Beachley.

At the New Passage Ferry the Severn is about 2 miles wide, though immediately downstream from the route of the ferry there is, on the Gloucestershire side, a considerable area of very shallow water which exposes the so-called English Stones at low tide. The waterway is only a quarter of a mile wide at low tide, through the deep channel near the Monmouthshire bank known as the Shoots. Here, however, the water is no less than 58 ft deep at low tide. It was probably the width and depth of the Shoots, and the difficulties anticipated in getting good foundations that led to the proposals of crossing the course of the Severn by tunnel rather than by a viaduct. Certainly the tunnel was no brainchild of a remote theorist. It was proposed by a very practical man on the spot, Charles Richardson, who was the Great Western resident engineer on the Bristol and South Wales Union Line. The Board called in Sir John Hawkshaw as consulting engineer, and on his advice backed by his experience in construction of the Metropolitan Railway, they decided to go ahead, and the Act was obtained in 1872.

There was something truly Brunellian in this vast project: in its very magnitude; in its heroic plunge into the unknown. There is something poignant about the outcome too, when for all the hazards, all the toil, all the anxiety and expense, the G.W.R. was saddled with an operating bugbear that had grown steadily more formidable as traffic to and from South Wales developed. It is easy to be wise after the event, but one feels that those responsible for the general conception of the tunnel and its gradients cannot have foreseen the enormous expansion of the coal traffic from South Wales direct to London, to Bristol and the West, and to the Salisbury line. At the time the tunnel was built the South Wales coalfield was primarily concerned with the export trade, but not many years were to pass before it was becoming necessary to double-head every mineral train through the tunnel. A stud of locomotives had to be maintained at Severn Tunnel Junction specially for assisting, while the heavy gradients leading into and out of the tunnel made it necessary to take all the usual elaborate and time-taking precautions with loose-coupled unbraked trains against the chance of the engines being overpowered on the steep descents.

It might seem graceless to preface an account of such an epic struggle against the forces of nature by suggesting it would have been better if the Severn Tunnel had never been built; but so indeed it appears today. From the railway point of view a bridge would have been far preferable, and although the crossing of the wide and deep channel of the Shoots would have given some problems to the engineers, it must be remembered that before the Severn Tunnel had reached a very advanced stage the Forth Bridge had been designed, and plans were actively in hand for its construction. At the Severn estuary the hazardous nature of the undertaking was fully realized, even to the extent of having a clause inserted in the Act of Parliament authorizing the work to the effect that it could be abandoned if the cost of construction and of excluding water should much exceed the estimates. The events of October 1879 might well have brought the Great Western near to thoughts of abandonment, and to considerations of other means of crossing the Severn, had not the catastrophe of the first Tay Bridge occurred in that very same autumn. At that time the full facts concerning the collapse of Bouch's viaduct were not known, and there were doubtless many who felt that what had happened on the Firth of Tay could equally well happen at the New Passage Ferry. Despite the almost insuperable difficulties it was better to go under, rather than over the estuary.

But from speculations on the trend of Great Western opinion I must retrace steps six years to the time when Charles Richardson began work on the Severn Tunnel. It was decided to carry the railway 30 ft below the river bed at the Shoots, and owing to its extreme depth at this point approach gradients of 1 in 100 from both the Gloucestershire and the Monmouthshire end would be necessary. Because of these long slopes down to the section immediately beneath the Shoots the tunnel itself was to be some 4¼ miles long, although the river is no more than 2 miles wide at the particular point. The original intention was to start work at the point considered most likely to cause trouble – beneath the Shoots – and proposals were made to sink shafts immediately on either side of the deep channel, boring down into the rock that was exposed at low tide. They would have had the advantage of reducing the length of the headings that would have to be driven from the foot of the shafts as well as making sure at an early stage in construction that all was well beneath the Shoots.

It was fortunate in many ways that the original proposal was abandoned – mainly on the grounds of high costs. The procedure actually adopted, namely that of sinking shafts on each side of the river beyond the reach of tidal water, eventually struck enough trouble as it was. Work began in 1873, with the sinking of a shaft at Sudbrook, on the Monmouthshire bank of the estuary; this was taken down to a depth of 200 ft and in so doing two separate springs were encountered. The first yielded some 12,000 gallons of water per hour, and the second 27,000 gallons. Cornish beam engines were installed to pump the water away, and it was indeed significant of the difficulties experienced in these preliminary stages, that it was nearly two years before the one shaft had been sunk to the level of the proposed tunnel, and that a heading on the line of the tunnel could be commenced. The scheme of operation was then to drive a heading or pilot tunnel, 7 ft square, along the line of the tunnel, which would be afterwards opened out to the full size of the finished tunnel.

From the foot of the Old Shaft, as the first sinking at Sudbrook was known, the 7 ft heading was commenced, eastward under the Shoots, in December 1874. More springs were encountered, yielding volumes of fresh water in driving through sandstone. Such was the volume of water to be dealt with, that with additional pumping machinery it was found necessary to sink a second shaft at Sudbrook purely for pumping purposes. Whereas the old shaft, used for men and materials, was lined with brickwork, the second shaft was completely lined with iron. Up to this point the difficulties, though numerous and frustrating, were dealt with as they were met. Richardson had to pile on more and more pumping capacity at Sudbrook, but the driving of the 7 ft heading went on, and by the middle of the year 1877 nearly a mile of tunnel had been bored under the river. In the meantime work had been going steadily forward from the Sea Wall Shaft on the Gloucestershire side. By the end of

September the distance between the two working faces had shortened to 130 yards. Other shafts had been sunk on the landward sides of the river, and altogether things seemed to be going forward in a very flourishing state.

Then came the event that might well have led to the abandonment of the entire tunnel. Suddenly, and without any previous signs or warning noise, there was a fall of rock at the foot of the Old Shaft, and water began to pour into the workings in such volume that the men took flight, and only just managed to escape with their lives up the Iron Shaft. Within a few hours the water level was within 50 ft of the top of the shaft! At first all concerned believed that the thing they had most feared had happened: that a fissure in the rocks had been struck and the river had broken it. Then, when conditions below had evidently become stable a descent was made into the Old Shaft, and it was then discovered that the flood water was not salt, but fresh! Where on earth had it all come from? No ordinary spring would gush water in such prodigious volume. Of course all work in the tunnel was stopped, while Richardson and his assistants thought over the twin puzzle of where the water came from, and how to get rid of it. It was at this stage that Sir Daniel Gooch himself took a hand, and he put Sir John Hawkshaw in direct charge of the whole job, from being merely a consultant. This was no slight upon Richardson, who remained as joint engineer, but a recognition of the emergency that had overtaken the work.

Rapid clues as to where the water was coming from were soon evident in the country north of Sudbrook, where the River Neddren ran dry for a distance of about five miles, and numerous local springs dried up. This river had flowed through a marshy district, and apparently there was a large natural underground reservoir, one end of which lay very close to the tunnel works at Sudbrook. The wall of rock left was evidently too thin to resist the pressure of the water and eventually collapsed. Interesting though it was to know where the water came from, nothing more could be done at the Monmouthshire end of the tunnel until the Big Spring, as it was called, was sealed off. The existing pumps were quite incapable of dealing with such a volume of water, and while consideration was given to extra power, plans were made for temporarily sealing off the Big Spring so that the water could be drained away and work recommenced in the tunnel.

It was at this stage that a contract was placed with T. A. Walker, of London, for completion of the entire tunnel. One looks indeed with interest to the man who agreed to take on the job at such an unpropitious moment, with the workings flooded and everything at a standstill. But Walker had been associated with Sir John Hawkshaw in some difficult underground railway jobs in London, and was apparently undaunted by the dismal prospects at Sudbrook. Hawkshaw decided to increase the depth of the tunnel beneath the Shoots from 30 to 45 ft, and this came to involve a steepening of the gradient on the Monmouthshire side from 1 in 100 to 1 in 90. From the viewpoint of the future coal traffic it was fortunate that the worsening of the gradient was in the direction of the empty wagon trains, although two engines would ordinarily be used – if for nothing else than getting the assistant engine back to Severn Tunnel Junction without separate occupation of a crowded line by light engine runs. But I am anticipating; the story has not yet progressed beyond that disastrous October of 1879, when all the tunnel works were completely submerged in water from the Big Spring.

Plans were made for impounding the flood water stage by stage; the first job was to get the Old Shaft clear, and two massive oaken shields were made to fit across the entrances to the 7 ft headings on either side of the shaft bottom. As the water was roughly 150 ft deep in the shaft these shields had to be placed in position by divers, and at that stage in history the equipment available to these men was somewhat primitive. And now Diver Lambert comes into the story. He was one of a small team engaged by Charles Richardson to get the oaken shields into position. It was an exceedingly difficult job to do, in pitch darkness, groping their way over tools and impedimenta left behind in the rush to safety when the waters of the Big Spring broke in; but the job was done, and with the installation of additional pumps the water was gradually cleared from the Old Shaft to an extent that exploration of the flooded headings could be started. The difficulties involved will be more vividly realized when I add a full year elapsed between the inrush of the Big Spring and the clearing of the Old Shaft. The next stage was to pump out the water from the long 7 ft heading that extended right under the river, and to within 130 yards of the heading driven from the Gloucestershire side. Fortunately an emergency headwall had been built across the heading, closed by an iron door. In the panic of October 1879, however, this door had been left open, and the task for the divers was to get it closed.

Of the man chosen to essay this ghastly job Charles Richardson's description cannot be bettered: 'His name is Lambert, a fair-haired man of few words, but of great courage.' The task ahead of him was to make his way alone for nearly a quarter of a mile along an underground passage 7 ft square, in darkness, dragging the air pipe that fed his breathing apparatus behind him. It was not a smooth, finished tunnel through which he had to grope his way but a rough working heading, in which tools and fallen rock were strewn across his path. Two other divers helped him, one to feed the air pipe round the sharp bend from the bottom of the Old Shaft into the heading, and another, stationed some distance along the heading, to help in feeding the air pipe forward. In the rough and uncertain conditions in the heading the utmost care had to be taken with the air pipe, for a fracture or a leak would have meant death to Lambert. At his very first attempt this brave man got within 70 ft of the door, but could drag the air pipe no further, and had to make a perilous way back. So far as his own safety was concerned this return walk was even more hazardous, because the returning bend of the air pipe caught up on every conceivable obstruction.

The standard contemporary diving equipment having been thus proved impracticable an attempt was next made with the Fleuss apparatus, which consisted of a self-contained oxygen supply in a vessel strapped to the diver's back. The inventor himself went to Sudbrook, and descended the Old Shaft in company with Lambert. Having seen the conditions below he is reported to have said that even if he were offered a sum of £10,000 he would not attempt to make his way through the heading and try to close the door. Lambert immediately offered to make another attempt, using the Fleuss apparatus himself, but there was a good deal of controversy and bargaining with the engineers before Fleuss would agree to apparatus being used by another diver. Then, after familiarizing himself with the gear, Lambert made another attempt; he reached the door, and did some preliminary jobs before closing it. These took so long that he feared the oxygen supply in the Fleuss apparatus would be exhausted, and returned to the surface.

Finally, on November 10th, 1880, Lambert again reached the door, closed it, shut down the flap valve and screwed down the sluice valve, hard. This time he had been under water for eighty minutes, but after his return, to the dismay of everyone concerned, the pumps did not immediately begin to have any appreciable effect on the water level. It seemed an analogous case to the building of the Liverpool and Manchester Railway embankment across Chat Moss. Just as George Stephenson had gone on tipping and tipping into the bog without any sign of a solid embankment rising, so Richardson went on pumping at Sudbrook. More pumps were added, and after a solid month of work the water level in the heading was reduced sufficiently for the foreman of the pumps to make his way to the headwall door. It was then discovered that by some unlucky freak of non-standardization one of the sluice valves had a left-hand instead of a right-hand thread, and Lambert instead of screwing it down hard had opened it to its fullest extent! Once this wretched sluice valve was properly closed the water was easily mastered, and temporary headwalls, massively built in brick and cement, sealed off the Big Spring from the tunnel workings and enabled the engineers to take stock of the whole situation.

Meanwhile Diver Lambert, whose courage had written such a shining page in Great Western history, disappears from the scene as quietly and unobtrusively as he had entered upon it. Many years after the Severn Tunnel was completed, in July 1901 to be precise, one of the Dean 7 ft 8 in. 4-2-2 express engines No. 3055 *Trafalgar* was renamed *Lambert*. As a connoisseur of all things concerned with the London and North Western Railway, and having in mind the felicitous way Crewe had of naming engines after current events and personalities on the line, I had assumed for many years that here was a parallel case of the Great Western, and that engine No. 3055 had been named after the hero of the Severn Tunnel. Only a short time ago, however, I was reminded that the Great Western had a General Manager by the name of Lambert, and that as the 3051–3060 series of Dean 'singles' already included *Grierson* and *Wilkinson*, not to mention two directors in the persons of *James Mason* and *Walter Robinson*, it is much more likely that engine No. 3055 was named in honour of Henry Lambert, whose tenure of office connected those of Grierson and of J. L. Wilkinson – 1887 to 1896.

Trouble in the Severn Tunnel was by no means over with the sealing off of the Big Spring. The next setback occurred at the Gloucestershire end, in April 1881. Although much of the estuary bed is exposed at low tide there exists the Salmon Pool, immediately off-shore, and beneath this the depth of solid ground to the roof is the least of any point in the tunnel. Here there was a sudden inrush of salt water which was traced to the development of a fissure in the rocks forming the river bed. The actual trouble-spot was discovered by the novel method of getting a chain of men to join hands and wade, shoulder to shoulder, across the Salmon Pool; when one of the men suddenly disappeared beneath the water the fissure was discovered! The man was quickly extricated by his mates on either side, and the bed of the pool was then overlaid with quantities of clay. Curiously enough this particular mischance was repeated, on a smaller scale, as recently as 1929, when train crews reported that jets of water 'as big as a man's fist', were flying horizontally across the tunnel. This also was traced to a fissure in the rocks, though in this modern instance things were made easier for the engineers by the rocks concerned being uncovered at low tide. The actual spot was discovered at high tide, by the existence of a small whirlpool in the water.

Following the sealing up of the fissure at the Salmon Pool progress was steady with the works for more than two years, save for a fortnight in the winter of 1881 when a period of exceptional frost brought most of the work to a standstill through the non-arrival of coal for the pumping engines. During all this time, however, the problem of the Big Spring had not been finally solved. The section of the heading beyond Lambert's door was still sealed off, and full of water, with the sheer weight of water likely to burst its bonds at any time. To describe in any detail the further adventures, if I may call them so, that Hawkshaw and Richardson had with the Big Spring before the tunnel was finally completed would take a whole chapter of this book. October seemed to be the black month in the construction of the Severn Tunnel, and the year 1883 saw yet another tremendous inrush of water from the Big Spring into a special heading driven to try and by-pass Lambert's door, which was impossible to move under the weight of water.

This inrush took place on October 10th, and as if this were not enough, no more than a week later during the night of October 17th a tidal wave swept up the Severn estuary, burst the river banks, put out the fires of the pumping engines, flooded the workmen's cottages and poured in a torrent down the Old Shaft. If the shaft had not marked the very lowest spot of the tunnel all the men below would undoubtedly have been drowned. As it was, much of the tunnel had been enlarged to its full size, and fully lined. Even so the water rose to within 8 ft of the roof, and 83 men had to take refuge on the timber stagings erected for the bricklayers. These men were rescued by lowering a small boat end-on down the shaft, launching it on to the flood-water, and then rowing towards the distant stagings. Even this had its difficulties, for cross-stagings barred the way for the boat and the rescuers had to saw their way through. The situation at the end of 1883 was disheartening in the extreme. It was evident that imprisonment was not the answer to the Big Spring; pumping capacity had to be provided to deal with the continuous extraction of an enormous volume of water.

So there was built up the very large pumping station at Sudbrook, with its enormous Cornish beam engines, which until recently were

undoubtedly the greatest among the lesser-known sights of the Great
Western Railway. There is another pumping station at Sea Wall, on
the Gloucestershire side, and between them these stations have
dealt with water up to the colossal maximum of 36,500,000 gallons
per day. During the constructional work, as more and more pumps
were installed, so the danger from disaster from the Big Spring
receded. In September 1884 the sluices in that critical headwall
were gradually opened, and the imprisoned water allowed to flow
down in a controlled manner; the heading was cleared, and in 1884
the month of October was one of triumph instead of disaster. In his
diary for October 27th, 1884, Sir Daniel Gooch, then 68 years of
age, has this entry:

'I went this morning to the Severn Tunnel. Lord Bessborough met me
there, and we inspected the surface work, and after lunch went below. It
fortunately happened that the headings were just meeting, and by the time
we had finished lunch the men had got a small hole through, making the
tunnel open throughout. I was the first to creep through, and Lord
Bessborough followed me. It was a difficult piece of navigation, but by a
little pulling in front and pushing behind we managed it, and the men
gave us some hearty cheers. I am glad I was the first to go through.'

Two more years were to pass before the first revenue-earning train
went through the tunnel, and regular passenger working began on
December 1st, 1886. It is pleasant to know that Sir Daniel Gooch,
who was associated with the Great Western from its earliest days,
lived to see so great a work in full operation. At the beginning of this
chapter I wrote that the whole project was almost Brunellian in its
conception. It was no less Brunellian in the long succession of disheartening setbacks encountered on the way. But whereas Brunel
failed with the Atmospheric, with the *Great Eastern* steamship, and
ultimately and posthumously with the broad gauge itself, the
engineers of the Severn Tunnel succeeded. One feels that this might
not have been so had it not been for the unshakeable resolve of Sir
Daniel to see it through.

XII

The End of the Broad Gauge

To say that the ultimate extinction of the broad gauge was inevitable might seem nowadays to be dangerously near to a platitude. But in the late 'sixties of last century, despite the collapse of its brief penetration into the Black Country, and despite the chequered career of the Oxford, Worcester and Wolverhampton which turned the flank of the entire broad gauge position north of the main line at Didcot, there were undoubtedly some in high positions on the Great Western Railway who still retained some lingering hopes of hanging on to what remained in South Wales and in the West Country. Apart from this, there were many among the directors who were quite convinced that it was impossible to equal the best broad gauge express schedules with narrow gauge locomotives. But however much the old faith might linger at Paddington or Bristol the attitude of businessmen and traders was far otherwise. Sir Daniel Gooch put the matter fairly and squarely at a General Meeting of the Company on March 2nd, 1866:

'There is no doubt it has become necessary for us to look the matter of the narrow gauge fairly in the face. We have had within the past few days a memorial signed by nearly every firm of any standing in South Wales wishing that the narrow gauge might be carried out in their district. It is also pressing upon us in many other districts, and it will be necessary for us now to consider how this matter should be dealt with. That it will be a costly question there can be no doubt. We cannot look at it without seeing that it involves a large expenditure of money. How best to meet and deal with that expenditure is a question the Directors will have to solve, and that probably before we meet you again.'

In recent years some of the best patronized and most profitable services worked by the Great Western Railway were those between London and South Wales, and it is interesting to see that the first proposals for conversion of the gauge on a large scale concerned the lines between Gloucester and Milford. In the meantime the report of a Royal Commission on Railways, appointed in 1865, had issued its report, and it included this paragraph:

'We are of the opinion that the continued existence of the double gauge is a national evil. We think it worthy of consideration whether it may not be desirable to require the Broad Gauge to be put an end to; and, as the evil has arisen to some extent from the proceedings of Parliament, whether a loan of public money should not be granted for that purpose, on the principle we have suggested for advances to Irish Railway Companies.'

This report was issued in 1867, but no action was taken to implement this pointed suggestion so far as the broad gauge was concerned. Events were moving to force the hand of the Great Western, and from this time onwards it became largely a matter of providing the money necessary to do the job, and of organizing the actual work along the line. Very wisely, conversion operations were commenced on no more than a limited scale. In 1868 it was announced that a start would be made with the complete conversion of the broad gauge line between Hereford and Grange Court. At the same time it was proposed to lay in mixed gauge between Grange Court and Gloucester, and from Gloucester southwards to Standish Junction so as to provide a continuous line of narrow gauge rails from Bristol over the Midland Railway to Standish, and thence via Gloucester and Grange Court to link up with the important narrow gauge line running from Shrewsbury down into South Wales. At that time, of course, the Severn Tunnel had not yet been built, and there was not a through north to west route via Pontypool Road. It is interesting, however, to see the importance attached to the Grange Court–Hereford link in 1868, in view of its use today as a relief route for the north to west expresses on Sundays when the Severn Tunnel is closed for maintenance work.

The line from Grange Court to Hereford provided an interesting and exacting 'curtain-raiser' to gauge conversion on the grand scale. The line was single-tracked for 21½ miles, to Rotherwas Junction, just outside Hereford. South-eastwards to Ross-on-Wye the line was fairly straight, cutting clean across the extremely winding course of the River Wye in a series of viaducts and short tunnels. From Ross, however, the line has to make its way through the eastern hills and woodlands of the Forest of Dean; there is a stiff climb out of Ross to the summit point at Micheldean Road, and the curves are constant and severe all the way from Ross to Grange Court. It is a fascinating and beautiful stretch of railway, and logging this part of the run on a Sunday North-to-West express has many times provided me with a pleasant change from the straightforward speeding of main line travel. It is usually necessary to provide pilot assistance for the hilly section through the Forest of Dean, and it was always an added interest in the days when Hereford used to turn out a 'Bulldog'

4-4-0 to couple on ahead of our train engine. A special stop was made at Mitcheldean Road to detach the pilot.

But in gossiping of my own travelling experiences I have drawn very many years ahead of the gauge conversion, which was actually carried out in August 1869. The line was closed entirely from Sunday, August 15th, during which time the passenger service was provided by a number of London omnibuses hired for the occasion. The public announcements gave warning that the railway service would be suspended for about a fortnight, but so smartly was the work done that narrow gauge trains began running on Friday, August 20th. The work of conversion was made more difficult because of the varieties of permanent way included in this short line. It would seem that it had been used for experimental purposes, and within its 21½ miles were to be found examples of Brunel's longitudinal 'baulk road', conventional cross-sleepered track with standard chairs and bull-head rails, and even some lengths of Barlow rail. It was not just a case of cutting the cross-transoms of the 'baulk-road' and slewing the rails across; the sharply curved sections involved much cutting of the rails, and the labour involved, in the open air, was considerable.

The organization of the work had been carefully thought out beforehand, and the experience of doing it was invaluable when it came to the far larger conversion operations undertaken in 1872 and 1892. On the Grange Court–Hereford line the target aimed at was four miles to be completely converted in a day. On each length the line was divided into quarter-mile sections, and to each of these sections a gang of 20 platelayers was allocated. Each day the work went on from dawn to dusk, and platelayers, foremen, and engineers alike lived on the job throughout. A lengthy 'work train' was assembled at the Hereford end, containing sleeping vans, blacksmiths shops, stores, tools, travelling kitchens, and an office for the engineers. At the start of the operation it stopped each quarter of a mile from Rotherwas Junction, setting down the gangs at the appointed lengths, and then drawing just ahead of the four-mile section to be converted that day. This work-train provided the headquarters for the whole job, and each day it moved four miles nearer to Grange Court. At the end of each day a narrow gauge train from the Hereford end worked its way through the newly completed section, picking up the platelayers from their various quarter-mile lengths, and bringing them to the broad gauge work-train which was their place of rest for the night. And at 4 a.m. next morning the broad gauge work-train started out on its next four-mile journey. One can imagine with what pride and satisfaction this immense caravan of a train was photographed on its arrival at Grange Court on August 20th.

The next conversion, that of the entire South Wales main line, together with the connecting line from Swindon to Gloucester, was a colossal undertaking, and it was programmed for April and May 1872. In all there were 188 miles of double track and 48 miles of single track, which, together with sidings, made a grand total of nearly 500 miles of broad gauge railway to be converted. In this case there could be no question of closing the line while the job was done. What was decided upon was to do the up line and the down line separately, resorting to single-line working during the period of conversion. Two separate operations were provided for, one dealing with the line between Grange Court and New Milford, and the second covering the line between Swindon and Gloucester. The short section between Grange Court and Gloucester had been laid with the mixed gauge at the time that the Hereford line was converted. The South Wales main line was of course not carrying anything like the traffic that is handled today, particularly in freight, but even so during the period of conversion the passenger service had to be much reduced.

Experience on the Grange Court–Hereford line had shown that a tremendous amount of time could be spent in altering point and crossing work by 'knife and fork' methods on the actual site, and throughout the length of the South Wales main line a great deal of work was done prior to that eventful April of 1872 in making up new narrow gauge points and crossings, and having them ready at the various stations and junctions. On the curves the outer rail would be moved inwards, and to avoid the loss of time due to cutting to the new lengths, each curve was carefully surveyed beforehand, and a sufficient number of shorter rails was provided on each site so as to make up the exact length of the new outer rail. Fortunately all the Barlow rails that were at one time installed west of Swansea had been renewed and replaced with cross-sleepered track, though the conversion of some 40 miles of the latter was to prove one of the most laborious tasks of all, because the chairs were all fixed to the sleepers by fang bolts.

The alteration of the old Brunellian 'baulk-road' was really a simpler matter, providing the operation was well planned in advance. On the Grange Court–Hereford line, for example, it had been found that the actual amount to be sawn off each cross-transom varied slightly, because of slight differences in the width of the timbers. It became necessary therefore to measure individually every transom between Grange Court and New Milford, and to mark on each one the exact point at which it was to be cut. Then, the cross-bolts had become weathered, and much time and trouble had been expended in getting the nuts unscrewed. On the South Wales main line every cross-bolt was examined and oiled before the time of changeover to make sure no time was wasted in disconnecting. These details reveal the extent to which the operation was planned beforehand. By comparison with those responsible for locomotives, the civil engineers of a railway do not come prominently into the news once a railway is built, and in this respect it is a pleasure to mention the names of engineers primarily responsible for this gigantic work. W. G. Owen was the Chief Engineer of the G.W.R., and to exercise general supervision on site he appointed J. W. Armstrong, Divisional Engineer, Hereford, who had the invaluable experience of the Grange Court–Hereford conversion; under Armstrong the work was in charge of the local divisional engineers: W. L. Owen from Grange Court to Cardiff; John Lean from Cardiff to Milford.

The practice of having a single work-train moving gradually through the section would obviously not be applied to such a long stretch as that from Grange Court to Milford; instead central depots were set up at intervals along the line which provided temporary headquarters for the gangs, and avoided the loss of time that had been incurred between Hereford and Grange Court in moving men and tools daily by train. Tuesday, April 30th, 1872, was zero hour, and that night the passage of a broad gauge train from Milford was the signal that the up line was closed, and handed over to the engineers for conversion. To provide facilities for traffic working on the down line only, under 'single-line' conditions, passing places were set up at no more than thirteen stations between New Milford and Grange Court. These were, Haverfordwest, Whitland, St. Clears, Carmarthen Junction, Llanelly, Landore, Neath, Bridgend, Llantrissant, Cardiff, Newport, Portskewett and Lydney. Before the actual conversion, work had commenced in getting every broad gauge vehicle and engine not immediately wanted in South Wales away to Swindon either for scrapping or converting. As a former locomotive engineer Gooch had been worried as to whether there would be enough narrow gauge stock available afterwards, and at one point had hesitated about going ahead with such a large amount of conversion at one time. But Joseph Armstrong merely said: 'You alter the gauge, Sir Daniel; I'll have the engines ready.'

The up line was ready for narrow gauge trains on Sunday, May 12th, and by then it was becoming evident that Swindon could not accommodate the vast conglomeration of broad gauge rolling stock that was coming in. The Berks and Hants line was changed over to single-line working between Newbury and Hungerford, and its down line used as a dump, eight miles long, for unwanted broad gauge wagons. Apart from the Great Western's own wagon stock there were no fewer than 1682 broad gauge wagons in South Wales belonging to private owners. While traders had been ready enough to condemn the broad gauge, when it came to the practical aspects of the conversion they were by no means ready to co-operate. The railway company, with the innate courtesy always characteristic of the G.W.R., asked for disposal instructions for these wagons. Some owners were awkward; others ignored the communication, but in any case the wagons one and all had to be worked eventually to the premises of their owners. Then, of course, the private sidings were choc-a-bloc with useless wagons, and still more kept arriving. Again the G.W.R. sought disposal instructions, and in the absence of anything definite they were just pushed off the line out of the way. In one case, a particular owner's field was full of broad gauge wagons spread out fanwise like locomotives round a turntable!

On Saturday, May 11th, 1872, the last broad gauge trains ran in South Wales. What a day it must have been! As soon as each train had completed its advertised journey engines and stock had to be worked eastwards, to Gloucester at least, if not to Swindon; otherwise it would have been trapped, and unable to be moved. The 12.40 p.m. from Gloucester, due at New Milford at 8.50 p.m. was the last train through, and less than half an hour later this train started back, empty, followed shortly by the very last broad gauge movement in South Wales. This was a pilot engine carrying inspectors who distributed to stationmasters and all concerned notices to the effect that all broad gauge stock had been removed, and that the broad gauge down line was forthwith being handed over to the engineers for conversion. The engine used – and no doubt it had been specially chosen for the sad task of closing down broad gauge working in South Wales – was the 6 ft 6 in. 2-4-0 passenger engine *Brunel*. The first narrow gauge train to go through was the 12.50 a.m. down night mail from Gloucester, in the early hours of May 12th, 1872. The down line was finished ten days later, and normal service was then restored.

Immediately this was finished a large force of platelayers was dispatched to the Gloucester–Swindon section, and work commenced on exactly the same general lines. Such was the speed of the work that the up line was ready on Sunday, May 26th, and on the following Wednesday, with the down line completed also, normal service was restored. While the section between Swindon and Gloucester had remained exclusively broad gauge, the narrow gauge locomotives and stock required for South Wales had been worked round from Swindon via Oxford, Worcester and Hereford. This was possible because the mixed gauge had, in the meantime, been laid in between Didcot and Swindon. This latter work was completed, without any interruption of normal traffic, by February 1872, so that by the end of May 1872 through narrow gauge trains could be run between Paddington and New Milford. The estimated cost of the conversion, as laid before the shareholders in 1870, was the sum of £402,000, divided in the proportion of £226,000 for permanent way and other civil engineering work, and £188,000 for rolling stock.

Once South Wales had been dealt with attention was next given to all the branches, and subsidiary lines lying to the south of the London–Bristol main lines: the Berks and Hants, the Wilts, Somerset and Weymouth, and the Avon Valley line through Bradford-on-Avon. To give narrow gauge access to the Weymouth line mixed gauge was laid in on the main line between Swindon and Thingley Junction, also between Bathampton and Bristol. From the viewpoint of permanent way costs this was an even bigger task than that of South Wales, and amounted to the sum of £290,000. Actually the laying in of mixed gauge between Thingley and Bathampton was included in this scheme, and by the middle of August 1875, with the conversion of the short branch from Chippenham to Calne, there remained only two short branches of purely broad gauge in the domains of the Great Western Railway as it existed then. These were the lines from Twyford to Henley-on-Thames, and the line of the independent Faringdon Railway which joined the main line at Uffington. These two were converted in 1876 and 1878 respectively.

With the conversion of the Henley branch, completed in March 1876, the Great Western itself had become to all intents and purposes a narrow gauge line, and the broad gauge was retained between Paddington and Bristol only for the convenience of maintaining through express services to the West of England which ran over the tracks of the purely broad gauge companies beyond Bristol. As already told, however, the lines in the West Country were all absorbed into the Great Western in 1876. Before this, the Bristol and Exeter had decided to lay the mixed gauge over the entire main line, while the West Cornwall Railway had been mixed gauge for many years. Nevertheless, some of the most interesting and picturesque years of the broad gauge lay ahead, for with the amalgamations of 1876 the Great Western express engines began working through to Newton Abbot, and Gooch's beautiful eight-footers became as familiar objects on the Dawlish–Teignmouth sea wall as they had hitherto been at Paddington, Reading and Swindon. It was of course no more than a swan-song, but it is pleasing to recall that it took place in the lifetime of Sir Daniel himself, whose death did not take place till October 1889.

Despite the impending end of the broad gauge a new West of England express was put on in 1890, the 'Cornishman', leaving Paddington at 10.15 a.m. and due into Penzance at 6.57 p.m.; but five years earlier the Board of the Cornwall Railway had suggested the complete abolition of the broad gauge. At the request of the Great Western Board Grierson drew up a comprehensive report covering all aspects of the change, and this was laid before the Board in April 1886. Times were bad, and money scarce, and these circumstances strengthened the natural reluctance of the Great Western Chairman and Directors to part with something that had meant so much to the company, and so it came that Sir Daniel Gooch was spared the task of signing the death warrant. The decision was taken in February 1891, and May 1892 fixed as the date for the final conversion. On the main line west of Exeter there existed just 100 miles of purely broad gauge line. With the various branches the route miles totalled 171 miles. In view of the interest surrounding the final conversion, the actual sections concerned on the main line are listed herewith:

Section	Double line m. c.	Single line m. c.
Exeter—City Basin Junc. *		1 25
City Basin Junc.—Dawlish	10 58	
Dawlish—Parsons Tunnel		1 32
Parsons Tunnel—Rattery	19 37	
Rattery—Hemerdon		11 20
Hemerdon—Tavistock Jc.	4 34	
Millbay Station	10	
Keyham Junc.—Truro		50 78

*The line was double here, but the down line was mixed gauge

In addition to the above there were the important branches from Newton Abbot to Kingswear, and from Truro to Falmouth, making for another 26½ miles of route. From the accompanying table it is interesting to see that the section between the Rattery and Hemerdon signal boxes, on the South Devon Line, was single line at the time of the conversion of the gauge. This section included the original single-tracked bore of the Marley Tunnel just beyond Rattery Box, and the five lofty timber viaducts, namely Glaze, Bittaford, Ivybridge, Blackford and Slade. Then again, except for a very short stretch immediately beyond Plymouth, the main line of the Cornwall Railway was single-tracked throughout. The Kingswear branch of the South Devon Railway was double-tracked only as far as Torquay. The existence of these lengthy stretches of single line entirely precluded use of the methods used in South Wales, which had involved closing one line entirely while the work was being done. In the West of England there would have to be *some* period when some parts of the line were closed, but the interruption of traffic could not possibly be for long in any one case.

Louis Trench, the Chief Engineer, decided to do the whole job *in a single weekend*. After the most careful examination of all that was involved, and of the burdens that would fall particularly upon the Plymouth Divisional Engineer, T. H. Gibbons, it was planned that the broad gauge service would end on the evening of Friday, May 20th, 1892, and that the whole group of lines would be open for the resumption of traffic on the narrow gauge on Monday, May 23rd. Only on the Saturday and Sunday would South Devon and Cornwall be without trains, and during that time the service between Exeter and Plymouth was to be maintained by running over the London and South Western Railway. The Cornish mails were to be conveyed by sea on the Saturday. Quite apart from the engineering work the traffic arrangements had to be planned to the last detail, and a special working book of 55 pages was issued to the staff at the end of April, followed by a further 30-page booklet of local instructions for the men immediately concerned from the Divisional Superintendents at Bristol, Exeter and Plymouth.

The task of evacuating all broad gauge stock from the far west was a far bigger undertaking than the similar operation in South Wales because of the prevalence of so much single line. No goods traffic for Cornwall was sent forward from Exeter after the night of 17th May. Then there moved west a procession of engines and brake vans to bring all the goods rolling stock out of Cornwall and South Devon. On the Wednesday prior to the great changeover the surfacemen's specials began to move westwards, and on the Thursday trains from Chester, Crewe, New Milford, Tondu, Bristol, Weymouth and Paddington arrived at Exeter. A total of 3,400 men were brought in from all parts of the Great Western system to reinforce the local platelayers. The business of moving the men and all their heavy tools and equipment was complicated by the fact of all trains from the far ends of the line being narrow gauge. Only that from Bristol was broad gauge, and this latter was the only one on which the men did not have to change at Exeter. The scenes of ordered animation at St. David's station, with train after train of navvies arriving and changing from narrow to broad gauge vehicles for the continuation of their journeys can be well imagined.

In such a gigantic operation no time could be wasted in moving men about from place to place during the actual work. Accommodation was found for them immediately adjacent to the sections of line on which they were to work for those eventful two days. The grand total of 4,200 men massed in Devon and Cornwall for the job were organized in gangs of 20, and each gang had a mile of plain line to convert. Sleeping arrangements were organized to the last detail, in goods sheds, station buildings, and where nothing else existed, in tents erected at intervals along the line. The men brought their own food but the company provided cooking appliances everywhere, with liberal supplies of oatmeal. The work of converting goods yards and sidings did not wait for the main line 'zero hour'. At Brent, for example, the goods yard was completely changed over to narrow gauge by the early evening of Friday, May 20th. On the sections of line equipped with cross-sleepered track the engineers had profited by the difficulties experienced in South Wales by laying chairs in advance at the correct narrow gauge position; then all that had to be done was to knock out the keys, lift the rails into the new position, and key-up once more.

In the meantime those with cherished memories of the broad gauge gathered at the principal stations to see the last trains go through. In our own times many enthusiasts have travelled far and wide to photograph or ride in the last trains over branch lines about to be closed, or on the last occasion that famous services were worked by steam. Much the same sentiments were felt and expressed at the end of the broad gauge. The Rev. A. H. Malan whose beautiful photographs adorn so many of these pages had by that time moved from Teignmouth to Shropshire, but he travelled to Weston-super-Mare, and revisited his old photographic haunts at Worle and Uphill Junctions, to photograph the very last broad gauge expresses to and from the west. He has told of the procession of surfacemen's specials travelling slowly on the down line, and of his own apprehension lest empty bottles might be hurled at his head! From the photographic viewpoint the last days were disappointing; although fine, he records that it was cold and very windy. One of the curiosities of the photographic records of the broad gauge is the picture, so many times titled as the last broad gauge down train passing through Sonning Cutting, which actually shows an *up* train!

On Friday, May 20th, the last through broad gauge train from Paddington to Penzance was the 10.15 a.m. 'Cornishman', hauled from Paddington to Bristol by the 4-2-2 engine *Great Western*. A crowd assembled to see her off, and the engine was drawn up specially far ahead of the usual starting point to be photographed from several angles. In front of her were grouped a number of officials including the veteran George Armstrong, and his nephew John Armstrong who was then Divisional Locomotive, Carriage and Wagon Superintendent in London. That day the 'Flying Dutchman' ran no farther than Plymouth, and the very last broad gauge train to leave Paddington was the 5 p.m. This train was hauled by *Bulkeley* as far as Bristol, while the *Iron Duke* had the task of hauling this last broad gauge down express forward from Bristol to Newton Abbot. It was probably a great disappointment to the Rev. A. H. Malan that the 'Dutchman', on its last down trip on the broad gauge, was hauled not by a Gooch 4-2-2 but by a Dean 7 ft 8 in. 2-2-2 'convertible', – an engine that eventually became a member of that most beautiful of Great Western engine classes, the '30XX' 4-2-2s.

In the meantime broad gauge engines, carriages and wagons scheduled for scrapping had been arriving at Swindon. Some fields between the works and the M.S.W.J. line had been bought and 15 miles of sidings laid to accommodate all this condemned rolling stock. By midday on Saturday, May 21st these sidings were completely filled with an extraordinary collection of locomotives and carriages. The vast assembly was photographed officially from many angles, and must have formed a veritable treasure trove for any fascinated by broad gauge lore, for it contained many vintage specimens of ancient and obscure carriages. The site of these sidings, when eventually cleared, was partly occupied by the great new erecting shop, 'A' shop as it is known, brought into service in 1902. Beyond 'A' shop, the remainder of the ground to the M.S.W.J. line – 'the dump' – has ever since been the graveyard of super-annuated Great Western locomotives.

Down in the West, the work of conversion went like clockwork. The weather, though cool and windy, remained fine, and by Saturday some parts of the line were already finished, and narrow gauge engines were on the line, testing the track. This had been made possible by sending a number of engines on broad gauge crocodile trucks to Newton Abbot beforehand, so that they could make their way along the line as soon as parts were finished. It is indeed amazing to recall that on Saturday evening the work was sufficiently complete for a narrow gauge test train to work through from Exeter to Plymouth. It is not surprising, however, that much of the conversion work still remained to be done on the Sunday, but the entire regular service of passenger trains was recommenced on Monday, May 23rd. This opening day was the occasion of a gesture as bold as it might have seemed risky. Because of the great speed at which the conversion work had been done the most profuse instructions were issued to enginemen to run with the utmost caution over the 'new' portions of the line; but the men on the first narrow gauge up 'Cornishman' were determined to show what could be done. That train kept exact time from Truro to Plymouth, and ran so well afterwards as to reach Paddington 4 min. early.

This gesture was not repeated for a long time afterwards. Consistent late running continued throughout the month of June, and in July the schedules were eased out to the extent of 20 to 30 min. extra time between Exeter and Penzance. This aftermath of the great conversion, far from detracting from the magnitude of the job done, merely serves to emphasize the achievement. The relaying of 177 miles of track in two days was a feat without parallel, either before or since. All the additional surfacemen were returned to their home stations on Tuesday, May 24th, and the local men then had the task of going systematically through the converted lengths and working all of it up to first class standards. It is not surprising that it took many months to finish the job. The achievement of 1892 may be compared statistically with the two previous conversions:

Year	Track miles converted	Time taken. Days
1872	424	28
1874	247	17
1892	177	2

Such was the end of the broad gauge. The Gooch 4-2-2 engine *Lord of the Isles* and the historic *North Star* were saved from the general slaughter, and preserved at Swindon Works until 1906. In that year, however, Churchward decreed that they should be scrapped because they were occupying valuable space in the works. So vanished the last appreciable relics of a great era on the G.W.R.

XIII

Coaching Stock

IT was the Duke of Wellington, the 'Iron Duke' of the Peninsular War, of Quatre Bras and of Waterloo after whom so many British locomotives have been named, who at first deplored the construction of railways because their existence would facilitate the movement of the lowest classes, and particularly of trouble-making radicals, from one part of the country to another. The early railways, by the primitive and exposed nature of the accommodation provided, certainly seemed to be doing all they could to *discourage* third class travel, and that discouragement was nowhere more pronounced than on the broad gauge routes of the Great Western. In the early days third class passengers were just not wanted. The wealthy merchants and shipowners of Bristol saw no need for artisans, labourers and vagrants to travel about at all, and Charles Saunders in his timetable arrangements was careful to see that the running of trains conveying third class passengers did not take place at times likely to interfere with or cross the paths of the crack expresses. In fact, every effort was made to keep them out of sight at such times.

This attitude had its effect upon the Great Western carriage design from the outset. First class passengers were conveyed in the greatest comfort that the railway coach builder of the day could contrive; second class was spartan, yet tolerable, while when Gladstone's Act of 1844 compelled the railway companies to provide sheltered accommodation, the Great Western, like many another railway, displayed pure 'cussedness' in its reaction. One can almost imagine the attitude: 'Right; if we must provide a roof and sides we'll do so. There's nothing in the Act to say we must provide *windows*'! The Great Western built some travelling boxes containing ten plank seats fixed transversely, and each intended to seat six persons. There were some small sliding shutters in the sides that could be opened, and a number of slats, Venetian blind fashion, by way of ventilation; but there was no lighting, and incredible to relate only one door on each side of the carriage. Just imagine a crowd of passengers entering by the one door, and then having to scramble over the planks, among all the other passengers *in the dark* to try and find seats!

Left: Iron plated third class carriage of 1846 for Parliamentary trains.

Below left and below: First class carriage, 1838.

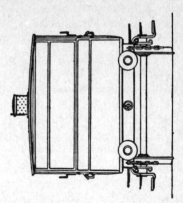

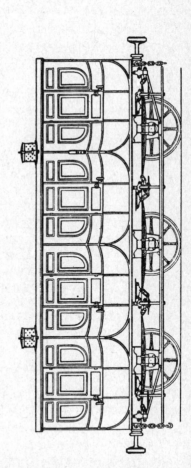

The drawing on the previous page shows an improvement on the above arrangements. In this grim, iron-plated carriage, there was at least a door for each compartment, and four little windows in each door. But a further curiosity was to seat a brakesman among the passengers in the middle of the carriage. This fellow did at least have a primitive lamp above his head so that he could see something of what he was doing, but he was required to hear rather than see, and apply the hand brake when the driver gave the appropriate code upon the engine whistle. The Great Western, as in so many other things, stood apart from the practice of other British railways in building six-wheeled carriages from the very outset. This was done at Brunel's recommendation, and was a measure of the higher standards of permanent way he expected to maintain with his famous baulk-road. Carriages for first, second, and third-class passengers were alike in this respect, and also in the unusually large diameter of the wheels.

A further drawing shows one of the original first class carriages, used from the opening of the line in 1838. No pains were spared to make these vehicles as comfortable as possible. Each compartment seated eight passengers, and the seats were amply upholstered and trimmed in leather. The windows were fixed, but louvre-type ventilators were placed over each window. At first they had no lighting, but oil-lamps were introduced after a few years of service. An interesting feature included in some of the compartments was an intermediate partition, which in effect divided them into four-seat compartments. The door connecting the two sides had a window in it, but absolute privacy could be secured by the parties on either side of the door by pulling down a spring roller blind. The British love of privacy, or isolation when travelling, could not be exemplified better than by these compartments, which are said to have been very popular with small family parties in shutting them off from any contact with their fellow travellers.

Apart from the experimental eight-wheelers put on to the Paddington–Birmingham service during the brief period in which it was broad gauge, and known as the 'Long Charleys', six-wheelers remained standard on the broad gauge sections of the G.W.R. until the Dean narrow-gauge eight-wheelers of 1874, also tried first on the Paddington–Birmingham–Birkenhead service. These fine vehicles were also adapted to run on the broad gauge. On the narrow-gauge at an earlier period the Great Western inherited a miscellaneous collection of four-wheelers from some of the constituent companies, but an exception to the general run of six-wheelers on the broad

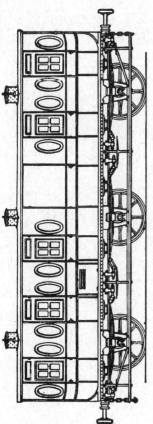

Left: Second class carriage, Bristol and Exeter Railway.

Below: Broad gauge 40 ft. composite coach; wide body (two 'first'; three 'second'), 1874 design.

gauge were the so-called 'posting carriages' designed by Brunel. One of the points he constantly stressed in favour of the broad gauge was that the extreme width enabled comfortable coach bodies to be constructed *between* the wheels, thus enabling the wheels themselves to be larger than would otherwise be possible, and give smoother riding in consequence. The posting carriages, however, seem to have been the only passenger vehicles on this principle, and although they were intended to be exclusive to the last degree they did not prove very popular.

Contemporary writers have told of the elegance with which these vehicles were fitted up, but in all probability it was the 'open-saloon' type of accommodation that was disliked. The general design was most curious. The bodies were wide in their upper portions, though waisted below to clear the large wheels. There were very large windows in the bodies themselves, extending to the full height and width of the wide portion above the waist, and these posting carriages are of historic interest in being the first British railway carriages to have clerestory roofs. There were windows throughout the length of the clerestory and the roof was so low that a standing passenger could look out of these windows! Inside two large U-shaped sofas were provided, giving seating for 18 first class passengers, but despite this most unusual provision of glazing the arrangements for ventilation were bad. There were no louvres as in the ordinary 'firsts', no venetian slats, and nothing more than one small drop-light in each of the two doors.

The clerestory roof, which was to become so characteristic a feature of Great Western coaching stock both broad and narrow gauge, was introduced by William Dean in the late seventies of last century, following quickly after Clayton's application of it on the Midland. Some of the first to be seen in the West Country were full-width broad gauge sleepers, put on to the night trains between Paddington and Penzance in 1877. These were six-wheelers, 29 ft long and 10 ft 6 in. wide. As sleeping cars they were a failure, largely because the folding beds were placed close together, and first class passengers objected, as Hamilton Ellis has put it: 'to sleeping in close-packed rows like recumbent cod on a fishmongers slab'. But the general form of the body was to set the fashion for several years, and it was to be seen in various forms of saloon, and in that popular vehicle of the period, a tri-composite with luggage compartment included. It is also natural to find, among special G.W.R. vehicles, a hounds van – appropriate enough to a railway that gave special attention to the needs of the more aristocratic of its patrons.

The first Great Western eight-wheelers, other than the 'Long
Charleys' of 1852, were not bogie carriages. They were 43 ft long and
had six first class compartments, and were carried on two groups of
four wheels which had a limited amount of side play in their bearings.
This arrangement did not last long; instead the Great Western
adopted the so-called 'Dean bogie', which was not really a bogie at

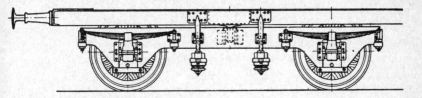

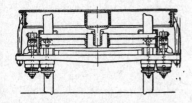

The Dean carriage bogie.

all in the ordinary accepted sense. The Dean bogie, no less than
Webb's radial axles on the L.N.W.R., provides a typical example of
the individualism of the old British railway companies before the
grouping of 1923, manifested in a resolute refusal to adopt a good
practice successfully introduced by another company. In this case it
was the carriage bogie introduced on the American Pullman cars on
the Midland, and used by T. G. Clayton in his own bogie stock built
at Derby. Dean's centreless bogie was no less successful, though one
feels its use would be confined to a railway having none but the
finest of alignment and track maintenance.

The principle of this 'bogie' can be followed by reference to the
accompanying drawing. The bogie frame carries the axle-boxes
rigidly mounted to it. The axle-boxes are contained within horn-
plates extending down from the solebars of the carriage, but they have
a liberal amount of side play. The amount of side play is controlled
by the peculiar method of suspension from the main frames. Hanger
brackets are suspended from the solebar, and the connection
between these and the laminated bogie springs in all four cases by a
link on a hemispherical bearing block. Any side movement of the
bogie would cause the vertical links to tilt, and the resistance to
tilting would exercise control upon the amount of side movement the

bogie would take up. This arrangement was used for many years on
the Great Western, and an adaptation of it provided a very neat
solution to the problem of fitting the new 7 ft 8 in. 2-2-2 express
engines of the '30XX' class with bogies, after the derailment of the
Wigmore Castle in Box Tunnel. The full story of this particular episode
is told in the succeeding chapter.

While some of Dean's new eight-wheeled coaches were built to the
full width permissible on the broad gauge, the time of complete
conversion was by that period always looming in the minds of Great
Western engineers, and many eight-wheeled clerestory carriages
were built new as convertibles with narrow gauge bodies, but
mounted on broad gauge bogies, and having wide footboards
outside. The full-width broad gauge coaches were 10 ft 6 in. wide
overall, and seated first class passengers four aside in great comfort.
Even though these carriages were made full width, they also were
designed so as to be readily convertible to narrow gauge. As it
eventually worked out, the end bulkheads and internal partitions
were cropped, and the actual job of conversion carried out in a
relatively short time. As for those with narrow bodies, the arrangements for conversion were planned with such precision as to permit
of bogie coaches being done six at a time, and all within the astonishing time of half an hour. On arriving in the specially equipped
changing shed the bodies were raised by hydraulic jacks, the broad
gauge bogies run clear, and the narrow gauge ones brought in
underneath.

At the time of the conversion of the gauge the Great Western
clerestory carriages had reached the zenith of their decoration. It
was not merely a case of 'chocolate and cream'; the lining was
elaborate and colourful, and as there are many enthusiasts today
who strive to recapture the beauty of the old railways in perfect scale
models I am including, by courtesy of Mr R. A. Smeddle, the Chief
Mechanical and Electrical Engineer, of Western Region, the
accompanying drawing showing not only the colours but also the
exact dimensions of the various bands of lining and shading. This
lovely finish was continued until the early nineteen-hundreds, when
the basic colour was changed from chocolate and cream to lake. The
luggage vans which ran in both broad and narrow gauge expresses
were all flat roofed. As a schoolboy I had a train of Great Western
clerestory carriages in Gauge 1, lithographed tin plate, in chocolate
and cream with full lining, and this train included a full van with
clerestory roof. So far as I can trace no such vehicles ever existed on
the line, though there were some clerestory-roofed T.P.O. vans, used

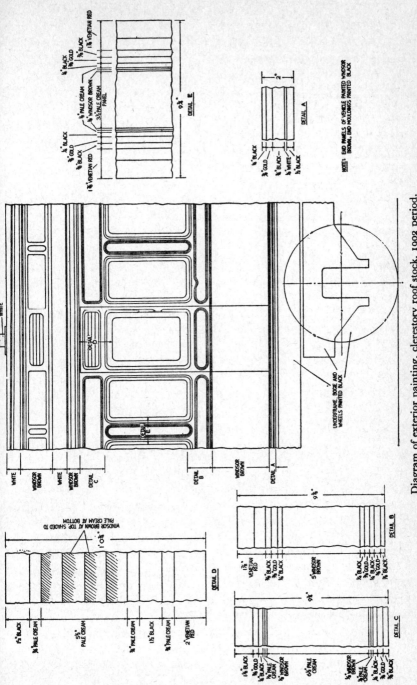

Diagram of exterior painting, clerestory roof stock, 1902 period.

on the Penzance postal train, and on the Ocean Mails from Plymouth and Fishguard.

Although the Great Western traffic requiring sleeping cars was very small compared with that of the East Coast and West Coast routes to Scotland, in the 'eighties of last century, Swindon design so far as sleeping cars were concerned was far in advance of that of the northern companies. While Dean's first essay in this direction was not a success, his new 'sleepers' of 1881 proved the true fore-runners of the modern sleeping car. The northern companies persisted at this stage in arranging their berths longitudinally, but Dean retained the transverse berths of his earlier 'fishmonger's slab', while dividing the car into sections containing two berths at the most in one compartment. The traditional luxury of accommodation for first class passengers on the broad gauge led Swindon inevitably to the fact that if acceptable night travel was to be provided, it was no use trying to pack the maximum of sleeping passengers into the minimum of space. The dead weight per passenger must go up. Dean's first full transverse sleeper of 1881 was a convertible: narrow gauge body, on a broad gauge frame, with broad gauge bogies. The later vehicles which it was possible to convert at such speed had narrow frames, wide footboards, and wheels outside the frames when running on the broad gauge.

I have written that Dean's 'sleeper' of 1881 was a 'full transverse' vehicle. This is not strictly true, for while there were eight beds arranged transversely four more were tucked in longitudinally at the ends. In 1890 some new sleeping cars were introduced into the Paddington–Penzance night service, which were 50 ft long and had seven double berths, all entered from a side corridor running from end to end of the car, or from individual doors to each two-berth compartment on the non-corridor side. The vehicle was corridor only in that the passage provided access to the lavatories at each end; there were no gangway connections to other parts of the train. The Great Western never introduced the hazards of upper and lower berths in their 'sleepers'. It would be interesting to know how many passengers were actually tipped out of bed from some of the long-itudinal upper berths on the night Anglo-Scottish expresses! In the 50 ft Great Western 'sleepers' of 1890 the sides were bellied out between the doors to give additional width, and for that reason the cars were always known at Swindon as the bay-window type.

Having reached the year 1890, it is time to say something of the development of continuous brakes on the G.W.R. The increased traffic, and gradually increasing speeds of the seventies was making

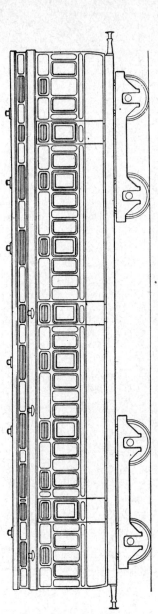

Above: Transverse berth sleeping car of 1881. Narrow body, and shown with narrow gauge bogies.

Below: Dean's corridor composite coach of 1900 design. Three first and four second class compartments.

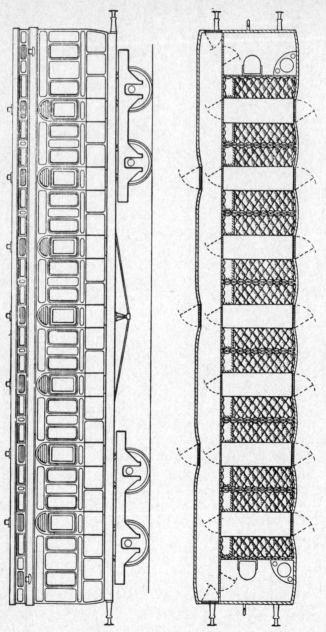

Dean's broad gauge convertible corridor sleeper, of 1890.

senior railwaymen much more 'brake conscious', while the introduction of the Westinghouse automatic air brake into this country brought a realization of how inadequate most of the existing arrangements on British railways actually were. At once the automatic air brake had its champions in Great Britain, but a far greater number of engineers and railway administration opposed it partly on grounds of expense, but no less on the grounds of its American origin. For a time English inventors were trying to devise other forms of power brakes, and to try and prevent the situation becoming quite chaotic in the diversity of brakes proposed, and on trial, the Board of Trade suggested a series of trials of the different forms of brake in comparable running conditions. The result of this was the famous, though inconclusive series of trials near Newark on the Nottingham–Lincoln line of the Midland Railway. But so far as the present story is concerned the trials were no more than incidental, because the Great Western stood completely aloof, and sent no train for testing.

The trials were generally favourable to the Westinghouse, though as a brake the simple non-automatic vacuum showed up well, and had the advantage of less apparent complication and cheaper equipment. The non-automatic brake had, however, the grave defect that in the event of part of the train breaking away, or becoming in any way disconnected from the engine, that part was completely bereft of any power brake. At first the Midland seemed inclined towards the Westinghouse brake, and it is probably true to say that if that great company had made it their standard the majority of railways would eventually have followed. Instead, a number of points of serious dispute arose between the Midland Railway and the Westinghouse Brake Company, and instead of adopting the air brake Derby set to work to produce a satisfactory alternative to it. For a time many of the leading railways were using a non-automatic type of vacuum, but from a time very soon after the Newark trials William Dean felt that the Great Western should have an automatic brake. Trials were made of the Sanders apparatus, and then in 1880 he decided to initiate a development of his own. The project was given to Joseph Armstrong's fourth son, also named Joseph, but always known on the G.W.R. as 'Young Joe' to distinguish him from his illustrious father. To collaborate with Joe Armstrong from the carriage side Dean appointed a young engineer who had come to Swindon from Newton Abbot after the absorption of the South Devon Railway, in 1876, and was then an assistant to the Carriage Works Manager. His name was George Jackson Churchward.

Joe Armstrong was one of the most brilliant inventors in the locomotive engineering profession. Many years later Churchward was talking in a reminiscent mood to R. J. Armstrong, and said: 'If your Uncle Joe had lived, I should not be occupying this house today as Locomotive Superintendent; he was a far cleverer man than I.' Joe Armstrong was killed on the line at Wolverhampton, shortly after midnight on New Year's Day 1888, at the early age of 31; but before that, with the aid of Churchward, he had made a major contribution to Great Western engineering practice in his development of the automatic vacuum brake. Armstrong's brake arrangement included two novelties: the elimination of the small ejector previously used for maintaining vacuum while running, and the designing of an extremely neat combined large ejector and brake application valve for mounting on the backplate of the locomotive firebox. The latter became a standard fitment and formed part of the equipment of Swindon built locomotives, until the last engines of Great Western design had been completed.

The elimination of the small ejector was made possible by the introduction of the vacuum cross-head pump. This not only achieved an economy in steam consumption, but it made possible the maintenance of a higher degree of vacuum than is ordinarily practicable with the usual types of ejector. One of the criticisms always levelled at the vacuum brake, even in its most modern form, is of the very low pressure-difference that it can provide. To compensate for this the cylinders have to be very large. On other railways trains were run with 20 in. of vacuum, whereas with Joe Armstrong's cross-head pump 25 or even 26 in. could be maintained with a consequently much more powerful brake. On the Great Western, thanks to the foresight of Dean, and to the fruitful collaboration between Joe Armstrong and Churchward, the automatic vacuum brake reached its most effective and puissant form, while in Churchward's time its efficiency was still further enhanced by the development, by C. K. Dumas, of the direct admission valve. That, however, is a story for the later volume, though it further serves to show the high priority given to brake equipment at Swindon.

The 'brake question', which was to prove so trying and embarrassing a time for many a great British railway, was largely settled on the Great Western some years before the final abolition of the broad gauge, and returning more particularly to the story of carriage design, it is to record that Dean scored another 'first' with the construction of the first-ever all-corridor train to be seen in Great Britain. This was completed at Swindon late in 1891, and went into regular service between Paddington and Birkenhead in 1892. The complete train consisted of five vehicles, of which one was a 40 ft flat-roofed van, not connected to the rest of the train. The four corridor carriages were all of the 50 ft bay-window type – one each for first, second and third class passengers, and a brake third in rear. Excepting the latter vehicle each carriage included both compartment and 'open' sections, and a most inconvenient feature from the operating point of view was that the gangway connections were at the side, exactly in line with the corridor. This did not matter so long as the set was kept together, but when the corridor stock began to come into general use, the vehicles were apt to become turned round in traversing some of the more complicated sections of the system and a centre gangway became essential. Although the passenger accommodation was gangwayed throughout the connecting doors were kept locked, so that second and third class passengers could not walk through to the first class carriage. Only the guard had access throughout.

Following this pioneer effort the use of corridor stock spread rapidly on the Great Western. The bay-window design was abandoned, and in the ten years from 1893 to 1903 many variations of the familiar clerestory vehicles appeared from Swindon works. (See diagrams on pages 161 and 166). Smokers were not permitted in the ordinary compartments. Instead, open sections with centre corridor were provided for first, second and third class passengers. The dining cars were as long as 55 ft 8 in., and were first class only, though in these no opportunity was taken of providing larger windows. They had the same sized windows as in ordinary compartment stock, with three small windows to a table and its opposing chairs. The arrangement of the windows was, however, no more than an incidental and mainly external detail. In ordinary stock and diners alike the accommodation was very comfortable, and many vehicles were electrically lighted. The first corridor train of 1891 also had quite an advanced form of passenger communication whereby a tug on the cord could produce a partial application of the vacuum brake.

So, by the turn of the century, the principal expresses of the Great Western had assumed a very handsome and uniform appearance, through the widespread use of the new clerestory roofed stock, and this chapter may well be concluded by a reference to the narrow-gauge 'pride of the line', the 10.35 a.m. 'Cornishman', and predecessor of the Cornish Riviera Express of our own times. The 'Cornishman' was originally a broad gauge train, put on in 1890, and leaving Paddington at 10.15 a.m. When it became possible to omit

the refreshment stop at Swindon the train was accelerated, leaving
Paddington at 10.35 a.m. but maintaining the same arrival times at
Bristol and points west. The popularity of this service increased to
such an extent that in 1896 it was frequently necessary to run a
relief, and the bold step was taken of running this advance section
non-stop to Exeter, 194 miles in 223 minutes. With a load of nine of
the new bogie corridor coaches, including a dining car, this
represented quite a task for one of the Dean 7 ft 8 in. 'single' express
locomotives. The regular 10.35 a.m. had an additional stop at
Bristol.

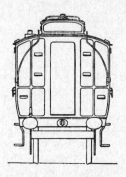

The End

Dean's corridor composite
coach of 1900 design (see
page 161).

XIV

Dean Locomotives and their Work

AFTER the conversion of the gauge there was an interesting and picturesque interlude before the modern Great Western of the twentieth century began to emerge. This interlude was no more than brief, yet it was characteristic of the old G.W.R., and in it the stately, leisured splendour of the broad gauge moved into a phase of even greater outward elegance. It was a phase in which the glittering turnout of express locomotives was accentuated many times by the crowning feature of polished brass domes, expanding to huge proportions in the 7 ft 8 in. singles, and in the ever-memorable 'Dean Goods'. In the nineties even the most enthusiastic backer of the Great Western could hardly have contended that it was a fast line. Until 1895 the bugbear of the enforced refreshment stop at Swindon remained, and the best express running was probably that of the Birmingham trains, which of course then travelled via Oxford.

So far as the principal express services were concerned the Great Western, like the Great Northern of those days was a 'single' engine line. 2-4-0s were used on the West to North route via the Severn Tunnel, west of Newton Abbot, and on subsidiary lines like that to Weymouth, but between Paddington and Wolverhampton – via Banbury or Worcester – Paddington and Newton Abbot, Paddington and Cardiff the 'singles' reigned supreme. In addition to the Dean 7 ft 8 in. 4-2-2s of which there were eventually 80, the various 2-2-2s of the 'Sir Alexander' and '157' classes took a very active part. Strictly speaking the 'Sir Alexanders' should not come within the scope of this chapter heading, as the original design was prepared under Joseph Armstrong; but they were so essentially of the same locomotive family, and were continuing to do such good work well into the present century that it is both convenient and appropriate to include them. Then, although I have no actual records of their running, there were the two short-lived 7 ft 8 in. 2-2-2s, Nos. 9 and 10, which were rebuilt as 7 ft engines in 1890.

Engine No. 9 used certain parts from an unsuccessful 4-2-4 tank engine, and was peculiar in having the eccentrics for driving the Stephenson link motion *outside*. No. 10 was a new engine built in

1886, and is important as the prototype of the entire range of Dean's later locomotive designs. The novel feature of engine No. 10 so far as Swindon was concerned lay in the positioning of the slide valves underneath the cylinders. The arrangement originated on the Brighton, with Stroudley, and has the advantage that the valves drop off their faces when steam is shut off, and by the elimination of this item of sliding friction enables the engine to coast freely. On the other hand the exhaust passages are lengthened considerably as compared with those of an engine having valves on top of, or between the cylinders. Dean did not adopt this arrangement direct from Stroudley, as it were, but more probably through the influence of James Holden, who had been principal assistant at Swindon. When Holden went to the Great Eastern in 1885 to succeed T. W. Worsdell, he adopted the Stroudley valve arrangement on his excellent 'T19' class 2-4-0s, the first of which came out in the same year as Dean's No. 10 on the G.W.R. The difference was that Holden went straight ahead with a large class, whereas at Swindon the application was experimental until the '30XX' class was turned out, beginning in 1891.

Thirty of these latter engines were built as 2-2-2s, and of these eight were originally convertibles for use on the broad gauge. The very beautiful final version of this class, with the 4-2-2 wheel arrangement, came about through the derailment of No. 3021 *Wigmore Castle* in most alarming circumstances. This engine sustained a broken leading axle while travelling at full speed – not only so, but the mishap occurred in the middle of the Box Tunnel! Because of this experience it was decided to substitute a bogie for the leading axle, which, it was felt, was carrying too much weight. To fit a bogie, however, was easier said than done, for a conventional type with a centre pin supported on a stretcher between the frames would have blocked access to the steam chest covers and the valves beneath the cylinders. The problem was solved by the adaptation of the Dean centreless bogie used on the Great Western carriage stock of the period. This arrangement provided a thoroughly reliable method of transferring the weight of the engine to the bogie, and at the same time one that permitted the easy removal of the bogie when access to the steam chests and valves was required.

The year 1894 saw the culmination of what may be termed the 'Dean style' in G.W.R. locomotives. In that year four 2-4-0s of varied origin were rebuilt as 4-4-0 versions of the '30XX' class, and they ranked with the latter as the most graceful of all Swindon passenger engines. These four engines, Nos. 7, 8, 14, and 16, were named after four great personalities of the past, namely, *Armstrong, Gooch, Charles Saunders* and *Brunel*. They had short smokeboxes like the 7 ft 8 in. singles, and boilers of the same type; but the cylinders were no less than 20 in. diameter by 26 in. stroke, and the boiler could not supply such cylinders satisfactorily. Thus despite their beautiful appearance these four locomotives were not very effective machines in traffic while they remained in their original form. In Churchward's time they were rebuilt to have the standard 6 ft 8½ in. coupled wheels (instead of 7 ft), fitted with domeless tapered boilers, superheaters, and 18 in. by 26 in. cylinders. As such they became members of the 'Flower' class, but were always distinguishable, apart from their names, by their curved outside framing.

Although it is far removed from the period immediately under review I may tell here of a personal experience connected with one of these engines. On a sweltering day in July 1925, armed with a lineside photographic permit, I was at Rattery, on the South Devon line. The signalman there was a friendly soul, and in between trains I was glad of the shade and cool of the signal box. Well, I had gone out into the sun, walked a little distance down the line to position myself for the next down express when the up line signals were pulled off. At that time, alas, my youthful enthusiasm was centred mainly upon the largest express locomotives. The 'Castles' were comparatively rare birds, and on that particular day I had 'copped' only one so far; even the up Limited, to my disappointment, being hauled by a 'Star'. So I was not interested in the approach of an up stopping train – until I saw the most curiously tall 4-4-0 engine. It was too late then to swing the camera round, for stopping train or not, *Brunel* – for such it turned out to be – was going like the proverbial bomb. The odd sequel to this story came after I had snapped the down express and walked back to the box. The signalman immediately quizzed me about 'that funny old engine with the curious name, *Burnell*' (sic)! A few guarded remarks from me revealed that here was an even greater curiosity, a Great Western man, a West countryman at that, to whom the name of the great Isambard K. meant nothing!

From 1895 onwards there was growing evidence of a change in the air at Swindon. Those who delighted in the almost perfect symmetry of line in the Dean 'singles' and in the four 'Armstrong' class 4-4-0s were perplexed at the curious effect produced by the rather aggressive extended smoke-boxes on the 'Duke of Cornwall' class of 5 ft 8 in. 4-4-0s, while a contemporary comment upon the 'Badminton' class 4-4-0s of 1897 ran thus: 'These engines are different in many respects from their predecessors. Once more we see a reversion to the double framing, but for the first time the Severn Tunnel route is treated to the sight of a bogie engine. A very large Belpaire firebox hardly improves the appearance of the engine, but gives ample grate area. The overhung springs and extended smokebox are far from pleasing features in the design, and here they are particularly aggressive. It is a curious anomaly that a line which possesses in its "singles" some of the handsomest engines in the world should produce coupled engines which can hardly be termed other than hideous'. In referring to the use of bogie engines on the Severn Tunnel route the writer was meaning the West to North service between Bristol and Shrewsbury. Even before the construction of the 'Badmintons' two Dean 7 ft 8 in. 4-2-2s were stationed at Ebbw Junction shed, Newport, for working the up Newport–Paddington non-stop, which at that time ran via Stapleton Road, North Somerset Junction and the old main line through Bath.

Although belonging to the nineteenth century and having all the embellishments if not all the grace of a 'Dean', the 'Badmintons' embodied the first fruits of Churchward's historic development in boiler design. The extended smokebox contained a large spark-arresting device, something after the style of contemporary American practice, while the severely functional shape of the firebox was merely the first stepping stone to the 'Camels', 'Atbaras', 'Cities', and ultimately to the 'Saints' and 'Stars'. The 'Badmintons' were excellent engines, and details are quoted later in this chapter of a very fast run with one of them over the West to North route. Their names were a miscellaneous lot, all new to the G.W.R., whereas the 7 ft 8 in. singles of the '30XX' class perpetuated most of the names previously borne by the Gooch's broad gauge eight-footers. The names not perpetuated were those of battles in the Crimean War, and the mis-spelt *Estafette*. All the others re-appeared: *Racer*, *Rover*, *Swallow*, *Hirondelle*, *Warlock*, *Tartar* and the rest, came to dignify the new narrow gauge engines.

Turning down to some actual performances on the road, the work of the 7 ft 2-2-2 singles may first be studied from the logs on Paddington–Oxford expresses detailed in Tables I, II, and III. With one exception all the runs included in this chapter are taken from the records of the late R. E. Charlewood, through the kindness of Mr G. J. Aston, the present owner of the original notebooks. The first of these, relating to the 8 p.m. down express when it included a 4 min. stop at Reading within an overall time of 82 min., includes a run with the unique 2-2-2 engine No. 160. This was a member of the

Dean '157' class of 1878–9, but it had been rebuilt at Wolverhampton
with a Belpaire firebox boiler and boiler mountings like the 7 ft 8 in.
singles. Seen broadside-on this engine, except for its sandwich
frames, looked like a slightly shortened version of the '30XX' class
in its 2-2-2 days. She was handsome, but in a compact, stocky kind
of way. Her work on the 8 p.m. down, as shown in Table I, was not
exactly heroic. The check at Southall cost about 2½ min. in running,
after which speed never reached as much as 60 m.p.h. to Reading,
and the train was a minute late in arriving. The station stop was
extended from 4 to 6 min., after which rather better work was done,
regaining 1½ min. despite the relaying slack between Culham and
Radley. The arrival in Oxford was roughly a minute late.

TABLE I

G.W.R. 8 P.M. PADDINGTON–OXFORD

Run No.		Sch.	1. 160 * 155 155		2. 1127† 170 150	
Engine 2-2-2 No.						
Load to Reading, tons full						
„ „ Oxford „ „						
Distance Miles		Sch. min.	Actual m. s.	Av. Speed m.p.h.	Actual m. s.	Av. Speed m.p.h.
0·0	PADDINGTON	0	0 00		0 00	
1·3	Westbourne Park		3 07	—	—	
5·7	Ealing Broadway		8 48	46·5	9 39	—
			sigs		—	
9·1	Southall	13	13 00	48·6	13 27	53·7
13·2	West Drayton		20 03	34·9	17 59	54·5
16·2	Langley		23 32	51·6	21 08	57·2
18·5	SLOUGH	23	25 49	58·8	23 17	62·8
24·2	Maidenhead	30	31 56	56·0	29 13	57·7
31·0	Twyford	38	39 00	57·8	36 02	59·8
36·0	READING	44	45 03	—	41 39	—
2·7	Tilehurst	5	5 16	—	5 02	
5·5	Pangbourne		8 40	49·4	8 34	47·7
8·7	Goring		12 08	55·3	12 11	53·2
12·5	Cholsey		15 54	60·6	16 06	58·8
16·8	*Didcot East Junc.*	21	20 17	58·8	20 34	57·7
20·1	Culham		23 47	56·5	24 08	55·7
			pws			
22·3	Radley		26 18	52·7	26 32	55·0
27·4	OXFORD	34	32 20	—	32 19	—

* '157' class, with domed Belpaire boiler
† 'Sir Alexander' class

In column 2 of Table I, No. 1127, of the 'Sir Alexander' class, ran
much more smartly to Reading. The start from Paddington was
2½ min. late, due to the late arrival of the engine on the train; this
lateness was recovered, and Reading reached on time. With a load

of 170 tons the average speed of 59·7 m.p.h. from Langley to Twyford, gradually against the collar, was good work for an old single-wheeler with 18 in. by 24 in. cylinders. But the station staff at Reading once again exceeded their 4 min. allowance, and the train was sent on its way 1½ min. late. To Culham the subsequent running was very similar to that of No. 160, though with time in hand the driver of No. 1127 came very gently into Oxford, to arrive exactly on time. The tradition of lengthy station stops on the G.W.R., so frequently commented upon by travellers from other parts of the country, is a very old one. It is in evidence here, with short trains having little in the way of heavy intermediate traffic.

Table II includes details of two runs made after the evening service from London to Oxford had been changed to 7.30 p.m. and run down non-stop in 75 min. – not a very exciting average speed of 50·7 m.p.h. over a very good road. The revised working, however, included a slip portion for Reading, and the train often loaded up to

TABLE II

G.W.R. PADDINGTON–OXFORD (NON STOPS)

Run No.		1		2	
Engine 2-2-2 No.		157 *		999†	
Load to Reading, tons full		183		230	
„ „ Oxford „ „		135		170	

Distance Miles		Actual m. s.	Av. Speeds m.p.h.	Actual m. s.	Av. Speeds m.p.h.
0·0	PADDINGTON.	0 00		0 00	
1·3	Westbourne Park	3 19	—	3 37	—
5·7	Ealing Broadway	9 07	45·5	9 48	41·7
		sigs	—		
9·1	Southall	13 25	—	13 42	52·3
13·2	West Drayton	22 05	—	18 23	52·5
16·2	Langley	25 16	56·4	21 38	55·4
18·5	SLOUGH	27 27	61·2	23 56	58·7
24·2	Maidenhead	33 19	58·4	30 13	54·4
31·0	Twyford	40 23	57·7	37 41	56·0
36·0	READING (SLIP)	45 35	57·7	43 10	54·7
38·7	Tilehurst	48 15	60·7	45 57	58·0
41·5	Pangbourne	51 09	58·0	49 02	54·5
44·8	Goring	54 30	59·0	52 28	55·7
48·5	Cholsey	58 19	58·3	56 24	56·4
52·8	*Didcot East Junc.*	62 55	56·1	61 02	55·6
56·1	Culham	66 15	59·5	64 33	56·3
58·3	Radley	68 29	58·9	67 06	51·8
63·4	OXFORD	74 09	—	73 10	—

* '157' class, with domed boiler
† *Sir Alexander*

more than 200 tons. On the first of the two runs No. 157 got very smartly away from Paddington with 183 tons, passing Westbourne Park in 3 min. 19 sec.; but then she was brought to a dead stand at Southall West, and lost some 4 min. to Slough. Good work followed to Reading, with an average speed of 58·5 m.p.h. from Langley; after that, with the load reduced to 135 tons by loss of the slip portion, it was just a case of steady level-pegging at 56–60 m.p.h. to the out-skirts of Oxford, which was reached on time, after a late start of one minute. The net time was 69½ min., equivalent to an average of 54·7 m.p.h. start to stop.

The second run, with a load of no less than 230 tons, features engine No. 999 *Sir Alexander*. Again, the starting time to Westbourne Park is very smart, and praise must be given to the drivers who had acquired such skill in handling these old single-wheelers with the very minimum of slipping. It was an even greater art than might be imagined, because these engines slipped so smoothly and silently that at times it was almost imperceptible on the footplate – quite unlike the noise and racking that occurs when a coupled engine slips. On this run No. 999 was completely unchecked, and although she got away rather slowly after her immediate start out of Paddington the going was very steady and even. Although speed did not so much as touch 60 m.p.h. at any point there was a gain of 1¾ min. on schedule.

Next, in Table III, come two runs on the 2.12 p.m. from Oxford to Paddington, made in 1903, and allowed 73 min. for the non-stop run. Although the road is very slightly in favour of the engine and would account for the faster schedule of this up train, the 2.12 p.m. was in some ways a harder proposition. In this direction the Reading slip coaches could not be detached at full speed, because a crossover had to be made from the up through to the platform road. Engine No. 159, the first built of the '157' class, was on the job on the first run. She left Oxford 7¼ min. late, and with signals 'on' prior to the slack to detach the slip portion at Reading, and no particular effort afterwards, time was actually lost. The net time of 71¼ min. did not show very enterprising work in the circumstances.

By contrast No. 1124 of the 'Sir Alexander' class made some really spirited running, as detailed in column 2. For an old single-wheeler and a load of 210 tons the start out of Oxford was remarkable, with speed up to 60 m.p.h. in a little over 5 miles. Then came a whole succession of checks. The train had been kept on the relief line at Didcot East Junction, and was slackened to cross over to the fast line at Goring. Then came a reversion to the relief line at Reading West Junction, and finally back to the fast at Reading East Main. It was

TABLE III

G.W.R. 2.12 P.M. OXFORD–PADDINGTON

Run No.		1		2	
Engine 2-2-2 No.		159 *		1124†	
Load to Reading, tons full		215		210	
„ „ Paddington „ „		130		130	
Distance		**Actual**	**Av. Speed**	**Actual**	**Av. Speed**
Miles		**m. s.**	**m.p.h.**	**m. s.**	**m.p.h.**
0·0	OXFORD	0 00	—	0 00	—
5·1	Radley	8 56	—	7 53	—
7·3	Culham	11 27	52·5	10 04	60·4
10·6	*Didcot East Junc.*	14 57	56·6	13 13	62·8
14·9	Cholsey	19 50	52·8	17 38	58·5
				sigs	
18·7	Goring	23 49	57·2	21 25	—
21·9	Pangbourne	27 24	53·7	25 49	43·6
24·7	Tilehurst	30 31	53·8	28 54	54·4
		sigs		sigs	
27·4	READING (SLIP)	34 57	—	32 57	
32·4	Twyford	41 08	48·5	39 05	48·9
39·2	Maidenhead	48 16	57·2	45 16	65·8
44·9	SLOUGH	54 10	58·8	50 48	62·1
50·2	West Drayton	59 44	57·2	56 01	61·2
54·3	Southall	64 06	56·4	60 13	58·6
57·7	Ealing Broadway	67 35	58·5	63 39	59·5
		sigs		sigs	
62·1	Westbourne Park	72 49		67 54	
63·4	PADDINGTON	75 20		70 52	
	Net time	71¾		67	

* '157' class
† 'Sir Alexander' class

all very smartly done nevertheless, and the average speed from Cholsey to Twyford worked out as high as 48·8 m.p.h. Once clear of Reading No. 1124 galloped merrily along with her reduced load of 130 tons; and although Oxford had been left 3½ min. late there was a good chance of clocking into Paddington less than a minute late, despite all the crossing and re-crossing. There was a final check at Westbourne Park, and the eventual arrival was 1½ min. late. The net time of 67 min. showed most enterprising work.

We now move to the Bristol and Exeter road, and in Table IV are detailed three runs on the up 'Cornishman', made in 1900, and all with the Dean 7 ft 8 in. 4-2-2s. The non-stop timing of 88 min. for the 75·6 mile run had some very uneven point-to-point bookings intermediately. To pass Whiteball summit in 26 min. required some hard work. Although it is only in the last two miles that the gradient steepens to 1 in 115, the collar work is continuous from Exeter. The brief descents past Hele and Tiverton Junction give no respite, and merely enable a driver to gain a little speed to help him on the next stretch of climbing. Then comes the anomaly of 12 min. allowed for 10·9 miles of real racing ground down to Taunton, while the ensuing 25·1 level miles on to Uphill Junction were allowed 28 min. In these circumstances it is not surprising that the drivers of single-wheelers were inclined to take things quietly up to Whiteball, knowing that they could easily regain a few lost minutes afterwards.

Engine No. 3065 *Duke of Connaught* had not then achieved immortality in the locomotive world by her performances on the Ocean Mails, but on the run detailed in column 1 she put up some fine running. Things were taken easily to Whiteball, following a punctual start, but there was some really fast work down the Wellington bank. No maximum speed is quoted, but with an average of 76½ m.p.h. from Wellington to Norton Fitzwarren the top speed must have been very near 80 m.p.h., if not in excess of it. From being 3½ min. down at Whiteball the train was 2 min. early on passing Bridgwater. Good steady running at 60 to 64 m.p.h. continued over the long level stretches of the Somersetshire coastal flats, and despite a permanent way slack between Yatton and Nailsea Bristol was reached 3½ min. early.

As shown in column 2, No. 3055 *Trafalgar* did not do nearly so well. Exeter was left a minute late, but although the immediate start was better than that of the *Duke of Connaught*, and similar up to Whiteball, the subsequent work was not in the same class at all. Charlewood makes no mention of the weather on this trip. A cross-wind can be a serious hindrance over the completely exposed stretch of line from Durston to Flax Bourton, while a wet rail would set up that imperceptible slipping that could be a great handicap to a single-wheeler. Anyway, from whatever cause it may have been *Trafalgar* barely held her own, and I have included the run as an example as the less brilliant side of the Dean 7 ft 8 in. singles. The load was by no means excessive, and in any case the engine did quite adequately on the section where the load would have the greatest effect.

The last run in Table IV, with engine No. 3063 *Duke of York*, was a brilliant performance, with the heaviest load of the three. First of all, the hard booking up to Whiteball was practically kept, and the final minimum speed of 37¾ m.p.h. was first-class for a 'single' up 2 miles of 1 in 115. Speed then rose to 77 m.p.h. down Wellington bank, and despite a slight easing through Taunton the train was 4¼ min. early

TABLE IV

G.W.R. 3.7 P.M. EXETER–BRISTOL

Run No.			1		2		3	
Engine 4-2-2-No.			3065		3055		3063	
Name			Duke of Connaught		Trafalgar		Duke of York	
Load tons full			165		165		185	
Distance Miles		Sch. min	Actual m. s.	Av. Speed m.p.h.	Actual m. s.	Av. Speed m.p.h.	Actual m. s.	Av. Speed m.p.h.
0·0	EXETER	0	0 00	—	0 00	—	0 00	—
3·5	Stoke Canon		7 20	44·6	6 50	46·5	7 15	49·7
8·4	Hele		13 55	51·3	13 10	50·3	13 10	56·6
12·6	Cullompton		18 50	43·6	18 11	42·5	17 37	51·7
14·9	Tiverton Junc.	19	22 00	40·4	21 25	41·0	20 17	48·1
19·9	Whiteball	26	29 25	58·3	28 45	55·1	26 31	61·0
23·7	Wellington		33 20	76·5	32 53	66·5	30 15	75·9
28·8	Norton Fitzwarren		37 20	72·0	37 30	55·5	34 17	64·8
30·8	TAUNTON	38	39 00	63·3	39 40	57·1	36 08	58·1
36·6	Durston		44 30	61·2	45 45	56·2	42 07	59·6
42·3	BRIDGWATER	52	50 05	63·0	51 50	57·4	47 51	61·9
48·6	Highbridge		56 05	—	58 25	—	53 57	62·2
51·4	Brent Knoll		—	63·3	—	58·3	56 39	62·1
55·9	Uphill Junc.	66	63 00	63·7	65 55	50·8	61 00	58·8
63·6	Yatton		70 15	—	73 50	—	68 40	—
69·6	Flax Bourton		p.w.s. 77 15	—	80 40	52·7	eased 75 39	—
75·6	BRISTOL	88	84 25	—	88 25	—	sig. stops 85 35	—
Net times			83½		88½		82½	

passing Bridgwater. Although things were then so well in hand this driver continued in good style to the outskirts of Bristol, and even after two signal stops he was still 2½ min. early on arrival. This splendid run shows the Dean 7 ft 8 in. singles at their very best, with a good paying load. The actual train consisted of seven clerestory corridor bogies, and Charlewood records that as usual with the 'Cornishman' it was very full. The train hauled so well by the *Duke of Connaught*, run No. 1, consisted of six corridor bogies and one six-wheeler. In connection with the work of this class I am only sorry that I can find no details of down runs from Bristol to Exeter, which would include the far harder task of climbing from Norton Fitz-warren up to Whiteball summit.

Next we come to the 'Cornishman' east of Bristol, and Table V shows details of a typically good run with No. 3060 *Warlock*, with a

TABLE V

4.45 P.M. BRISTOL–PADDINGTON

Load: 7 corridor bogies, 175 tons full
Engine: 4-2-2- No. 3060 *Warlock*

Distance Miles		Sch. min.	Actual m. s.	Av. Speed m.p.h.
0·0	TEMPLE MEADS . . .	0	0 00	—
1·7	St. Annes Park		4 05	—
4·6	Keynsham		8 04	43·5
7·0	Saltford		10 50	52·1
10·5	Twerton *		14 05	64·6
11·5	BATH	15	15 49	34·5
13·8	Bathampton		18 49	46·0
16·5	Box		22 02	50·4
20·1	Corsham		27 45	37·8
24·4	CHIPPENHAM	31	32 51	50·6
30·7	Dauntsey		39 05	60·6
33·1	*Incline Box*		42 11	46·5
35·5	Wootton Bassett . . .		45 22	45·3
41·1	SWINDON	51	51 50	52·0
51·9	Uffington		62 29	60·8
58·0	Wantage Road		68 18	63·1
65·1	DIDCOT	77	75 10	62·2
69·9	Cholsey		79 33	65·5
76·9	Pangbourne		86 15	62·7
82·4	READING	96	91 50	59·2
87·4	Twyford	101	96 55	59·0
94·2	Maidenhead	108	103 42	60·1
99·9	SLOUGH	114	109 30	59·0
105·2	West Drayton		114 49	59·8
109·3	Southall	123	119 15	55·4
112·7	Ealing		122 53	56·0
117·1	Westbourne Park . . .		128 08	50·3
118·4	PADDINGTON	135	130 45	

*Now Oldfield Park

load of seven corridor bogies. The train had the very liberal allowance of 10 min. standing at Temple Meads, including a changing of engines, and in 1900 the non-stop timing to Paddington was 135 min. for the 118·3 miles – a leisurely timing of 52·6 m.p.h. But the running conditions were very bad on this occasion, with rain, hail and thunder all the way from Bath to Wantage Road. After that the weather cleared, but the train was running on time, and a substantial gain on schedule would have been possible in the concluding stages had it been necessary. In the early stages of the run, when the weather was at its worst, the accelerations from slacks and the ascents through Box Tunnel and up Dauntsey Bank were notably good. After Swindon no higher speed than 66 m.p.h. was reached at any point, while the average speed from Swindon to Slough was 61·2 m.p.h. This shows very even, consistent and commendable work.

Table VI brings us to the Birmingham service, and includes details of two non-stop runs, via Oxford, in days when the allowance was 140 min. for the distance of 129·3 miles, an average speed of 55·5 m.p.h. This was equal so far as average speed is concerned to the much publicized two-hour runs of later years on the Bicester route, though the latter, with permanent speed restrictions at Old Oak Common and High Wycombe, together with heavier gradients, was a harder run. The older route had only the slight slack at Didcot, and a heavier one through Oxford. Both runs tabulated were entirely without checks, and the drivers of *Fire King* and *Grierson* brought their respective trains into Snow Hill almost exactly on time. Intermediately there was a considerable difference between the running of the two engines. *Fire King* on a rough January day had to contend with a strong side wind and heavy rain all the way from Slough to Oxford. Things were distinctly better afterwards with the wind behind the train, and speed averaged 60 m.p.h. from Oxford to Leamington. Here the line is rising steadily from Kidlington to the summit point at Claydon Crossing, midway between Cropredy and Fenny Compton, after which there is a fast run down into Leamington.

Grierson, although running on a June day, fared no better for weather. It was wet, with a bad rail, and between Oxford and Banbury the engine was much hindered by hail and heavy side wind. Because of this the general performance north of Oxford was below that of the previous run, and speed fell to a minimum of 50½ m.p.h. beyond Cropredy. But this driver was evidently a pretty resolute type, as he took his engine hard down to Leamington, touching

TABLE VI

G.W.R. PADDINGTON–BIRMINGHAM (VIA OXFORD)

Run No.		1		2	
Engine 4-2-2 No.		3010		3058	
Engine Name		Fire King		Grierson	
Load to Leamington, tons full		155		170	
Load to Birmingham, tons full		135		130	

Distance Miles		Sch. min.	Actual m. s.	Av. Speed m.p.h.	Actual m. s.	Av. Speed m.p.h.
0·0	PADDINGTON	0	0 00	—	0 00	—
1·3	Westbourne Park		3 18	—	3 11	—
5·7	Ealing		9 07	45·4	9 13	43·9
9·1	Southall	12	12 49	55·1	13 03	53·2
13·2	West Drayton		17 26	53·4	17 33	54·7
18·5	SLOUGH	21½	22 57	57·7	22 48	60·6
24·2	Maidenhead	27½	29 20	63·5	28 45	57·5
36·0	READING	39	42 00	56·0	40 46	59·0
41·5	Pangbourne		47 51	56·5	46 18	59·7
48·5	Cholsey		54 44	60·8	53 15	60·4
52·8	Didcot E. Jc.	57	59 13	57·5	57 40	58·4
56·1	Culham		62 38	57·8	60 56	60·7
58·3	Radley		64 53	58·7	63 10	59·1
63·4	OXFORD	68	69 51	61·5	68 10	61·2
66·3	Wolvercot Jc.	72	73 27	48·3	71 18	55·3
69·0	Kidlington		76 19	56·5	74 05	58·2
71·0	Bletchington		78 26	56·8	76 20	53·4
75·1	Heyford		82 28	60·8	80 40	56·9
78·0	Somerton		85 13	63·3	83 41	57·8
80·2	Aynho		87 19	63·3	85 57	58·5
86·1	BANBURY	91	92 52	63·7	91 52	59·8
89·7	Cropredy		96 32	58·9	95 47	55·3
94·8	Fenny Compton		101 53	57·2	101 27	54·1
99·8	Southam Road		106 24	66·5	105 54	67·4
105·9	LEAMINGTON	113	112 25	60·9	111 34	64·7
107·9	Warwick		115 07	44·5	114 01	49·0
112·1	Hatton		121 04	42·3	119 35	44·2
116·3	Kingswood *		126 10	49·4	124 35	50·4
118·8	Knowle		128 59	53·4	127 27	52·3
122·2	Solihull	132	132 40	55·3	131 11	54·5
125·0	Acocks Green		135 16	64·6	133 50	63·5
127·0	Small Heath		137 03	67·1	135 39	66·2
128·0	Bordesley		138 05	58·1	136 42	57·2
129·3	BIRMINGHAM	140	140 03		138 34	

* Now Lapworth

75 m.p.h. after Southam Road, and passed Leamington 1½ min. early. The slack through that station was severely enforced on both runs, and the usual quick recovery followed on the favourable mile to the crossing of the River Avon before Warwick. Then comes Hatton bank, with its three miles of 1 in 108–103–110, not to

mention the sharp approach gradients. *Fire King* fell to 33 m.p.h. on this severe incline, but although the loads were now reduced to 130–135 tons *Grierson* did well to climb the bank at a minimum of 38 m.p.h. After that both engines ran well on the final gradually downhill stretch into Birmingham, and that villainous quarter-mile at 1 in 45 up through Snow Hill tunnel was rushed smartly.

On another occasion Charlewood joined the 4.45 p.m. from Paddington at Oxford, and clocked the excellent run detailed in Table VII. The engine, No. 3062 *Albert Edward*, slipped considerably in starting from Oxford, and speed had not risen above 50 m.p.h. until the miniature summit between Bletchington and Heyford had been cleared. After that No. 3062 continued splendidly up the continuing gradual rise to Banbury. The slipping of one coach there helped in the climbing to Claydon Crossing, but even with 170 tons the minimum of 51 m.p.h. before Fenny Compton was excellent.

TABLE VII

G.W.R. 6.12 P.M. OXFORD–BIRMINGHAM

Load: to Banbury, 195 tons full
to Leamington, 170 tons full
to Birmingham, 120 tons full
Engine: 4-2-2 No. 3062 *Albert Edward*

Distance Miles		Sch. min.	Actual m. s.	Av. Speed m.p.h.
0·0	OXFORD	0	0 00	—
2·9	*Wolvercot Junc.*		5 57	—
5·6	Kidlington		9 26	46·5
7·6	Bletchington		11 55	48·2
11·7	Heyford		16 27	54·3
14·6	Somerton		19 27	58·0
16·8	Aynho		21 42	58·7
22·7	BANBURY	28	27 50	57·7
26·3	Cropredy		31 56	52·7
31·4	Fenny Compton		37 51	51·8
36·4	Southam Road		42 30	64·5
42·5	LEAMINGTON	50	48 01	65·3
44·5	Warwick		50 08	56·9
48·7	Hatton		55 24	47·9
52·9	Kingswood		60 25	50·3
55·4	Knowle		63 22	50·9
58·8	Solihull		67 00	56·1
61·6	Acocks Green		69 40	63·1
63·6	Small Heath		71 36	62·0
64·6	Bordesley		72 41	57·6
65·9	BIRMINGHAM	78	74 36	

Downhill to Leamington speed was sustained at 72 m.p.h. for some distance. Charlewood comments that the engine was 'eased' off for

Leamington. It cannot have been much of a 'slack' for the next two miles on to Warwick to be covered in 2 min. 7 sec.! Hatton bank was taken at a minimum of 41 m.p.h. though now with a load of only 120 tons. Still, this was a good run, leaving Oxford 2½ min. late and arriving ¾ min. early.

Next comes a collection of runs up from Birmingham to Oxford on various trains, as shown in Table VIII. The 2-2-2 engine No. 162 *Cobham* was probably the best known of the '157' class, by her being the only one of her ten to be named. For some years she was driven by David Hughes, and made a great reputation on the Birmingham expresses. Run No. 1 in Table VIII was made with a light load on the 5.45 p.m. out of Snow Hill. Although leaving 3½ min. late things were taken very easily to Leamington, and only just keeping the 29 min. timing. But a remarkable effort was made up Southam Road bank. Here the gradient is 1 in 187 for 3 miles, and to pass Southam in less than 10 minutes was most unusual. Charlewood gives no maximum and minimum speeds, but after a couple of miles of level past Southam, the rise continues and includes 3 miles at 1 in 265– 251–239 past Fenny Compton. The average speeds quoted in the table are indicative of excellent work. The result of this was that nearly 3 min. were gained between Leamington and Banbury, and with further smart work after Aynho, Oxford was reached 1½ min. early.

Runs 2 and 3 were made on the up 'Zulu' leaving Birmingham at 2.44 p.m. At the turn of the century this train stopped only at Leamington, but slipped a coach at Oxford. It was in this latter that Charlewood was travelling on both runs. Schedule was then 29 min. start to stop from Birmingham to Leamington, and 50 min. for the 42½ miles onwards to Oxford. The 'Sir Alexander' class 2-2-2 No. 1116 had something of a task on this train with a load of 190 tons. A permanent way slack at Small Heath gave a bad start, but after that No. 1116 did wonderfully well. No more than a few seconds were dropped to Leamington, despite the initial check, the net time from Birmingham being about 27½ min. With so relatively big a load, for an old engine, the driver took things quietly up to Southam Road, but after that there was some fine free running down from Fenny Compton, with an average speed of 62 m.p.h. right through from Cropredy to Wolvercot Junction, and the Oxford slip coach arrived just inside time.

Engine No. 3070 *Earl of Warwick* made rather a patchy run with the same train. She made a grand start to Leamington, immediately wiping out the 2 min. lateness with which Birmingham was left.

TABLE VIII
G.W.R. BIRMINGHAM-OXFORD

Run No.		1		2		3		4	
Engine No.		162		1116		3070		3058	
Engine Name		Cobham		—		Earl of Warwick		Grierson	
Load		108		190		215		225*	
Distance Miles		Actual m. s.	Av. Speed m.p.h.	Actual m. s.	Av. Speed m.p.h.	Actual m. s.	Av. Speed m.p.h.	Actual m. s.	Av. Speed m.p.h.
0·0	BIRMINGHAM	0 00	—	0 00	—	0 00	—	0 00	—
1·3	Bordesley	2 26	—	3 01	—	2 55	—	2 59	—
4·3	Acocks Green	6 38	42·8	8 41 p.w.s.	—	7 13	41·9	7 30	40·0
7·1	Solihull	10 20	45·4	12 23	45·4	10 37	49·4	11 10	45·8
10·5	Knowle	14 25	49·7	16 19	51·8	14 17	55·6	15 12	50·6
13·0	Kingswood	17 09	54·8	18 48	60·3	16 39	63·4	17 45	58·8
17·2	Hatton	22 00	52·0	22 58	60·6	20 39	63·0	21 53	60·9
21·4	Warwick	26 18	58·6	26 49	65·5	24 20	68·3	25 40	66·6
23·4	LEAMINGTON	28 50	—	29 23	—	26 49	—	28 10	—
6·1	Southam Road	9 57	36·7	12 08	30·1	12 22	29·7	12 54	28·3
11·1	Fenny Compton	15 21	55·5	18 11	49·6	18 55	45·8	19 31	45·3
16·2	Cropredy	20 35	58·3	24 04	52·0	25 14	47·6	25 42	49·4
19·8	BANBURY	24 25	—	27 15	67·7	sigs 32 11	—	29 02	64·8
5·9	Aynho	8 10	—	32 31	67·3	38 43	54·1	34 26	65·6
8·1	Somerton	10 24	59·0	34 40	61·3	40 59	58·5	36 32	62·8
11·0	Heyford	13 09	63·6	37 25	63·3	43 42	64·3	39 11	65·7
15·1	Bletchington	17 01	63·7	41 25	61·5	47 39	62·3	43 07	62·7
17·1	Kidlington	18 58	61·5	43 23	61·2	49 36	61·5	45 06	60·4
19·8	Wolvercot Junc.	21 27	65·0	45 49	66·6	52 03	66·2	47 35	65·3
22·7	OXFORD	25 50	—	49 50	—	55 57	—	51 13	—

*Load reduced by slipping to 210 tons from Warwick and 195 tons from Banbury

Then, by comparison with No. 1116, the uphill work from Leamington was poor, and a bad signal check at the junction with the Great Central line just outside Banbury seemed to take all the heart out of the driver, and it was only after Somerton that some reasonable speed began to develop once again. As it was the Oxford slip coach arrived 6¾ min. late. The last run, with No. 3058 *Grierson* was on the 7.50 p.m. up, which slipped coaches at Warwick and Banbury. The Warwick slip was indeed a curiosity, with a booked stop at Leamington only two miles further on. The train left Birmingham 5½ min. late, and with this substantial load nothing appreciable was recovered: 50 sec. to Leamington and 47 sec. to Oxford.

Among Charlewood's records there is one on the 4 p.m. up non-stop from Snow Hill to Paddington with engine No. 3075 *Princess Louise* and a load of 120 tons. But no enterprise whatever was shown in combating a succession of checks, and 7 min. was lost on the schedule of 140 min. On another run he joined the up 'Zulu' at Leamington. This train was allowed 122 min. for the 105·9 miles to Paddington. Another of the 4-2-2s, No. 3004 *Black Prince*, had a load of 192 tons, reduced to 167 tons by slipping at Oxford and 144 tons at Reading, and again there was no enterprise shown on the foot-plate. Leamington was left a minute late; two slight checks were experienced, and Paddington was reached 2¼ min. late. From a study of these runs it is evident that even in the days of spotlessly clean engines, and brass domes that shone like gold, one found the same difference in temperament among drivers that exists in our own enlightened days – some men making it a point of honour to recover lost time, others seeming to take almost as much care in not gaining the slightest amount.

Last of all we must leave the single-wheelers and repair to Shrewsbury for a run over the North to West line. I must explain at once that this was no ordinary run. Twice a year it was the custom to hold wool sales in the Corn Market at Bristol, and special trains were run from Bradford for the convenience of the Yorkshire buyers. For this special traffic the Great Western and the North Western went into partnership against the Midland, and some fast running was made by both sides. The Great Western share was to run the 119·3 miles between Shrewsbury and Bristol in 2 hr. 27 min. – 28 min. faster than the best ordinary trains. The load on this particular occasion was one of five coaches, weighing 127 tons tare, and one of the new 'Badminton' class 4-4-0s No. 3301 *Monarch* was on the job. This run was recorded from the footplate by Mr A. G. Robbins, and the accompanying log and detail are taken from a very comprehensive article he wrote for *The Railway Magazine* in 1899. The details of the runs on two successive days are given in Tables IX and X.

On the southbound journey the special left Shrewsbury 2½ min. late, and there was thus every incentive to make up time, even on this fast schedule. At the start the engine was inclined to prime, so things had to be taken easily on the first stages of the 12 mile climb to Church Stretton; but speed rose to 53 m.p.h. on the easier stretch past Dorrington. Then unfortunately there came a relaying slack in the middle of the longest pitch at 1 in 90–100, and speed had not recovered to more than 35 m.p.h. when the summit was passed. Some fast running followed, with maximum speeds of 78 m.p.h. at Craven Arms and 77 at Onibury, but speed had to be eased somewhat round the curve at Ludlow, and thereafter the pace on generally favourable gradients was no more than ordinarily fast. Nevertheless the overall time of 55¾ min. was immeasurably faster than anything regularly scheduled over this route, and meteoric compared with the pedestrian booked times of today.

TABLE IX

G.W.R. SHREWSBURY–HEREFORD
The Wool Buyers' Special

Load: 5 coaches, 127 tons tare, 135 tons full
Engine: 4-4-0 No. 3301 *Monarch*

Distance Miles		Actual m. s.	Speeds * m.p.h.
0·0	SHREWSBURY . .	0 00	
2·0	*Milepost 2* . . .	4 53	—
4·3	Condover . .	8 55	36
6·4	Dorrington . . .	11 17	53
9·3	Leebotwood . . .	15 07	40½
—		p.w.s.	30
12·8	CHURCH STRETTON	20 47	—
15·4	Marsh Brook . .	23 30	66
19·9	CRAVEN ARMS . .	27 12	78/72
22·9	Onibury . . .	29 36	77
25·3	Bromfield . .	31 34	69
27·5	LUDLOW . . .	33 29	60 (slack)
32·1	Woofferton Junc. . .	37 32	72
35·2	Berrington . . .	40 26	60
38·4	LEOMINSTER . . .	43 21	69
40·8	Ford Bridge . .	45 28	65
43·5	Dinmore . . .	48 06	60
46·8	Moreton-on-Lugg . .	51 07	68
50·0	*Milepost 50* . . .	54 12	60
51·0	HEREFORD . . .	55 47	

*From readings at each milepost

TABLE X

G.W.R. HEREFORD–SHREWSBURY
The Wool Buyers' Special

Load: 5 coaches, 127 tons tare, 135 tons full
Engine: 4-4-0 No. 3301 *Monarch*

Distance Miles		Actual m. s.	Av. Speeds m.p.h.
0·0	HEREFORD . . .	0 00	—
1·0	*Milepost 50* . . .	2 12	—
7·5	Dinmore	9 30	54·2
—		p.w.s.	5
10·2	Ford Bridge . . .	12 45	
12·6	LEOMINSTER . .	16 35	37·6
15·8	Berrington . . .	20 05	54·8
18·9	Woofferton Junc. . .	23 03	62·5
22·0	*Milepost 29* . . .	25 40	71·2
23·5	LUDLOW . . .	27 20	54·1
28·1	Onibury . . .	31 40	63·8
31·1	CRAVEN ARMS . .	34 40	60·0
35·6	Marsh Brook . . .	39 35	55·0
38·2	CHURCH STRETTON .	42 47	48·8
41·7	Leebotwood . . .	45 55	66·8
44·6	Dorrington . . .	48 20	72·2
46·7	Condover . . .	50 05	72·1
51·0	SHREWSBURY . .	55 45	

Net time 53 min.

On the following day Mr Robbins could not record more than a few of the mileposts, as by that time darkness had fallen, and the art of speed recording by the rail joints had not been taken up. Nevertheless, the average speeds quoted in Table X give evidence of some excellent running, particularly on the stiff pull up to Church Stretton from Craven Arms. The engines normally used on the West to North expresses were the efficient 2-4-0s of the '3232' class, having 6 ft 6 in. coupled wheels, cylinders 17½ in. dia. by 24 in. stroke. These engines were built at Swindon in 1892, but their stay on the North to West expresses was relatively short. In 1898 they were replaced on the best trains by the 'Badmintons'.

XV

Prelude to a New Age

THE last years of the nineteenth century were some of the most vital in the entire history of the Great Western Railway. The Victorian era in England was rising to its crowning crescendo of glory as the time approached for the celebration of Her Majesty's Diamond Jubilee, and so far as railways were concerned the outward sentiments of the period were brilliantly epitomized in the new Royal Train which the Great Western built to take the Queen and her suite from Windsor to Paddington for the Diamond Jubilee celebrations in May 1897. No expense was spared in the construction of that beautiful six-coach train, though the Queen's own special requirements gave William Dean and his carriage staff some of the biggest 'headaches' they had ever had in coach construction, and the result was one of the oddest vehicles ever to run in this country in relatively modern times.

When the Board of the G.W.R. announced their intention of building a sumptuous new Royal Train Her Majesty gave the Company to understand that personally – in modern parlance – she couldn't care less, provided always that the carriage in which she had previously travelled on the Great Western remained unaltered. Having survived the first shock of this august command the most careful and discreet enquiries elicited the fact that it was not the actual vehicle to which the Queen was so attached, but her own private apartment. Here indeed was a problem, for the old Royal saloon of 1874 was, by the standards of 1897, quite an antiquated vehicle, which would have looked entirely out of place in the magnificent new train that Swindon had been instructed to build. Dean himself stated the problem clearly in an interview he gave to Herbert Russell, an early contributor to *The Railway Magazine*:

'We had therefore to rebuild the carriage without disturbing the Royal apartment, and I may say that this task has presented the greatest of our difficulties in the whole undertaking. We could far more easily have built an entirely new coach. The midship section, containing the Queen's compartment, had to be removed in its entirety from the original frames; and by the time we had lifted it, and deposited it in safety on the ground, we looked with some concern at the empty cask-like structure, which it seemed impossible could ever be restored to its former condition.'

How the task was done was a masterpiece of carriage designing and building, though when finished the Queen's saloon stood out from the rest of the new Royal Train through having a plain, semi-eliptical roof, while the remaining five vehicles were clerestory-roofed. Even so these five were apart from general Great Western standards. The clerestories were curved down at the ends after the fashion of the London and North Western dining and sleeping cars. The new Royal Train was electrically lighted, except for the Queen's own saloon. In her own compartment Her Majesty would not even have gas lighting, let alone electricity. As Dean expressed it: 'The Queen prefers the softer glow of an oil lamp.' She was equally insistent that the speed should not exceed 40 m.p.h. at any point. Again to quote Dean himself: 'Our standing orders were never to exceed forty miles an hour. Whisper it not, but Her Majesty does occasionally go nearer sixty than forty miles an hour, doubtless without observing it, for if there is one point in which the Great Western Railway has always excelled more than another it is in the smoothness of running.'

Two of the 7 ft 8 in. bogie singles were set aside for the Royal Train workings in connection with the Diamond Jubilee; Nos. 3041 and 3071. The former was originally named *Empress of India*. This, while significant in every way, was perhaps not quite appropriate enough to an event which was especially dear to the Mother Country, and so engine No. 3041 was renamed simply *The Queen* and as such she worked the Royal Train. The second 4-2-2, No. 3071, was named *Emlyn*, after Viscount Emlyn the Chairman of the Great Western Railway and afterwards Earl Cawdor. Engine No. 3071 was advance pilot to the Royal Train, and it was indeed appropriate that an engine bearing the name of the titular head of the G.W.R. should have led the way, as it were, on so memorable occasion. Engine No. 3041 carried, on each side of the smokebox and on each side of the tender, a superb representation in relief and full colour of the Royal arms. These beautiful pieces have been used subsequently for many other Royal train occasions, and they are preserved with great pride in the headquarters of the locomotive department at Swindon.

While the majority of Great Western officers looked back with the keenest regret to the passing of the broad gauge, there is no denying that it had been a millstone round their necks for the last thirty years of its existence. While the broad gauge had remained there was the strongest disinclination to develop fast and enterprising services on the narrow gauge parts of the line. In his classic work of 1889 Foxwell wrote of the Great Western:

'This is the largest English line as regards extent in miles, and the second largest in regard to traffic. But its proportion of express-running is still very unsatisfactory. The greater part of its three main routes is blessed with extremely easy gradients, hence the speed of its best trains is very high; and, as there are so few of these quick trains, they are particularly crowded. From time to time as years pass on, this company with timorous hand adventures on a new express, which is instantly filled; yet they will not try the experiment on a bolder scale, and face their rivals with a serious express programme. However, during the last thirty years the history of the Great Western has been one continuous ascent towards financial prosperity, and, now that its fortunes are consolidated, it will perhaps wake up to a sense of its position, and determine to give the public no more doles, but an express service organized and worthy of the largest line in the kingdom. It is in many ways such a great line that its meanness in the matter of quick trains is the more incongruous; thus twenty years ago its Exeter expresses ran at the same speed as now – only a shade slower than the quickest Great Northern run today; and again, no company has anything to be so proud of as the Severn Tunnel. The Great Western is a very solid line, and makes its progress in a solid style; doing some great things and many small, but all alike with the immovability of Jove.'

Yet despite the preferential treatment given to the broad gauge expresses the average speed of the best expresses from Paddington to Wolverhampton and to Birkenhead was actually higher than that of the best trains to and from Plymouth. No less excellent from the narrow gauge point of view was the West to North express service between Bristol and Crewe, via the Severn Tunnel. The average overall speed, including stops, of the six trains on this service was $38\frac{1}{2}$ m.p.h., whereas the six London–Plymouth expresses averaged exactly 40 m.p.h. Foxwell continued:

'If the Great Western were aggressive or energetic like other lines, it would see plenty of fresh enterprise lying ready to its hand. There is no reason why, if it ran more expresses to the North, it should not secure a more equal share of traffic between London and Birkenhead, while the same venture would yield a similar increase as regards Birmingham, Wolverhampton, etc. And now that it has the stimulus accruing from joint mileage over the "Severn Tunnel route to the North", might it not re-establish under happier auspices the service lapsed between Weymouth and Cherbourg? Then the "Irish boat trains" should be promptly accelerated to do the journey between Milford and London in 7 hours (which would be only 40 miles an hour), not merely for the sake of more tourists in summer, but in deference to neglected Swansea, if not with an eye to the development of future "transatlantic" exploits. Again, with a little dash, the company might in time make *Barmouth* as great a source of profit as Scarborough is to the Great Northern. Scarborough is 230 miles from Kings Cross; families are taken there in five hours with only *two* stops. Barmouth is only 20 miles farther from Paddington, yet the quickest time is 7¾ hours, and there are a dozen stoppages. It is true that when there we have something infinitely lovelier than Scarborough; but what a fraction of the crowds that swamp Scarborough ever visit the panorama of the Mawddach. Some companies are born to a rich seaside traffic, as was the Great Northern; some, like the Great Eastern, achieve it by persistent enterprise, and the Great Western waits dozing till the traffic shall be thrust upon it.'

It is curious to find this distinguished writer concentrating so much attention upon the Cambrian coast. Had Brunel's proposal for the Irish Mail route been adopted, with Port Dinllaen as the packet station, instead of Holyhead, and a magnificent broad gauge route via Worcester, Ludlow, Newtown and Dolgelly, it is quite probable that Barmouth, Portmadoc, Criccieth and Pwllheli would have attained the eminence, as holiday resorts, that Prestatyn, Rhyl, Colwyn Bay and Llandudno enjoy today – and been completely spoiled in consequence!

Looking back upon the 54 years of the broad gauge Great Western men felt very keenly that there had never been any real chance to develop its potentialities. The Gauge Commission did their best to kill it outright, and although the death sentence was not endorsed, either by the Board of Trade or by Act of Parliament it was, in actual fact, no more than deferred. No significant development of broad gauge locomotives took place after the introduction of Gooch's famous 8 ft 4-2-2s in the late 'forties, and from being the mightiest express engines in the country they were gradually eclipsed until in 1892 they were among the feeblest. With Great Western finances in the parlous state they were for so many years there was no case for development, and when the long-deferred rise to prosperity began in earnest it was too late. The broad gauge was not only condemned by the Gauge Commission, its end had been decreed in the Board Room at Paddington.

It is interesting to pause for a moment to try and imagine the kind of twentieth century express passenger locomotive Churchward would have built for the broad gauge, and the heights of luxury and spaciousness to which carriage design might have risen. When British locomotive and carriage designers had entered upon the exacting race in amenities the restraining effect of the narrow gauge was felt acutely. The Great Western would have had an over-whelming advantage. But though regrets for the broad gauge were profound and essentially practical no time was wasted in brooding over the glories of what might have been. Once the broad gauge had gone it seemed that the management determined to take the new era as a challenge. Deprived of the great initial advantage over all others that they had inherited from Brunel, there seemed on all hands a resolve to regain the lead. The result was two decades of intensely exciting development in almost every aspect of railway working, and while the actual achievement belongs to the twentieth century the new teams were built up, the plans were laid, and the first stages got under way while the crack trains still continued to run their leisured way, while the Dean locomotives touched the pinnacle of their elegance, and while the Victorian era moved towards its close.

It is interesting to look back to the men who set this great resur-gence in motion. At the very head of affairs, as Chairman of the Board, was Viscount Emlyn, a man of great vigour and business ability. He took over the office in 1895 and was the first Chairman for nearly thirty years who had not previously been an executive officer of the Company. Sir Daniel Gooch had been succeeded by Frederick Saunders, nephew of the great 'Charles A', and he in turn had succeeded his uncle as Secretary of the Company. On the traffic side the resurgence had begun in 1888 when the conservative and unprogressive G. N. Tyrrell had been succeeded as Superintendent of the Line by N. J. Burlinson; but it was T. I. Allen who came in the wake of Burlinson's improvements and laid the foundations of a train service worthy of the Great Western and of the new century. Allen became Superintendent of the Line in 1894, and the third major change came two years later when Henry Lambert resigned the office of General Manager, and was succeeded by J. L. Wilkinson. The latter most able officer had joined the Great Western as a boy in 1863, but his service with the company had been broken for three years in a manner that was to be followed in later years by one of the greatest London and North Western General Managers.

Between 1885 and 1888 Wilkinson was General Manager of the Buenos Ayres and Pacific Railway, just as Sir Guy Calthrop became later. Wilkinson returned to Paddington as Chief Goods Manager, but it was from 1896 onwards when the triple association of Emlyn, Wilkinson and Allen had really got into their stride that the Great Western began to blaze a new trail worthy of the most thrilling pioneer days of Brunel and Gooch. At Swindon Dean continued in office, though by that time the influence of Churchward was becoming more and more evident, while in civil engineering the Company was fortunate at this stage in having a man of outstanding ability and strength of character in James Inglis. At the same time the chain of command still had many points of semblance to the days of Charles Saunders. Chief Officers like Inglis, Dean, and afterwards Churchward regularly attended at Board Meetings, and took their instructions from directors responsible for their particular branches of the business rather than from the General Manager. This state of affairs was to have some serious repercussions in later years.

And so, in the nineties, while Allen continued and greatly intensified Burlinson's efforts to smarten and speed up the train service, plans were laid and Parliamentary sanction obtained for a general streamlining of the main traffic routes of the Company. Not for nothing did the wits of the nineties aver that the initials G.W.R. stood for 'Great Way Round'. The West of England main line ran via Bristol; the line to South Wales, although greatly improved by completion of the Severn Tunnel, still had to pass through Bath and the congested eastern outskirts of Bristol; while finally the line to Birmingham, Shrewsbury and Birkenhead went by way of Oxford. With increasing congestion on the main line east of Didcot a policy of widening to provide four running lines had been decided upon in 1873, though because of financial stringencies and the heavy work involved in the widening of the Wharncliffe Viaduct at Hanwell, the work had stopped short on the east side of Maidenhead bridge in 1884. But as all the long distance traffic for London had funnelled into the main line by Didcot the provision of quadruple tracks over the entire 53 miles between this junction and Paddington was considered essential, and work began upon the heaviest section of all, between Maidenhead Bridge and Reading, in 1890.

Far from having any apprehension over Brunel's beautiful elliptical arched bridge over the Thames, its design was followed exactly in the widening works of the nineties, but apart from this some of the most interesting engineering work – from the viewpoint of present day practice – was carried out in widening the long cutting between Maidenhead and Twyford. Here there were many overbridges, and over the double-tracked broad gauge line single brick-arched structures had sufficed. The building of a second arched opening alongside was evidently considered to involve too much in the way of excavation, with a deviation in the new lines to pass round the wide and heavy piers. Accordingly it was decided to remove the old arches altogether, and replace them with new steel girders to span all four tracks and obviate any need of a central pier. In recent years the demolishing of old brick-arched bridges by explosive has, by the publicity given to it, attracted a good deal of public attention; but in the 'nineties, all the old bridges in the Shottesbrook cutting were demolished in this way.

No less interesting was the method of erecting the new steel girders. Occupation of the running lines for any appreciable time by large travelling cranes or work trains was evidently considered out of the question, and so these massive girders were raised and swung into position with no more elaborate equipment than a vertical pole and a 'block and tackle'! The photographs reproduced facing pages 161 and 192 give a vivid impression of the magnitude of this undertaking, and studying these one can well appreciate how much depended upon the skill and diligence of the foreman in charge of the operation, and no less upon every man concerned. The widened lines between Maidenhead Bridge Junction, as it had been known, and Reading were brought into service in June 1893. Much of the work west of Reading had been completed earlier, and at the end of July in that same time the widening was complete to Didcot, save for a section through Reading itself. Here the old station, with its quaint track layout, was in course of complete rebuilding, and this latter work was not finished until 1899.

The Paddington–Didcot widening and the reconstruction of Reading station was no more than one part of a great 'modernization plan', calculated to sweep away for ever the leisured and roundabout travelling that had been for so long traditional of the Great Western. Already great centres of traffic lay in the Black Country and South Wales, while the new management of the G.W.R. descried that all the ingredients of vast summer holiday business lay *not* on the Cambrian coast, as suggested by Foxwell, but in Devon and Cornwall. In modern railway business of the kind now envisaged the old roundabout routes just would not do, and so the new plan involved the construction of direct routes, cutting out all the deviations and avoiding the congestion and delay to through trains from local and conflicting movements which, though important and revenue earning in themselves, were unconnected with the longer distance traffic.

So far as express passenger traffic was concerned the Great Western began to embrace the principle of long non-stop runs, to give passengers pleasant and undisturbed journeys, and to simplify and speed up the operating. The first of the new 'cut-off' lines to be considered was a direct result of the success of the Severn Tunnel.

Since its opening traffic had increased to an almost embarrassing extent, and at one time during the 'nineties there were suggestions that it might have to be doubled! Part of the trouble arose, however, from the fact that all London-bound traffic from South Wales that passed through the tunnel had also to pass through Bristol. In 1895 what was called the South Wales and Bristol Direct Railway was promoted, leaving the old main line at Wootton Bassett and running almost due west through a countryside hitherto untouched by railways to make a triangle junction with the existing Bristol and South Wales line on the high ground between Bristol and the coastal flats. So far as through traffic to and from London was concerned it would avoid the steep descent from Filton, avoid the slow running between Lawrence Hill and St. Anne's Park and avoid the Box Tunnel and Wootton Bassett inclines.

The Great Western management of that period was thinking of far more than traffic to South Wales in building the Badminton line. In the very first article in the first number of *The Railway Magazine* J. L. Wilkinson, the General Manager, gave an interview to the Editor of this new journal, and after discussing the possibilities of the London suburban traffic G. A. Sekon asked:

'You have other possibilities of expansion of traffic within the range of practical politics I presume, Mr Wilkinson?'

'Certainly', the General Manager replied. 'For instance, sooner or later—and perhaps sooner than many expect—Milford will become *the* port for dealing with an extensive oversea traffic, which traffic the Great Western Railway will be glad to accommodate. When the time comes, it is possible that the Paddington–Milford boat specials may be the "crack" trains of the world.'

As will be shown in the second volume these aspirations did not work out quite as intended, but in the meantime the direct line to Birmingham was beginning to take shape. Down to the year 1897 a chain of branch lines between Maidenhead and Kennington Junction had provided a somewhat circuitous alternative route to Oxford, via Wycombe, Princes Risborough, and Thame. The entire route was single-tracked, and included heavy gradients and a rather poor alignment in its passage through the Chiltern Hills. The central portion of this route, from Wycombe to Princes Risborough, lay roughly on a direct line from Acton to Banbury, and the first stage in a shorter route to Birmingham was to build a new and almost straight line from a junction a mile east of Acton, to High Wycombe. A Bill for the construction of this line was promoted in 1897. However well this new line might have been built, the old single-tracked branch through the Chilterns was anything but suitable for inclusion in a new main line, and the expense of modernizing it might well have proved prohibitive, running concurrently with so many other improvement schemes.

The statesmanship and farsightedness of the Great Western management of those days then came prominently into evidence. The Great Central Railway London Extension was then in course of construction, and in the nearness of the new line to their own, at Banbury, the Great Western saw an opportunity of realizing an ambition dating back to the Battle of the Gauges – namely an outlet to North Eastern England. It was at the suggestion of the G.W.R. that the Great Central included the branch from Culworth Junction to Banbury in their great southward drive, and the G.W.R. agreed to loan the necessary capital to build the branch. The cordial relations between the two companies then came to the assistance of the Great Western further south. When the London Extension of the Great Central was first promoted access to the Capital was to be obtained over the Metropolitan Railway. This was easily arranged because Sir Edward Watkin was Chairman of both companies. After his resignation things were not quite so friendly, and the Great Western, sensing the insecurity felt by the Great Central in their dependence upon the Metropolitan, dropped a few careful hints about the advantages of an alternative route. So there came, in 1899, the incorporation of the Great Western and Great Central Railways Joint Committee, with powers to do three important things:

1. To purchase the existing G.W.R. line between High Wycombe and Princes Risborough, convert it to double track and bring it up to first class main line standards.

2. To purchase from the G.W.R. that portion of the recent authorized Acton–Wycombe line lying northwest of Northolt.

3. To build a new line from Princes Risborough to a junction with the G.C.R. London Extension at Grendon Underwood Junction.

By this arrangement the Great Western got the Great Central to share in the cost of building a major part of the new short route to Birmingham. With the Acton–Northolt piece constructed only the 18¼ mile 'cut' across virgin country from Ashendon Junction to Aynho Junction remained to be built solely at Great Western expense. This latter section was not authorized and built until some years later.

The 'cut-off' schemes that were to assume the greatest prominence in the eyes of the public, however, were those concerned with the shortened route to the West of England. Before the end of the nineteenth century work had at last started on this great project, which had more than once been authorized by Parliament, but had been allowed to lapse. The Great Western Board gave the 'right away' in 1895, and the full scheme involved the following works:

1. Doubling the Berks and Hants line between Hungerford and Patney.

2. Building a new line between Patney and Westbury.

3. Building a new line between Castle Cary and Langport, on the Durston and Yeovil branch.

4. Doubling this latter branch between Langport (Curry Rivel Junction) and Athelney.

5. Building a new short cut between Athelney and Cogload Junction (avoiding Durston).

And so the great conception arising from the Battle of the Gauges, the short route to the West that was partly Great Western and partly Bristol and Exeter, at last became a reality. All in all it was probably a better route than the 'Exeter Direct', which would have short-circuited the Bristol and Exeter altogether, and which would have blocked the South Western advance into Devon. The 'Exeter Direct', while serving Yeovil, would have had all the heavy climbing of the present Southern main line, via Crewkerne and Honiton. Instead the new Great Western line to the west had a splendid run from Castle Cary down to the Athelney marshes, and only the Whiteball ascent, which is not to be compared for gruelling difficulty with the climb from Seaton Junction to Honiton Tunnel.

The last trunk route to be constructed, again by connecting up a series of branches, was the north to west line from Birmingham to Bristol, though this was so essentially an affair of the twentieth century as to be held over to the second volume of this book. But whether it was on the Badminton line, on the G.W. and G.C. Joint, on the Langport 'cut-off', or on the Honeybourne and Cheltenham the object was the same, to cut out the complications of long distance travel, and provide smooth, undisturbed journeys for the passengers. In the late 'nineties there were signs on every hand of a new race for railway supremacy in Great Britain. It was not another contest in speed like 'Kinnaber', of 1895. The sparks from that memorable affair were barely down, it is true, but now it was a race for supremacy in popular favour, and in that respect the Great Western approached the end of the nineteenth century with a large amount of leeway to make up. Its leisured first class patrons were probably satisfied, but the enterprising management was now doing everything in its power to encourage third class travel.

The race in amenities was on. The Great Western could not afford
to match the luxuries provided on the Anglo-Scottish expresses, and
the building of vastly heavy twelve-wheeled stock at Wolverton,
Doncaster and York found no echo at Swindon. In speed the northern
lines had left the Great Western far behind, but little by little there
came evidence that the successors of Brunel, Gooch, and Saunders
were beginning to assert themselves; water troughs were laid down
at key points, and by the year 1897 the Great Western could claim
the longest non-stop run in the world, that of the 10 a.m. London
express from Cardiff, which ran non-stop over the 143·5 miles from
Newport to Paddington via the Severn Tunnel and Bath. During the
summer the advance portion of the 10.35 a.m. down 'Cornishman'
ran non-stop over the 193·9 miles from Paddington to Exeter. As yet
the speeds were not high, by the standards of the North Western and
of the Caledonian; but it was no more than a beginning, and a very
good beginning at that. The cult of the long non-stop had an
immense publicity value at that period. The Race to the North had
brought tremendous publicity and prestige to the railways engaged,
and for the first time in history railways generally began to advertise
their achievements to the public in general.

On the Great Western the lion's share of the most spectacular
non-stop running fell to the Dean 7 ft 8 in. 4-2-2s, and while the trend
towards an entirely new age was unmistakable the working methods
still remained what could well be termed 'leisured Victoriana.' The
Newport–Paddington non-stop was a case in point. I am not
suggesting that the running of the 10.18 a.m. up was anything but a
very good locomotive achievement in itself, but to run that one train
two 4-2-2s were stationed at Ebbw Junction, Nos. 3006 *Courier* and
3042 *Frederick Saunders*. Each engine had its own crew, and no other,
and they ran the train on alternate days. Each day the second 4-2-2
stood pilot until the 'non-stop' was away, and then it took a stopping
train to Gloucester. The days of common-user and intense utilization
were still far ahead, and it is almost a platitude to add that engines
engaged on such top-link duties were as carefully maintained as they
were immaculately cleaned.

Even as *Courier* and *Frederick Saunders* were running the Newport
non-stop, however, the 'Badmintons' had arrived on the scene, and
shocked those who saw in them a sharp decline in the aesthetic
beauty of Great Western locomotives. The 'winds of change' were
blowing still more strongly at Swindon, and the year 1898 was to
bring the 'Atbaras'. If the 'Badmintons' had surprised and shocked,
the 'Atbaras' left the aesthetes speechless, almost to the extent that

Bulleid's 'Q1' 0-6-0 horrified us all in 1942! With the 'Atbaras', however, the stage was set for the 'Cities', for *Albion* and *North Star*, and for the famous twentieth century development that was to lead to *Caerphilly Castle* and *King George V*. Indeed, with all the great new civil engineering works authorized and with the completion of the 'Atbaras' at Swindon, the prelude was virtually ended. The new age on the G.W.R. was about to begin.

Index